AMERICAN SOCIETY FOR I̶̶̶̶̶̶̶̶̶
1625 PRINCE STREET
ALEXANDRIA, VA 22314
(703) 519–6200

Supervisory Survival

A practical guide for the professional survival
of new, experienced, and aspiring law
enforcement supervisors.

Compiled and Edited by

Ed Nowicki

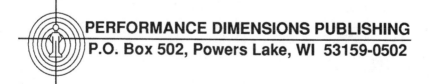

PERFORMANCE DIMENSIONS PUBLISHING
P.O. Box 502, Powers Lake, WI 53159-0502

Supervisory Survival

A practical guide for the professional survival of new, experienced, and aspiring law enforcement supervisors.

Compiled and Edited by
Ed Nowicki

Published by:

PERFORMANCE DIMENSIONS PUBLISHING
a division of Performance Dimensions, Inc.

P.O. Box 502, Powers Lake, WI 53159-0502, U.S.A.
Phone (414) 279-3850

Copyright © 1993 by Performance Dimensions, Inc.
First Printing: April 1993
Printed in the United States of America

Library of Congress Cataloging-in-Publication Data

Supervisory survival : a practical guide for the professional survival
   of new, experienced, and aspiring law enforcement supervisors /
   compiled and edited by Ed Nowicki.
       p.   cm.
   Includes bibliographical references and index.
   ISBN 1-879411-23-7 (pbk.) : $17.95
     1. Police--Supervision of.   2. Police--Supervision of --Study and
  teaching.   I. Nowicki, Ed, 1947-
HV7936 . S8S86   1993
350 . 74 ' 068 ' 3--dc20   93-4274
                                           CIP

Dedication

This book is dedicated to all new, experienced, and
aspiring law enforcement supervisors.

Epigraph

*"There are people, who, by their sympathetic attractions, carry
nations with them, and lead the activity of the human race."*

— Ralph Waldo Emerson

Foreword

Supervisory Survival is must reading for anyone who is, or desires to become, a supervisor. It deals with the essence of supervisory methodology. Today's supervisor must deal with the dynamics of individual personalities and complex street conditions unheard of some years ago. Supervisors need every tool possible in their arsenal.

Today's supervisor must deal with some law enforcement officers who have gone through grade and high schools and still cannot differentiate between a subject and a verb in a basic sentence. Yet, these officers are expected to write concise and clear reports that spell out the elements of a crime, probable cause, and describe what they have observed.

Composing simple but professional memos and letters causes concern for many officers and supervisors. Stan and Dean Berry in their chapter on *Writing Professional Memos and Letters* guide us through the functional process of planning, organizing, and writing clear and understandable letters and memos. They help to take the pain out of the process.

Many agencies require their supervisory personnel to conduct basic internal affairs investigations. However, rarely do they train or instruct them on how to deal with the basic problems associated with sustaining a disciplinary action through the courts or before an arbitrator at a hearing. John Blume in his chapter on *Internal Affairs Investigations* guides the new supervisor through the process and provides valuable insight.

Wally Bock discusses the qualities inherit in a good supervisor in his chapter on *How to be A Super Supervisor*. Good supervisors are not born, they are made. They are people who learn the tools necessary to lead people. Mr. Bock shares with us his formula for success.

Effective supervisors must be effective communicators. Many supervisors are not effective leaders and trainers simply because of their inability to communicate. They don't understand the nature and essence of communication as an art. Robert L. Bonshire, Jr. in his chapter on *Organizational Communication* does a fine job of telling us how to communicate and why it is so important to the organization's efficiency and effectiveness.

All we ever do is done through either written or verbal words. In either case, communication never takes place unless both the sender and the receiver of the communication receive and understand the true nature of the message. Supervisors who do not possess good communication skills, or who communicate poorly, will be doomed to mediocrity as leaders.

Stephen M. Bunting in his chapter on *Training Safety: A Supervisory Responsibility* points out clearly the need for supervisors to be concerned with officer safety issues, not only for the officer's sake, but for the public at large. Today, due to the litigious nature of our society, we are sued too frequently for negligent training. Supervisors need to know and understand the importance of their roles as trainers.

Michael J. Carpenter in his chapter dealing with *The New Supervisor* points out the painful reality that good law enforcement officers may not possess the skills necessary to become good supervisors. Good supervisors work at developing these skills and Mr. Carpenter provides a road map for all new supervisors to follow.

Someone once said that to be a good supervisor requires many skills, any of which could constitute a lifetime study. Law enforcement officers – by the nature of their jobs – are observers of life. They see people at their best and at their worst. No supervisor can do a good job without some knowledge of psychology. Dr. James T. Chandler in his chapter on *The Psychology of Supervision* brings to the reader a practical formula for success with employees.

Every supervisor will, at some time in their career, have to deal with the media. Care needs to be exercised to insure that the rights of all citizens are dealt with in a fair and equitable fashion. How we express ourselves to the media sets the tone of our organizations. We need the media to help us carry forward our message on crime. Thomas Christenberry in his chapter on *Dealing With the Media* helps new supervisors understand their role as supervisor in relation to the media.

Robert C. Crouse in his chapter on *Performance Appraisal: The Key to High Performance* deals with the skills and tools that supervisors need to raise employees to their true potential in any organization. Supervisors dread doing an employee appraisal, but good supervisors understand that the appraisal process is a day to day learning evaluation that leads to a better understanding of employee behavior.

Supervisors must know how to develop a plan and carry it out. Gorden E. Eden, Jr. points the supervisor in the right direction in his chapter on *Planning*. He creates a building block to understanding the planning process.

Ginny Field opens new doors for supervisors by describing their role as editor in her chapter on *Supervisory Editing*, and David M. Grossi reinforces the supervisor's role in officer survival in his chapter, *The Supervisor's Role in Officer Survival Training*.

Supervisory Survival is free of complicated rhetoric and does not engage in boring and lengthy explanations of basic and simple concepts. It is easy to read, easy to understand, and can be used as a quick guide reference on general principles. It is "boiler plate" material that will help new, as well as experienced, supervisors get off to a good start or stay on the straight and narrow in a very important role.

— James J. Carvino
Chief of Police
Boise (ID) Police Department

Introduction

The Supervisory Survival Program

Supervisory Survival is not your typical book on law enforcement supervision. It is not filled with strange theories and radical insights on law enforcement supervision, nor is it written by pure academics who only know how to spell experience. It is meant to be a part of each law enforcement supervisor's professional library.

Supervisory Survival, was selected as this book's title because law enforcement supervisors must survive the demands of their role as supervisor in addition to other officer survival concerns. The first-line supervisor has an extremely difficult role within the organization. They can be sandwiched between loyalty to their subordinates and their duty to carry out administrative directives. They must be able to balance their loyalty and responsibilities to each in a professional and responsible manner – not an easy task!

Law enforcement supervisors must possess a working under-standing of the duties that their subordinates are required to perform. They must also possess the additional skills needed to function prop-erly as a supervisor. In addition to being a law enforcement officer, they must also be a motivator, disciplinarian, trainer, evaluator, leader, counselor, referee, and amateur psychologist. Therefore, survival for supervisors is more than surviving the streets. They must also be able to professionally survive the many demands of being a law enforcement supervisor.

This book was written for new, experienced, and aspiring law enforcement supervisors. It can be considered a comprehensive law enforcement supervision training program in book form. As you read these pages you will see that there is no other supervisory book like this one!

Supervisory Survival was not entirely written by professional writers. Although writing ability was an important consideration in assembling this cadre of contributors, being an expert was the primary consideration for selecting the author of each chapter. Twenty-three different author/experts contributed chapters to this practical and in-sightful book.

Since it is virtually impossible for one author to have all the necessary skills or experience for each chapter, a recognized ex-pert/practitioner developed one chapter on a specific topic. Each of these expert/practitioners is well-known and respected for their knowledge about the material contained within their chapter.

Supervisory Survival contains some of the most relevant information available to law enforcement supervisors. Each author's expertise was attained through education, training, and practical experience.   The chapters include a wide range of topics: Internal Affairs Investigations, The Psychology of Supervision, Writing Professional Memos and Letters, Dealing With the News Media, Sexual Harassment, Supervisory Liability, and others relevant topics.   Beyond theory, *Supervisory Survival* is a "how to" book.

Within the pages of this book, you have a comprehensive law enforcement supervision training program.   This program will provide you with information on how to professionally survive the demands that may be placed upon you.   These demands, in one way or another, all relate to your law enforcement supervisory duties.   Department policies, rules, regulations, and personal preference may affect the way you choose to use this information in carrying out your duties.

You may want to begin reading the first chapter and continue to read each following chapter until the entire book is completed.   Or, you may want to selectively read chapters based on your perception of personal importance.   There is no correct way to read this book.   You may even choose not to read certain chapters, because you don't care for what the author has to say, or because you already have strong opinions about a topic.   How you choose to use the information contained in this book is entirely up to you, but *do* use the information.

You may completely disagree with some of the information contained in some of these chapters, since there may be other alternatives or insights that were not covered by the author.   If this is the case, then *Supervisory Survival* made you conscious of the fact that you do not agree, so you learned something from the chapter anyway.   In fact, many of the authors in this book do not totally agree with each other on some of the information contained in *Supervisory Survival.*

Keep an open mind with the motivation to learn and you will receive maximum benefits from this book.   Your professional survival is not only important to you, but it is important to your family and friends, your subordinates, your supervisors, your community, and your department.   As a law enforcement supervisor, you can no longer just think officer survival;   you must now think *Supervisory Survival!*

— Ed Nowicki
Police Training Specialist
Milwaukee Area Technical College

Warning—Disclaimer

The information displayed in this book are intended to assist the law enforcement supervisor. It is not the intention of the authors, publisher, or any of their agents to encourage persecution of any single person, group, organization, or religion who are free to express themselves under the protection of the First Amendment of the Constitution of the United States.

This book is designed to provide information in regard to the subject matter covered. It is sold with the understanding that the authors and publisher are not engaged in rendering legal or other professional services. If legal or other professional assistance is required, the services of a competent professional should be sought.

It is not the purpose of this book to reprint all the information that is otherwise available to the authors and publisher, but to complement, amplify, and supplement other texts. You are urged to read all available material and to learn as much as possible about officer safety and survival and to tailor the information to your individual needs. For more information, see the "Suggested Reading" section at the end of this book.

Every effort has been made to make this book as complete and as accurate as possible. However, there may be mistakes, both typographical and in content. Therefore, this text should be used only as a general guide and not as the ultimate source of supervisory survival. Furthermore, this book contains information on supervisory survival only up to the printing date.

The purpose of this book is to educate, inform, and stimulate thought. The authors and Performance Dimensions shall have neither liability nor responsibility to any person or entity with respect to any loss or damage caused, or alleged to be caused, directly or indirectly by the information contained in this book.

If you do not wish to be bound by the above, you may return this book to the publisher for a full refund.

Contents

Contents

Supervisory Survival

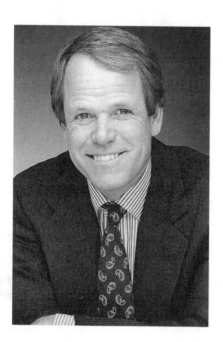 

Stan Berry   Dean Berry

Mr. Stan Berry has a B.A. from the University of Minnesota and an M.A. from Yale University. He is the co-author of Action Writing for the '90s and Business Grammar & Style, and the Law Enforcement Resource Center's two video series, Report Writing and Writing Skills for Command Personnel. He is an active member of the American Society of Law Enforcement Trainers (ASLET).

Mr. Dean Berry has a B.A. and an M.A. from the University of Minnesota. He is the Author of A Workbook of Writing Models; The Officer As Writer; and Report Writing and Writing Skills for Command Personnel. He is the co-author of the Law Enforcement Resource Center's two video series, Report Writing and Writing Skills for Command Personnel. He is also an active member of the American Society of Law Enforcement Trainers (ASLET).

Chapter 1

Writing Professional Memos and Letters

by Stan Berry and Dean Berry

Most law enforcement supervisory personnel write occasional memos and letters to their officers, peers, residents, or other agencies. During the years that the authors have conducted writing seminars for corporations, associations, and public agencies, they have critiqued thousands of memos and letters. Some were written well. Some were barely readable. Almost all could have been improved. The same is true for the memos and letters written by law enforcement personnel with whom they have worked.

In this chapter, the authors briefly define business writing and offer suggestions for planning, organizing, drafting, and revising memos and letters.

Definition

When asked what makes for good memo and letter writing, supervisor participants in writing seminars typically answer, "Conveying as much information about a subject as you can." "Writing in a professional, academic style," or "Writing clearly and concisely."

Each of these definitions has important elements of what business writing is, but they miss the target. They miss the one essential focus of what you are trying to accomplish when you write memos and letters.

The authors' definition of business writing is simply WRITING TO GET THINGS DONE. When you say, "taking care of business" or "getting down to business," you imply doing things.

The closer you stay to this definition, the more effectively you will write. When you sit down to write, one of the first questions you must ask yourself is, "Exactly what am I trying to get done with this document?" You will answer this and other questions during your planning stage in the writing process.

Planning

Thinking Process

Many supervisors say that they tend to write off the top of their heads. They have only a general idea of what they want to say when they begin to write.

Many begin their memos and letters using a **thinking** rather than a **reporting process**. Many times they aren't sure exactly what they want to say, so they start someplace safe. They start with what they know, which is usually some background information. It's sort of a warm up to get things going.

Once they get moving, they are likely to consider the options for, say, solving a problem. If alternatives have already been tried, they often think these should be explained, too. Finally, they arrive at a solution. They usually present this to the reader in the form of a request, policy, recommendation, or conclusion.

This works moderately well as a **thinking** process, but not very well as a **reporting** process.

Using the thinking process when writing leaves readers in the dark about what you really want until they reach the conclusion, way at the end.

Reporting Process

Using the reporting process when writing tells readers what they want to know as they begin to read. Other material, such as background information, comes later.

The most effective steps in the reporting process are actually just the opposite of that in the thinking process. In the reporting process, you tell the reader at the beginning of the document the *purpose* of the document and what you expect of the reader.

Most seminar participants report that as readers they give a memo or letter just three to five seconds before deciding to act on it, to file it, or to put it aside for further attention. Most readers want to know immediately what, if anything, is required of them.

Using the reporting process rather than the thinking process puts the purpose of the document right up front.

Writing for the reader doesn't just happen. Your writing will be more effective if you spend two or three minutes before you begin to write, asking yourself questions such as these:

❑ What do I want to get done by writing this memo or letter?

❏ How much detail does the reader need?

❏ What questions will the reader have about the issue?

❏ Is there a deadline involved?

Jotting down and organizing your thoughts takes very little time for a routine memo or letter, but the payoff is great. You'll write in half the time, and your document can be read in half the time. And the reader will know exactly whether an action is needed, and if so, when.

The authors suggest the simple five-step planning process that follows:

Step 1. Define your purpose. Put your desired outcome in the form of an action statement. This statement will form the content of your opening paragraph.

Step 2. Determine what information the reader needs to know to act on the memo or letter.

Step 3. Sort your information into categories. Although the topic will usually determine the categories, frequently used categories include:

❏ recommendation

❏ background or rationale

❏ action

Make these sorted categories the main points of your memo or letter. Having this structure will save you a great deal of time when you begin to write.

Step 4. Write a draft of your document. Having completed steps 1, 2, and 3, this step is easy to do. Simply put the ideas into complete sentences.

Step 5. Revise and polish your draft into a final copy.

These five steps break any writing job down into simple sequences of steps. The process can become second nature almost immediately.

Organizing

The authors suggest two formats to use in organizing your writing. The first format is for the whole document; the second, for paragraphs.

Format for the Whole Document

An effective format to follow in your memos and letters is the authors' three-part model.

≫ **Part 1. The opening.** Put into paragraph one the purpose of the document. It might be to inform, to instruct, to thank a person, or to ask for information. Try to avoid the tired and wordy opening, "This memo is for the purpose of . . ." Instead, simply use the opening sentence(s) to state the purpose or the action desired.

Example:
I recommend that all future classes of fewer than 40 people be held somewhere other than in our department training room.

≫ **Part 2. The Body.** Use paragraphs 2, 3, and so on to give background, to explain the rationale for what you have stated or asked in the opening, to give instructions, etc.

≫ **Part 3. The Closing.** Use the final paragraph to express good will or to set a deadline for action, and the reason for the deadline.

Example:
Please let me know by June 5, Jane, whether you agree with my recommendation. We can then be ready to schedule the Quality Initiative training.

You can use this three-part model for ninety-five percent of your writing. It is simple, it gives a structure to your documents, and it makes them easy to read.

Format for Paragraphs

Most paragraphs in Part 2, or the body of your document, are connected units of thought. Each paragraph deals with one main idea, which is usually expressed in the opening sentence as a forecast.

Usually, the paragraph contains facts or details which support or explain the main idea.

    Examples:
The sound facilities are bad for small groups. (forecast)

The microphone does not work consistently. One of the speakers makes a buzzing noise. The room's acoustics are poor, as well. (details)

The training room also has a poor geographical location. (forecast)

In the afternoon, the sun transforms the room into an oven. (details)

Many physical aspects of the room are not ideal for small classes. (forecast)

The room is so large that small classes feel swamped. Since the chairs are bolted to the floor, they cannot be moved into small groups. (details)

Writing a Draft

    When writing your draft, you can tell how well you have planned your document. If you experience a "flow" as you write, you have planned well. If you stop frequently to determine what you want to say next, your planning probably was incomplete.
    Regardless of how well you have planned, though, try to write your draft quickly. You can revise it later if you need to.

The Subject Line

    Start your draft by writing a subject line which has two uses. You can use it to forecast the overall contents of the memo or of the long, involved letter. You can also use it to get obvious and unnecessary expressions out of the memo itself.

    Example of forecasting:
The subject line, TRAINING ROOMS, announces the topic. Yet, the reader is not given much of a clue as to what to expect in the memo.

The subject line, RECOMMENDATION FOR A CHANGE IN TRAINING ROOMS, announces the topic but also tells the reader that you are going to talk about changes. The readers know what to expect as they begin to read.

A second use of the subject line is to get unnecessary and obvious expressions out of the letter or the memo itself. Openings such as, *We are in receipt of your letter dated . . .* or *We wrote to you on . . .* serve little real purpose.

You can easily put this type of information into the subject line:

Subject: *Your letter of June 1, 19XX, Requesting Information About Our Drug Abuse Program*

Supervisors sometimes feel that these types of openings provide a safe formula to give their writing an official or business-like tone. Others use them out of habit, just as a way to get started. Still others feel that they provide a polite, harmless introduction to their readers.

The effect of these kinds of openings, though, is to start your letter on a flat, bland note that does nothing to help the reader.

Opening and Closings

As you write your draft, let the purpose of your letter determine its opening. The three most frequently used opening:

Definite Statement. Make a definite statement when, for example, you are referring to previous correspondence or when the purpose of the letter is to share information.

Example:
Our department presently does have an effective drug prevention program.

or

You will want to know about two crucial changes in our ABC policy.

Question. Ask a question when that fits the purpose of the letter.

Example:
Could you give us some help as we modify our Procedures Manual?

Good will. Express good will when that is the purpose of your letter.

Example:
Thank you for supporting our proposal at the supervisors' meeting yesterday.

You now have three ways to open your letters. Let's look at ways to close.

The three recommended ways to close are easy to remember. They are the same as the ways to open.

How often have your eyes skipped over the words,

Your prompt attention to this matter is greatly appreciated.

This is a week ending compared to the definite statement:

Please let me know by June 5, Jane, if you agree with my recommendation. We can then be ready to schedule the Quality Initiative training.

The second type of closing is to ask a question:

Can we meet at noon on Wednesday, Bob, to decide on the policy change?

And the third type is to express good will:

Thanks again, Bob, for your help.

When you let the PURPOSE of your letter determine its opening and closing, you use a powerful tool for reaching your desired outcome, instead of raising a lifeless barrier to the reader's interest.

Headings and Bullets

When writing your draft, use headings to make your categories obvious and bullets (dots and hyphens) to make your ideas stand out.

Headings

Date: *June 1, 19XX*
To: *Jane Able*
From: *Tom Baker*
Subject: *Recommendation for a change in training rooms*

Recommendation

I recommend that all future classes of fewer than 40 people be held somewhere other than in our department training room.

Rationale

Our room is inadequate for a number of reasons.

The sound facilities are bad for small groups. The microphone does not work consistently. One of the speakers makes buzzing noise. The room's acoustics are poor, as well.

The training room also has a poor geographical location. In the afternoon, the sun transforms the room into an oven.

Finally, many physical aspects of the room are not ideal for small classes. The room is so large that small classes feel swamped. Since the chairs are bolted to the floor, they cannot be moved into small groups.

Action

Please let me know by June 5, Jane, if you agree with my recommendation. We then can schedule the Quality Initiative classes.

Bullets

> *Date:*   *June 1, 19XX*
> *To:*   *Jane Able*
> *From:*   *Tom Baker*
> *Subject:* *Recommendation for a change in training rooms*

I recommend that all future classes of fewer than 40 people be held somewhere other than in our department training room.

Our room is inadequate for a number of reasons.

> ☐ *The sound facilities are bad for small groups. The microphone does not work consistently. One of the speakers makes a buzzing noise. The room's acoustics are poor, as well.*

> ☐ *The training room also has a poor geographical location. In the afternoon, the sun transforms the room into an oven.*

> ☐ *Many physical aspects of the room are not ideal for small classes. The room is so large that small classes feel swamped. Since the chairs are bolted to the floor, they cannot be moved into small groups.*

Please let me know by June 5, Jane, if you agree with my recommendation. We then can schedule the Quality Initiative classes.

Revising

Some of your memos and letters are more important than others and are worth revising. As you revise, ask yourself these questions:

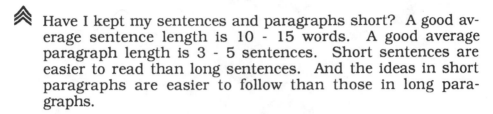

Have I kept my sentences and paragraphs short? A good average sentence length is 10 - 15 words. A good average paragraph length is 3 - 5 sentences. Short sentences are easier to read than long sentences. And the ideas in short paragraphs are easier to follow than those in long paragraphs.

Have I started most of my sentences with the subject of the sentence, thus staying in the active voice?

Have I used informal, rather than formal, language? Informal language is almost conversational, whereas formal language is similar to that used in textbooks.

You write more emphatically if you write *use* instead of *utilize*, *help* instead of *assistance*, *begin* instead of *commence*, and *next* instead of *subsequent.*

Have I checked my spelling, punctuation, and grammar? If you don't have computer software to do this, use a dictionary to check your spelling.

Have I been as concrete as possible in my language use?

Have I included all the information the reader needs?

Have I set a friendly tone to help get the results I want?

Should I have someone else review the memo or letter before I send it?

In conclusion, the writing skills which the authors have suggested will ensure that you will write in a professional, current style. Using these skills will also help you obtain the results you want from your writing.

John Blume

Mr. John Blume is a full-time instructor at the Institute of Police Technology and Management in Jacksonville, Florida. He develops and presents training programs in personnel administration, supervision, management, executive development, instructor techniques, field training officers' programs, internal affairs, and traffic management.

Mr. Blume's police career was twenty years with the Ohio State Highway Patrol. In his last position, he was responsible for personnel counseling and the evaluation systems for both uniform and civilian personnel. He also was involved in the development and presentation of supervision and management training programs at the North Carolina Justice Academy in Salemburg, North Carolina.

Mr. Blume graduated from Ohio Dominican College in Columbus, Ohio, with a B.A. degree in Criminal Justice Administration and from Central Michigan University, Mount Pleasant, Michigan, with an M.A. degree in Management and Supervision.

Chapter 2

Internal Affairs Investigations

by John Blume

Officers assigned to a specialized Internal Affairs Division are generally trained in internal affairs policies and procedures, and how to conduct an administrative investigation, as well as techniques for interviewing. Yet, many departments, because of organizational structure or due to limited resources, use supervisors to investigate officer misconduct. These supervisors frequently do not receive the same level of training.

This chapter addresses issues and techniques supervisors need to be familiar with prior to conducting an administrative investigation. Needless to say, not every issue or technique related to these investigations can be addressed. For this reason, to enhance your skills, you are encouraged to go beyond these pages and seek additional knowledge and training.

Review the Complaint

Once the complaint has been assigned for investigation, review it for completeness. Determine if the complaint is clear; if inconsistencies exist; and if the questions who, what, where, how and why are answered. If any area of the complaint is not clear or information is missing, contact the person who received the complaint for clarification.

It may be necessary to phone the complainant for further details. Eventually the complainant will be interviewed and it is best to enter the interview knowing as much about the complaint as possible. When much of the actual interview is centered on gathering information which should have been known prior to the interview, the complainant may question your competence.

If the complainant alleges use of force, determine from the person taking the complaint or other law enforcement employees who may have observed the complainant, whether or not any signs of injuries were noted.

Planning the Investigation

A supervisor wouldn't counsel or discipline an employee without first considering a plan of action. Neither should an administrative investigation begin without first developing a plan for the investigation. At the very least, do the following when developing a plan of action:

 Consider the possibility that criminal misconduct may be an issue. If criminal misconduct does exist, seek guidance from a higher authority, such as the administrator, legal adviser, or other person with the responsibility of making decisions in this area.

If the decision is made to conduct both a criminal investigation and an administrative investigation, use extreme caution so as not to violate the officer's rights. Legally speaking, it's easier and safer if the supervisor assigned to the administrative investigation does not conduct the criminal investigation. However, there are times when this is not possible. Never hold off seeking guidance or assistance when confronted with this issue.

 Keeping within the law of your state, municipality, Police Officer's Bill of Rights, or union contract, develop information around the complainant, witness(es) and accused officer.

☐ **Complainant** – Determine if the complainant has filed prior complaints, if the complainant or members of the complainant's family have been arrested by, or received citations from the accused officer or other members of your department. It's not unusual for citizens to lodge complaints out of retaliation.

☐ **Witness(es)** – If possible, determine the relationship between the witness(es) and the complainant. With the complainant, check for prior complaints, arrests, and citations.

☐ **Accused Officer** – Check to see if previous complaints have been filed against the accused officer, especially

complaints of a similar nature. If I.A. Officers were
polled concerning this issue, there would be a difference of opinion;   some saying previous complaints are
not a valid issue, and others saying they are. Be guided
by your department's policies, union contract, or Police
Officer's Bill of Rights, which may address this issue.

Review all available physical evidence. Administrative investigations can be difficult because many times there is a
lack of physical evidence. Examples of physical evidence
which may be available are: telecommunication tapes, departmental reports, photographs, laboratory results, medical
records (obtain a medical waiver when necessary), weapons
and ammunition. Determine the importance of existing
physical evidence and how it can be effectively used in the
investigation.

Schedule the sequence and location of all interviews. When
practical, the order of interviews should be complainant,
accused officer, and witness(es). Each case will be some-
what different, but the above order will serve as "building
blocks" for the gathering of facts and information.

Some departments, because of their Police Officer's Bill
of Rights, or a clause in an existing union contract require
the investigator, prior to interviewing the complainant, to
provide the accused officer the opportunity of making a
written statement.

By following this recommended order of interviewing,
you will have the opportunity to address all allegations as
well as uncover any inconsistencies. Also, by scheduling the
complainant's interview prior to the accused officers', additional facts, witnesses, or evidence may become known.

Make every attempt to interview the accused officer at
the department during the officer's regular duty hours.
Likewise, interview the complainant and witness(es) at the
department. Schedule interviews with the complainant and
witness(es) at their convenience. If they cannot or won't
come to the department, you go to them. Don't refuse to interview witnesses who can't or will not come to you.

Develop a list of questions for each interview.

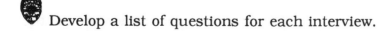 **Complainant** – Design questions for this interview which
are directed at gathering facts concerning the specific
allegations, specific actions of the accused officer, spe-

cific language used by the accused officer, the identification of additional witnesses, and language and actions of the complainant during the alleged incident. In addition, if inconsistencies are uncovered in the reviewing stage of the complaint, develop a series of questions which address and clarify these inconsistencies.

There are several categories of complaints which call for a high level of specific questions to be asked; i.e., sexual harassment and excessive use of force complaints. Design these questions so they will illicit responses which describe the exact language and actions exhibited by the accused officer.

The mere fact that a complainant alleges sexual harassment because an officer told an off-color joke is not good enough. Ask the complainant to state the words used by the accused officer, or if this is uncomfortable, to write the words in a formal statement. Likewise, don't allow the complainant to stop at stating, "The officer struck me." Design questions that will force the complainant to describe the act of striking.

☐ **Accused Officer** – Design these questions so the officer has an opportunity to deny or affirm each specific allegation stated in the complaint. In addition to addressing the allegations, use questions which cause the officer to describe and explain his or her actions and conduct. If the questions for the officer are developed after the interview with the complainant, include questions which will assist in clarifying inconsistencies in the complainant's statement.

☐ **Witness(es)** – This interview is extremely important to the complainant, the accused officer, and the investigation itself. A well thought out question list can go a long way in clearing up cloudy issues and inconsistencies in statements made by the complainant or accused officer. Develop questions which provide facts and information concerning what the witness heard and saw and if the witness was in a position to be sure of what was seen or heard.

A prepared list of questions serves as a roadmap for interviews. They build confidence, competence, and professionalism. Never begin an interview unprepared. The lack of prepared questions will result in an interview where loss of control is a real and serious concern.

Taping Interviews

A number of law enforcement agencies are developing policies and procedures for the taping of interviews associated with administrative investigations. Taping is to the advantage of all concerned parties. It is an excellent way to insure and display fairness, and a properly taped interview serves as documentation.

Before taping, ascertain what limitations or constraints are addressed in union contracts and existing laws, as well as departmental policies. If no limitations or constraints exist, do the following:

➤ Become familiar with the instrument to be used for taping. Test the equipment, including the microphone, to make sure it's operational.

➤ If taping is presently covered in your department's policy, or if the decision is made to begin taping administrative interviews, tape all interviews. Do not pick or choose which interview will or will not be taped.

➤ Prior to interviewing, advise the person to be interviewed of the department's policy concerning the taping of interviews. If necessary, state the reasons for taping: accuracy, fairness, and documentation. If the complainant or witness(es) will not give a statement on tape, document the refusal and go forward with the interview. It's better to forego the taping than not obtain a statement.

➤ Before questions are asked, open the interview on tape by stating the time, date, who is present in the interview room, the role of each person in the room, as well as the purpose of the interview.

➤ If there is a break given during the interview, document the break on tape by giving the present time and date, and that a break is being provided. Just prior to resuming the interview, state the time and date, and announce that the interview is resuming.

At the conclusion of the interview, announce that the interview is being concluded and once again announce the correct time and date. By following this procedure the tape will be properly documented and all time accounted for.

➤ The accused officer may ask for permission to personally tape the interview. Some departments permit it, others do not. Check departmental policy or seek guidance from the department's legal adviser.

 To prevent the possibility of taping over previous interviews which remain active, use a separate tape for each interview.

 Store taped interviews in a secured place, preferably in the Internal Affairs Division, if your department has one, until they are no longer needed. The length of time tapes remain in storage will depend on the appeal process or specific policies and procedures addressing this issue.

Principles and Issues Related to Administrative Interviews

 Enter each interview with the objective of gathering facts which can be used to conduct a fair, competent, and professional investigation.

 Show respect and empathy for all persons involved. Don't turn the interview into an adversarial conflict.

 Ask those being interviewed to relate the incident in their own words. Listen, don't interrupt. When you listen, project sincerity and empathy, and in addition, while listening you may be able to formulate important follow-up questions.

 After listening to the person's description or explanation of the incident, begin to use the list of questions developed for the interview. As the questions are asked, watch for non-verbal behavior which may be a clue to deception or fabrication. Also, be alert for inconsistencies in the statement and formulate additional questions for follow-up.

 Those questions directed to an accused officer must be narrowly and specifically related to the performance of his or her official duties. If the officer refuses to answer questions, he or she can be ordered to answer. However, the officer must be told that the failure to answer can result in departmental charges which could result in disciplinary action, including discharge.

You must also inform the officer that any incriminating statements will not be used against him or her in a criminal proceeding. However, they can be used against him or her in an administrative hearing (*Garrity v. New Jersey*, 385 U.S. 493, 1967).

If you are assigned to conduct both a criminal and administrative investigation, begin the criminal investigation first and read the officer his or her Miranda Rights prior to conducting the interview. If the officer waives his or her Miranda Rights and gives an incriminating statement, this statement can be used in an administrative investigation.

NOTE: Some state laws and union contracts may require that a *Garrity Warning* be given prior to any administrative interview; whether or not the officer cooperates in answering questions is immaterial.

 Putting a statement in writing can be difficult. Some departments require the interviewer to write the statement verbatim. This can cause the interviewer serious problems. If the interviewer spends too much time writing during the interview, less time will be devoted to listening to what is being said, and as a result important information or clues may be missed. It is possible to write the statement verbatim from the tapes, but this is very time consuming and it would probably result in time delay in obtaining the person's signature.

For the above reasons, it is recommended that you write the statement by paraphrasing and once written, read it back to the person interviewed. If the statement meets with the approval of the person interviewed, obtain their signature. If it doesn't meet with approval, agree on the needed changes, make the changes, and obtain their signature.

Concluding the Investigation

Review and weigh the pertinent physical evidence, all statements relating to the case, and additional facts gathered as a result of the investigation. After reviewing, determine the result of the investigation; then record the investigation by using the report format approved by the department.

If a procedure exists which calls for a letter of transmittal to be included with the investigative report, include in the letter a summary of the pertinent facts, and state your findings of the investigation. If a letter of transmittal is not required, state the finding under a specified caption within the investigative report.

Forward the investigative report to the person responsible for administrative investigations. In some departments this would be the chief administrator; in others it may be the commander of Internal Affairs or another designated officer.

Generally, a final decision concerning the findings of the investigation is made by a higher authority. Once a finding has been made, notify the complainant and accused officer of the outcome. Determine how your department's policy or procedure addresses the method to be used in handling these notifications. Some departments require a personal contact with the involved parties and others require notification by letter.

This chapter has stressed the techniques and principles which are necessary for conducting administrative investigations in a professional and competent manner. Citizens served by a law enforcement agency can and do expect law enforcement officers to exhibit conduct which exemplifies the highest levels of fairness, honesty, and integrity.

If complaints are taken lightly, or if they are not investigated properly, the reputation of the law enforcement agency and its individual officers may be severely damaged. In addition to the expectations of citizens, those officers finding themselves the subjects of an administrative investigation have the right to expect a fair and competent investigation.

Chapter 3

How to be A Super Supervisor

by Wally Bock

There are three steps to becoming a super supervisor. Find out who the great supervisors are, watch what they do, and try to be like them.

What follows is the result of a three year study of top performing police sergeants. But before we go on, you need to take a minute to link this to your experience. Identify great supervisors that you know, or know of. Think about how they do things. Then compare what follows with your own observations.

Who Are the Super Supervisors?

Our first problem was to figure out who to study. We selected two criteria.

The supervisors we looked at were highly rated by their departments. That is almost a definition of "top performing." However, that is not enough, because there are many supervisors out there with great ratings who simply are not credible with the troops. Management may think they're hot stuff, but the subordinates who work for them know better.

The supervisors we looked at were also highly rated by the subordinates who worked for them and by their peers. However, this is not enough by itself, because we might wind up with well-liked supervisors who aren't necessarily good supervisors.

What Are Super Supervisors Like?

The super supervisors we studied had the following six characteristics:

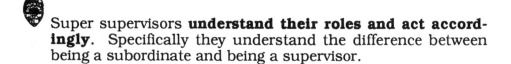 Super supervisors **understand their roles and act accordingly**. Specifically they understand the difference between being a subordinate and being a supervisor.

Super supervisors **are flexible**. They understand their subordinates and know when and where to use different supervision techniques. They have enough techniques and enough methods to deal with a variety of subordinates and situations.

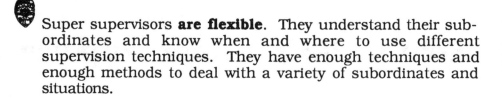 Super supervisors **are fair**. They are consistent in their reactions and discipline methods. Their subordinates know what to expect. They have a reputation for being trustworthy and for fair-dealing.

Super supervisors **are credible**. They know enough about their jobs and the jobs of the people they supervise to accomplish their missions without anyone getting hurt. The supervisors know what their reputations are and how that fits into the agency they work for. They also know how to use their reputations well in supervision.

Super supervisors **are good communicators**. They are good at both verbal and non-verbal communications. They get across key points and make sure their subordinates understand. They talk well, but they also listen well.

Super supervisors **balance today and tomorrow**. They know that today's job needs to be done, but they also realize that part of their job is training. They understand that the challenges of tomorrow will be different from the challenges of today.

Now let's look at the characteristics of the super supervisor in more detail.

Super Supervisors Understand Their Roles and Act Accordingly

When you became a first-line supervisor, the rules of the game changed. When you were a subordinate, you were rated on the basis of how well you worked. Generally if you wanted to produce more, to do better, to get more, you worked a little harder or you worked a little smarter. It was entirely under your control. Things are different once you become a supervisor. Now you're judged on the performance of your squad, team, or group. You're rated on how well your subordinates work. The power has shifted, and you no longer have control over direct production. The power, in fact, has gone to your subordinates because you are judged on what they do.

You must understand this in order to be an effective supervisor; that you don't have any real power. Oh, you can discipline your subordinates and fire them and the rest of it, but, as a practical matter, you can't make them do something they choose not to do if they are willing to take the consequences.

You must also accept the difficult parts along with the nice parts of the role. It's nice to have your subordinates look up to you and respect you, but the tough part of this job is telling your subordinates that they're doing a bad job and trying to get them to improve. This is one of the hardest things that any supervisor has to do, and it's just as hard for law enforcement supervisors as it is for bookkeepers and lathe operators.

One of the supervisors we interviewed put it this way. "Look," he said, "remember the first time you were out there by yourself on the graveyard shift and there was a guy weaving all over the road – looked like he was twice as big as you, and there wasn't any backup? You knew that you had to pull him over and deal with him. Or do you remember the first time you had to go to a bar fight by yourself? You were probably scared shitless, but you went ahead and did what had to be done. You have to do the same thing in supervision. When you've got a problem to deal with, whether it's a problem situation or a problem person, you've got to deal with it right then, no matter how uncomfortable it makes you feel."

To be a super supervisor, you must understand that your role is to get your subordinates to do a job that you will be rated on. The hard part is telling your subordinates that their performance needs improvement. And if you are going to be a super supervisor, you must learn to handle both of these tasks. There is no easy way to get better at this. You just have to handle each situation as it comes up.

Super Supervisors Are Flexible

You have probably heard the phrase, "different strokes for different folks," but it's more than that. It's very often, "different strokes for the same folks," but at different times and in different circumstances.

The super supervisors we talked to understand that not only is each officer different, but they are different in different aspects of their lives. You'll have officers working for you who are great at self-initiated activity, but they can't do good reports. Or officers who are fine in community relations, but they won't wear their hats when the chief tells them to. You will need to know how to deal with each officer in every situation.

In one way, being a law enforcement supervisor is great. Most people are in law enforcement because they choose to be. They want to be there and they want to do a good job. But they are all different. You must be flexible enough to deal with their differences and to use their strengths to help them do a better job.

This boils down to what I call the "Platinum Rule." You probably remember the Golden Rule, "Do unto others as you would have them do unto you." It's great and it's biblical, but in supervision the Platinum Rule is more important. "Do unto others in a way that they want to be dealt with."

Learn about your subordinates. Learn their strengths and weaknesses, their likes and dislikes. Then use that knowledge to deal with them more effectively.

Super Supervisors Are Fair

Fair is very often in the eye of the beholder. It is striking that the stories officers tell to describe their great supervisors are often about how their supervisors are fair in difficult circumstances. Subordinates don't expect their supervisors to treat people all the same way.

Subordinates expect their supervisors to treat them appropriately and consistently. Appropriately means that for each situation they expect the right treatment. If a subordinate is having trouble at home and is therefore having trouble doing the job, they expect the supervisor to know this and to account for it. They want their supervisor to go to bat for them when it's important and to protect them from the powers that be. They also expect their supervisors to be consistent; a similar type of action or behavior gets a similar type of response every time.

We found that great supervisors have different styles. We found yellers and screamers, supervisors with volatile, quick tempers, and supervisors who were more laid back and quiet. We found supervisors who gave some of the greatest ass chewings in the history of the planet described as great, as well as those who never gave an ass chewing, but just conducted a quiet performance review session.

What we found important was that great supervisors care about their subordinates. They love their people and are loved in return.

Super Supervisors Are Credible

You don't have to have been the best officer in a department to be a great supervisor, although it does help. But you do have to be knowledgeable enough so that your subordinates will trust you.

In your fist weeks in your new role as supervisor, all of your actions will be magnified. The first time you handle a tactical situation, your subordinates are watching for clues and they'll carry weight later.

One secret of great supervisors is that they understand they don't have to have all the answers. It is the great ones who are more likely to say, "I don't know the answer to that. Let's look it up in the legal guide."

There is nothing you can do about the reputation you already have, but you need to find out what it is. Take some time to talk to people you trust in the department. Find out how they see you and how they think others see you. Think about how you can use this information in your supervision. If there is one thing that separates law enforcement supervision from supervision in the private sector, it's the reputation thing. You must know what it is and how you can use it in your supervision.

One way you can improve your performance and reduce your chances of making a really big-time mistake is to play what-if games with yourself. Identify the situations that you might have to face, and then figure out how you will deal with them. Make checklists for yourself if it helps. Play mental what-if games. They will help you to be prepared when you have to face those situations in real life. And that, in turn, will help your reputation and credibility.

Super Supervisors Are Good Communicators

The great supervisors we talked to and heard about understand that communication doesn't happen at the mouth or at the pen; it happens at the eye and the ear.

Great supervisors give clear instructions and are active listeners. They take the time to find out if what they think they've said is what's actually been heard. They build review points into all their supervision to make sure that they catch errors early and correct them when they're small and easy. Someone once said that if you want to kill a bear, you'd better get it while it's a cub. Boy, is that true for supervision! Small problems are easy to deal with; big problems are not. If you let small problems get big, believe me, they'll eat you for lunch.

Great supervisors understand the power of praise and it may be the single most important training tool. People will crawl over broken glass for praise. Yet we don't give enough of it. One really great sergeant I know used to start every roll call briefing with something positive that someone on the squad had done. Sometimes it was two or three people. Sometimes it was the squad as a whole. Maybe they had handled a robbery in progress well the day before. There was always something positive to start the shift.

Make praise a part of your arsenal. Don't praise your people just for the sake of praise, but make sure they get praised and get praised frequently. Look for opportunities to praise!

Good communication also includes attention to the nonverbal parts of communication. Great supervisors pay attention to how, when, and where they talk to their subordinates. If they use their office for a meeting, they understand what kind of impact they want to create. They are alert to nonverbal cues in the course of the meeting. They use communication tools that are appropriate for the individuals they are talking to.

Super Supervisors Balance Today and Tomorrow

This seems to be a characteristic that sets great supervisors apart from ones that are okay or pretty good. Great supervisors want everyone who works for them to grow into ideal subordinates and ultimately into whatever they want to become in law enforcement.

They understand about getting the job done each day. One of the people we talked to called it "gettin the laundry out." Calls have to be answered, reports have to be done, and projects have to be completed, but accomplishing these missions is only one part of the supervisor's job. The other part is equipping your people with the tools and confidence they need to handle tomorrow's job.

We found that great supervisors were more comfortable with a broader range of styles, but they were considerably more adept at styles that gave their people a little freedom as they grew. Frankly, it doesn't take much brain power to closely supervise people who really don't know anything or to let the squad's stars who can do everything off on their own. However, it takes a great deal of courage, common sense, and attention to detail to let people try new things that they are not likely to do well. But that's what good supervisors do.

The great supervisors also pay a great deal of attention to what was going on in their communities. They were far more likely than their less excellent comrades to have a handle on population trends, to be up on new law enforcement techniques, and to be familiar with current events. After a while this quality of "being aware" became an indicator that we were dealing with super supervisors.

To get better at this, make it a point to read things other than training bulletins and *Law and Order*. Take the time to talk to people. Keep your eyes open for trends in your community. Then think about what it all means for you and your people.

Becoming One of the Great Ones

So, there you have it. It's simple, but it's not easy. The fact is that this is not rocket science. People know what makes good supervision. Then why is there so much bad supervision?

Good supervision is not intuitive. You don't come out of the womb, or even out of adolescence, knowing how to be a great supervisor. Good supervision is a set of behaviors, and learning them takes time and effort, just like learning to ride a bicycle, learning to swim, or learning to shoot a gun.

This means that you have to pay attention. It means that things will be harder and take longer at first even though they will come naturally later. Where do you start?

You start by learning to imagine good supervision. Identify good supervisors and talk to them about your supervision situations. You can imagine how good supervisors would handle the situations you face. You can imagine yourself as a great supervisor by mentally role playing your supervision situations.

Put together a self-development plan for yourself. Start by going back over our six characteristics and rating yourself on each one. Find someone who knows you and whose judgment you trust and have them help you.

Ask yourself four questions. Where do I want to be in five years? What do I do really well? What would I like to try? How should I go about improving what I do? Then use these questions to guide your development.

You don't get to be a great supervisor by just thinking about it. You have to go out and do it. You must understand the basics, but then you have to apply them – day after day after day, when it's easy, and when it's hard.

The payoff is being a great supervisor. It's making a difference to the people who work for you. It's making a difference in your community. And it's worth it.

About the Author

Mr. Wally Bock is a consultant and trainer based in Oakland, California. He works with law enforcement agencies to help them improve the quality of their management and planning.

Mr. Bock's firm offers the popular and effective Super Sarge Supervisory Skills program based on the material in this chapter. In addition they offer other courses in management and community policing as well as a complete series of publications and tutorials.

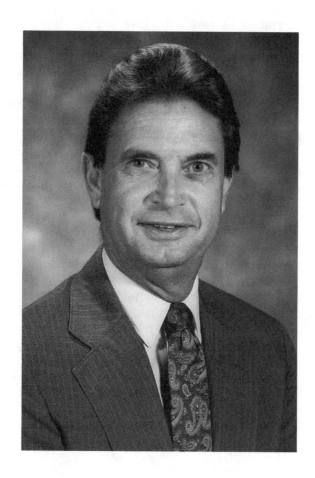

Robert L. Bonshire, Jr.

Mr. Robert L. Bonshire, Jr. is currently an instructor at the FBI Academy. He instructs in Public Speaking, Organizational Communication, Instructor Development, and Media for the National Academy.

Mr. Bonshire is a twenty-two year FBI Special Agent who served in Newark, NJ for two years and Minneapolis, MN fifteen years before joining the Academy faculty in 1987. He taught on the high school and university levels in Indiana before entering the Bureau.

Mr. Bonshire earned a B.S. degree in Secondary Language Arts and History, and an M.A. degree in Secondary Counseling, both from Ball State University in Muncie, IN. He has also earned thirty-nine hours toward an Ed.D. in Public School Administration.

Chapter 4

Organizational Communication

by Robert L. Bonshire, Jr.

Communication in any organization travels in many and diverse directions. Information must move in every direction among organizational members to enable that information to be shared. Information flows primarily in three distinct directions: downward, lateral, and upward – depending on the objective of the information. Information flows through formal channels and informal channels, adhering to the "chain of command" in formal channels and ignoring the "chain" in the informal channels.

We will examine these three directional flows – looking at the purposes, advantages, and problem areas of each.

Downward Communication

Downward communication consists of the methods by which information travels formally from a higher level to a lower level for the purposes of informing, directing, and controlling.

Daniel Katz and Robert Kahn wrote in *The Social Psychology of Organizations* that downward communication can be grouped into five general categories that serve the organization to

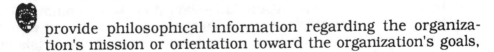 provide philosophical information regarding the organization's mission or orientation toward the organization's goals,

provide information which produces an understanding of the task and its relationship to other organizational tasks – giving rationale for the job,

provide information about organizational policies, procedures, and practices, provide specific task directives or instructions on how to do the job, and

 provide feedback on performance to subordinates.

Obviously, the above categories of information are primarily, if not entirely, "one-way," requiring no feedback from the receiver. This is where downward communication encounters its biggest problem. How does the sender know the message is received as intended?

A closer look at downward communication determines that the sender is primarily issuing instructions, explanations, rationales (answering the WHY issues), procedures, and rules and regulations by which the organization intends to meet its goals and objectives.

Other items of information distributed by the downward channels can include appraisals of employees and of the organization; support of individuals and their suggestions; announcements of interest, such as promotions and awards; personal achievements; employee family information; and other areas which promote the unity of the employees and the organization.

The primary advantage to downward communication is that the written downward message becomes an instant official record. Information in its original form can be captured for future reference and/or documentation.

Another advantage comes only with the verbal form of downward communication. Organizations must use strong downward communication in crisis situations. Management must give the information quickly and expect little or no feedback. Thus the sender must craft these messages in language that all receivers will understand immediately.

Experts believe that downward communication can provide immediate feedback. Senders should give feedback through oral messages and not with written messages. A written response could take too much time to be effective, and feedback to an individual is more effective if delivered face-to-face.

Downward communication has many problem areas. One area is that being primarily written and one-way, downward communication allows for little if any feedback to its message. As stated above, in some instances, no feedback is desired, i.e., the on-going crisis situation. But if the sender wants to make certain that the message is understood, the sender must be available to answer questions; otherwise, the message's meaning is left to the perception of the receiver.

Numerous organizations use videos to give downward communication as many employees grew up learning from the video. Smart leaders have learned to deliver their message via the most comfortable medium for the receiver. The sender must realize that videos are also one-way, giving the receiver no chance to ask questions of the message or the sender.

Another disadvantage comes when the downward message passes through the "chain of command." If the message is given orally by the various levels of the "chain," it can become diluted or distorted. Filtering, the changing of the intended message by adding personal interpretation of the meaning, deciding what is important and what is not important (gatekeeping), and even changing the wording, making it weaker or stronger to meet personal needs, is a reality. Even when people do not have an agenda to promote, classroom exercises in communication have determined that a message whispered from one person to another becomes almost unrecognizable after only three or four transmissions.

In some instances, gatekeeping is used to keep others from having information. This is usually done as a move for power. Information is power, and if the other person does not have the word, then they also may not have the power. Those with the information may be in a position of control.

Other hindrances to effective downward communication fall within the goal(s) of the communicators or the organization. If the goals of management, the organization, and the employee differ, the understanding of the message may, and probably will, suffer. Couple this problem area with the fact that bare information cannot communicate motivation or expectation, and the potential for miscommunication or non-communication arises.

Most organizations are saturated with information flowing in every direction. If the downward communication is too voluminous or written in hard-to-understand or ambiguous language, some messages could fail to achieve their intended purpose.

In addition to being saturated, the downward channels can also be very slow. Depending on the number of links in the "chain of command," the message may take days, and sometimes even longer, to reach its audience.

If Katz and Kahn are correct, messages intended to inform, direct, and control individuals and the organization must be crafted in understandable language and delivered in a timely fashion.

Lateral Communication

Lateral communication channels usually consist of informal methods by which information is shared for the coordination of tasks between individuals on the same hierarchical level of authority, although not necessarily of rank. Level of authority does not have to equate to rank structure.

Included in the lateral channels is the Grapevine. The Grapevine will be addressed later as a separate lateral communications entity, having its own information types, structure, and characteristics that differ from those of lateral communication.

Lateral communication's primary function is to coordinate and accomplish tasks. Richard Cheatham and Keith Erickson set out four parameters of lateral communication in *The Police Officer's Guide to Better Communication.* The four were

- ❑ relationship of tasks
- ❑ problem solving
- ❑ information sharing
- ❑ recognition of source of information as someone we know and trust

Other purposes of lateral communication found in a successful lateral system are resolving conflict (maybe identical to problem-solving), building rapport, and meeting the social needs of the individuals.

Much of the lateral information transfer happens among individuals or positions of similar status. This would be horizontal in nature. Information can also flow in a diagonal direction between unequal ranks or position, but between individuals NOT in a superior/subordinate relationship. This could be a Chief of Police exchanging information with a computer technician concerning a problem area in which both parties have an equal interest. The task is to solve a problem in a trusting environment with no concern for rank. In this situation, both individuals are on the same hierarchical level of authority.

Information shared within the lateral channels is usually accurate and timely. Inaccurate information that enters the channels is usually quickly detected and corrected due to the amount of valid information. Since information is used to coordinate a task, it usually enters the channel quickly.

Trusted information, the type usually found in the lateral channel, is transmitted rapidly between interested individuals. The information is considered reliable so recipients spend little time and effort trying to verify the message or the source. All communicators have the same goal or objective – getting something accomplished.

Lateral communication is used by all levels on the "chain of command," both within the organization and between organizations. Current multi-jurisdictional case work and managerial problem areas require law enforcement organizations to share information. Solving common problems requires decision-makers to have as much reliable information as possible.

A strong lateral communication system will enhance the downward and upward communication flow within any organization. Trust developed and maintained between individuals in the strong lateral system carries over to all other communication.

According to Valorie A. McClelland and Richard E. Wilmot in "Improve Lateral Communication," *Personnel Journal*, September 1990, "Organization departments communicate laterally with each other when a crisis or problem develops, but otherwise they rarely share information."

Students at the FBI National Academy have verified this statement when discussing lateral communication. Several have stated that friction develops between shift personnel when information is not disseminated between shifts and unnecessary or dangerous work is done because information is not shared. Conflict will occur, not because people share information, but because they don't.

Lateral communication has also been accused of being too fast. Sometimes the information is shared by one level without being shared by a higher level. This can give the appearance that the "higher-ups" are not keeping current on the information. This can be threatening, for such a perception can threaten their authority or standing.

Another potentially threatening aspect of the lateral system is the Grapevine. Grapevines are active at every level of the organization. Grapevines are rapid-paced and usually contain accurate, but often incomplete, information. Experts indicate that Grapevines are about 75% accurate. The "accurate, but incomplete" information within the Grapevine is easy to work with because those knowing the missing facts can provide the additional information, adding to the accuracy and completeness of the information.

Grapevines prosper because of the many social interactions and situations (shared interests) within the organization. Each individual participates in many Grapevines, with each Grapevine having its own cast of players. Although all individuals in the organization participate in Grapevines, few send the information. Most participants are receivers. However, some individuals are receivers in one Grapevine and senders in others.

Information is often placed in a Grapevine to test an idea. This use is valid if the purpose is legitimate. If the information is accurate and complete and the sender is seeking open and candid feedback to an idea, the use is appropriate. Sometimes information is fed into the Grapevine for "shock" purposes: to cause dissonance, to meet a personal agenda, to rile or irritate, or to cause confusion or disorder. This is not legitimate and should be avoided.

Rumors are also present in a Grapevine. Rumors usually contain inaccurate information and often result when individuals interpret perceived information. Not much positive can occur from rumors.

Susan A. Hellweg in "Operational Grapevines," *Progress in Communication Science*, Volume 8, 1987, indicated that three types of rumors exist in the Grapevine:

❑ Anxiety Rumors

❑ Wish Fulfillment Rumors

❑ Wedge Driving Rumors

 Anxiety Rumors are bits of information that cause individuals to become concerned over situations that affect their job and personal security. These rumors are laden with emotion, usually negative. Examples include a secret Internal Affairs investigation, reassignment, and new rules or regulations.

 Wish Fulfillment Rumors address the desires and fantasies that fill our ego-driven thoughts. Usually concerned with the positive area, these "happy" rumors often address promotions, reassignment to another position, wage increases, and other job satisfactions. These wishes could also involve "getting rid" of an undesirable partner, or even better, an unpopular supervisor.

 The opposite of the Wish Fulfillment Rumor is the **Wedge Driving Rumor**. *Wedge Driving Rumors* are "evil" devices that tend to disrupt the organization. Personal agendas are often the subject of these rumors – attempts to have individuals choose sides on an issue or to join on the side of another person's point of view or perception.

Bruce A. Baldwin addressed gossip in the workplace in "Gossip and the Grapevine," *USAir*, January 1991. Baldwin listed seven reasons for gossip:

- ☐   to win social recognition
- ☐   to gain personal advantage
- ☐   to hurt or punish
- ☐   to enjoy and experience vicariously
- ☐   to test reactions
- ☐   to communicate indirectly
- ☐   to protect or warn

The first five reasons are not legitimate, positive reasons for placing such information into the organizational Grapevine. The last two could be considered legitimate reasons; however, the intent of the sender would need to be examined.

National Academy students suggested the following principles for leaders when they deal with inaccurate information, rumor, and gossip:

 Anticipate fears which can cause anxiety.

 Give people the facts through open communication.

Be truthful. Think of the future, not the immediate situation.

 Educate personnel concerning the negative aspects of false information that can destroy the organization.

 Take legal steps if needed.

If the first four steps succeed, then maybe the fifth step will never have to be taken.

As Paul R. Timm stated in *Managerial Communication: A Finger on the Pulse*, "Tap into the grapevine instead of wasting time trying to chop it down." This would really mean having a finger on the pulse. Leaders should use its positive aspects and immediately correct those aspects that will only cause harm to the organization and its people.

Lateral communication coordinates task accomplishment and unites individuals to work toward the goals and objectives of individuals, units, departments, and organizations. What an important place lateral communication has in successful organizations.

Upward Communication

Upward communication is more complex in an organization than many believe. The methods used to establish a strong upward communication flow vary as widely as the individual organizations using them. Information in the upward system travels from one level to a decision maker at some higher level in the "chain of command." These decisions can address organizational behavior, individual behavior, or both.

Participative decision-making and W. Edwards Deming's *Total Quality Management* are concepts widely accepted in organizations. The empowering of the employee to provide candid and accurate information and giving the employee a sense of ownership in the organization are concepts all organizations are implementing.

A two-sided contribution of upward communication messages is recognizing what is working, but also bringing about change in areas where organizational or individual behavior needs changing.

Upward communication addresses the questions, "How is the organization doing?" and "How am I doing?"

On management's side, the task is to listen to the answers to the above questions and to make correct and appropriate decisions to change organizational and individual behavior. The real task is to sort through all information and use aggressive managerial skills to make the correct decision: to receive, to decide, and to act.

Upward communication provides information of cares and concerns on job-related situations held by the employee. Employees could propose suggestions or innovative ideas as possible answers to perceived needs or problems of the organization. Feedback to the organization on policy, procedure, objectives, and goals also moves up the ladder. These answer the question, "How is the organization doing?"

Upward communication also provides feedback to individuals by which their behavior can be assessed. This could be an appraisal as to "How you are doing." This feedback could also be a request for answers to the question, "How am I doing?"

Information in these messages also expresses ideas for change, feelings of satisfaction and dissatisfaction, indications of worker morale, innovative thinking, and sometimes singular ideas and information.

In her article, "Eager Lions and Reluctant Lions," *Forbes*, February 17, 1992, Toni Mack features Robert Horton, Chairman, British Petroleum (BP). BP was in financial difficulty when Horton was appointed Chairman, and he set as a goal to make BP quicker at recognizing and resolving problems and to be a smarter organization by releasing the ingenuity of its people.

Horten stated, "What this is all about is the simple belief that our people know more about their jobs than their boss or their boss's boss." Horton did not mean that decisions were not his, but that he had to listen to those who have current, first-hand information when making his decisions – that's upward communication.

Threat and risk accompany upward communication. Many upward communication methods go outside the "chain of command." Other upward communication methods require the decision be made by those individuals with decision-making authority at a level below the manager. Both involve risk for the sender and the manager.

Threat and risk-taking come in the area of listening. If you ask for candid feedback, you may get it. Problems and areas of concern will arise, suggestions will be made, and possibly, "whistle blowers" will surface.

The sender also feels risk. Those who send negative messages risk being perceived as troublemakers. The sender also might fear the politics of the department and fear loss of advancement opportunities. Receivers sometimes "kill the messenger." These are matters of trust and can be alleviated by the behavior of the organization and its individuals.

As in downward communication flows, distortion, dilution, and gatekeeping can enter and alter the original upward message. If the information is held by an individual, timeliness of the information reaching the receiver can be effected. These are two major hindrances which can enter the upward flow.

Upward communication flows not only within the organization, but also from the organization and into the organization. Information must flow from the organization to the entities which have decision-making powers for the organization, e.g., City Councils and other political bodies. Information also flows into the organization by the citizens and organizations for whom the organization is held accountable, e.g., the individual citizen and Citizen's Advisory Groups.

Upward communication comes in all names and configurations: advisory groups, annual reports, surveys, brainstorming sessions, committees, complaint procedures, community affairs, daily reports, employee councils, exit interviews, grievance procedures, inspections, incident critiques, management by walking around, meetings, newsletters, ombudsman programs, open door policies, quality circles, retreats, role reversals, suggestion programs, two-down interviews, and upward evaluations. These are some, but not all, of the ways information flows up into, within, and from the organization.

Strong upward communications methods place a dual responsibility on the manager. Managers must accept the challenge of upward communication messages and support the individuals sending the messages. Managers do not have to agree with or support the message, but they must affirm the system and the sender.

Accepting the challenge is listening to the message. Providing the support is keeping the lines of communication open and maintaining a trust with the senders which will ensure that senders will continue to use those open lines of communication.

Bruce Harriman wrote in "Up and Down the Communication Ladder," *Harvard Business Review*, that upward communication, with all its problems, is perhaps the most important type of organizational communication. If this is true, managers and organizations are obliged to provide opportunities for employees to be heard. In this way, all employees can make contributions to the growth and success of the organization and all its people, and lead-ers will make good decisions based on current, first-hand information.

Summary

The success of any organization depends on the flow of communication between its members and the flow of information between the organization and the many clients it serves. The success of the leaders of the organization depends on their ability to create an atmosphere wherein all members feel free to honestly and openly communicate with each other whether it be downward, laterally, or upward.

Acknowledgments

This author wishes to acknowledge those people who have written books and articles pertaining to organizational communication from which he has read and learned. He also wishes to thank those 573 law enforcement personnel who have shared their knowledge and insights while attending the FBI National Academy's Organizational Communication class.

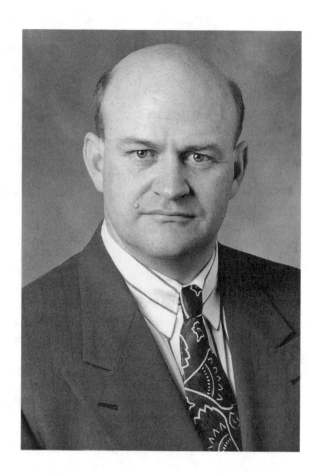

Stephen M. Bunting

Mr. Stephen M. Bunting is currently a Captain with the University of Delaware Police. He is a nineteen year veteran of law enforcement and has spent the last thirteen years with the University Police.

Mr. Bunting is certified to instruct firearms, defensive tactics, and officer survival. During the past 15 years he has trained thousands of officers from agencies of all types, including federal agencies, numerous state police agencies, countless city and county agencies, and officers from foreign countries.

Mr. Bunting is a founding director and the current Executive Director of the American Society of Law Enforcement Trainers (ASLET). He is a frequent lecturer to police recruits on coping with fear and danger in the police profession.

Chapter 5

Training Safety: A Supervisory Responsibility

by Stephen M. Bunting

One of the responsibilities of supervisors involves training the personnel who report to them. Thus, supervisors take on the role of training officers when the need arises. Often is the case too, where training officers, who are not supervisors, must exert a temporary supervisory role over trainees in the training class. Then there are supervisors whose primary function is the management of the training function. This chapter is written to assist those officers who are responsible for the safe training of law enforcement officers in whatever capacity they may be functioning.

Training law enforcement officers is a high liability function. Training officers are responsible for behavior that occurs in the training environment and then what occurs later in real-life as a result of that training. The very nature of the public safety mission is such that officers will be called upon to make split second decisions based on their training and experience, and further to react with trained responses to various stimuli. Officers will have to control violent individuals engaging in disorderly or life-threatening behavior. To train for this eventuality, the training must be realistic. Injuries are likely to occur in real life, and in training also, unless safety management is practiced.

Training officers should take heed from a celebrated training case known as *Saeger v. City of Woodland Park*. In short, an officer from Woodland Park attended basic police training at a nearby training academy. At that training academy, he was exposed to a training film that visually portrayed how NOT to do something. He later employed the technique he SAW incorrectly done causing the death of a citizen.

Training officers must never lose sight of the fact that 75% of all learning occurs through sight. Seeing something done incorrectly runs the risk of becoming learned as an incorrect response. Training officers should always use positive teaching methods and demonstrate correct performance rather than incorrect performance. The other lesson to be learned from the Saeger case is that the burden of the quality of the training belongs to the training academy and not necessarily to the employing agency. In short, training officers are responsible for the quality of training.

Another fundamental issue that permeates law enforcement and law enforcement training is that of proper documentation. In another celebrated case known as *Whiteley v. Warden*, a case that actually dealt with undocumented probable cause for an arrest warrant, the U.S. Supreme Court held that if it is to the agency's benefit and it is not documented, it did not happen. Thus, trainers must document all aspects of training or it will be ruled that the undocumented training or undocumented portions of the training did not occur. Training officers must be nearly fanatical when it comes to recording the training event. Undocumented training is no training!

Training officers must approach training with two goals in mind. One must be to provide the most realistic training possible and the other must be to do so with zero training injuries. Both are duties imposed by law. The Equal Employment Opportunity Commission (EEOC) requires that the incident of training must approximate the incident of encounter, thus realistic training. Tort law imposes a duty on training officers not to be negligent when it comes to the safety of those for whom they are responsible. Training officers can meet these goals, but whenever the two come in conflict, safety must always take priority.

To aid training officers in managing the training safety function, a ten-part training safety program is presented. Law enforcement has a long history of being reactive rather than proactive. Training officers must not wait for injuries to occur to employ this program. The program is proactive and is designed to work with any type of training program, but was intended for training in which the inherent risk of injury is high; firearms, physical training, defensive tactics, EVOC, etc.

 The first part of the ten-part program deals with what is called a **release of liability or hold-harmless agreement**. This document is nearly worthless to the training officers who engage in willful or wanton misconduct or gross negligence and thus causes an injury. The release does afford some protection in cases of minor or mere negligence on behalf of training officers when incorporated with other safety management practices. The release most certainly does not permit training officers to engage in dangerous training practices simply because the trainee has signed a waiver!

A proper written release of liability contains several key elements, many of which are common sense. The most often overlooked are the need to properly warn and the assumption of risk statement. The release should advise, in clear language, just what training activities will occur and further warn trainees with specific medical conditions to refrain from participation. Only when properly warned can a trainee intelligently assume the risk associated with that activity. Thus the statement that the trainee knows the risks and assumes those risks is important. This can be said in many ways, but must be said for the release to be effective.

A release is most important. It is not a complete defense, but an element in the total package of legal defenses. Many training officers don't feel a need to follow this practice thinking they train only officers in their own agencies and that workmen's compensation covers them. Workmen's compensation covers the injured employee up to certain prescribed limits and protects the employer from claims in excess of those limits. Some states permit third party claims in workmen's compensation cases. Simply put, the injured trainee could sue the training officer, yet they can't sue the employer! Training officers are well advised to determine the level of exposure under local law and to use release of liability forms whenever possible.

 The second part of the safety management program deals with **proper screening**. The trainee must be able to safely participate in the training activity. Some agencies have very good programs requiring annual medical exams and annual physical performance standards. In these cases, training officers can proceed with a fairly high confidence level that officers working active duty assignments can safely participate in most training activities. When these standards do not exist, and in some cases where entry level standards are minimal, the situation changes.

In cases where extremely strenuous activity is required, a physical examination may be required. Some programs may at least require a blood pressure check. The author recalls an instructor program where a blood pressure check revealed four trainees who were borderline emergency referrals and where one third of the class should have been on high blood pressure medication according to American Heart Association standards! If some kind of screening is not possible, then the training needs to be conducted at a level of physical activity where all participants can safely train.

If a trainee has a condition that enables that trainee to participate, but in a limited capacity or with some caution, a red-band marking system is recommended. If a trainee has a weak shoulder, the trainee would wear a red wristband on the injured or weak side. This alerts all participants in the class to exercise caution when working with this trainee.

 The third part of the program is **maintaining a safe training environment**. The training officer is responsible for the training environment that includes the facility and the equipment. There are two kinds of equipment, that which is furnished by the trainer and that which is furnished by the trainee. The training officer is responsible for both!

Training officers need to provide for adequate training space, ventilation, heating and cooling, water, telephone, first aid kit, sanitary facilities, etc. If at a range, an adequate backstop must be provided, safety zones must be kept clear, sharp objects on the ground must be removed, and if indoors, the ventilation system must be optimal. At driving courses, the surface must be inspected, the safety zones again must be clear, and emergency equipment must be nearby and fully functional.

Regarding equipment, safe training aids and props are a must. Dummy weapons are a must in handgun retention classes. In situations where simulation is required, various kinds of alternatives are available to make the training realistic yet safe.

Training officers should use the products that have been tested and are safe. Make absolutely certain no live ammo can get mixed in with "blanks" or cotton rounds. Inspect, double check, and triple check. Use rubber knives and not real ones. When using padded surfaces for striking, make certain the padding is not worn and that elbows, if exposed, are protected, etc. Make certain eye protection and hearing protection devices are used where necessary.

When trainees bring equipment to a class, the training officer must inspect it if it is to be used in the training. Firearms, impact weapons, holsters, etc. must be fully functional and not display any defects that could result in an injury. Court type shoes, not running shoes, should be used in defensive tactics or any type of training where lateral movement is required.

Training officers must develop checklists to assure that these conditions for safe training are met. It is the sure way to maintain a safe training environment and simultaneously fulfill the documentation requirement.

 Safety rules and procedures are the fourth segment of the program. They should be included in the lesson plan and presented to every class. The trainer must set the example and be the epitome of safety. Strict enforcement is a must and a notation should be made in the roster indicating the safety rules were covered.

 The fifth component is that of **adequate and proper physical preparation**. A basic rule of conditioning has to do with the specificity of conditioning concept. A person is only as strong or fit as what they do to get that way! The training officer must assess the training activity and prepare the trainee with a proper warm-up and stretching session specific to that activity.

Nearly every physical skills training session involves the rotation or bending of the lower back. In as much as lower back injuries account for the majority of disability claims, it makes good sense to always stretch this muscle group. Stretching improves performance and reduces the likelihood of injury.

 The sixth component is the **use of techniques and skills that are safe and effective**. Motor skills must be taught according to the proper and accepted sequence if they are to be safely taught. Speed and simulation work must be reserved for after proper form and technique have been developed through practice.

The training officer should proceed by introducing the skill, encouraging high repetition practice at a controlled speed, and finally introducing speed and simulation in what is called the perfection phase. Motor skill teaching is a most definitely a topic unto itself. Training officers engaged in motor skill teaching must learn to teach those skills properly.

The seventh component is probably the most important, certainly the most litigated claim in training injury cases. That component is **adequately supervising the class**. First and foremost, the training officer must be physically present. While that may sound simple, often is the case where the training officer slips out to handle a phone call, use the restroom, or perform some quick administrative task, all the while the class continues to practice. It is a training officer's duty to be present!

Supervision includes maintaining safe student to instructor ratios. For hands-on training classes where the risks are high, a 5 : 1 up to a 10 : 1 ratio is recommended. Some training commissions regulate this ratio and it is wise for the training officer to check. This ratio is necessary for both proper instruction and training safety.

The other aspects of supervision are monitoring for fatigue, injuries, unsafe conditions, etc. The training officer must maintain control and discipline of the class. Supervision of the class is one of the training officer's most challenging and most important duties.

 The eighth component deals with **injury management**. Even the safest training program devised can have an injury occur! Planning and preparation are paramount to manage this situation if it occurs. The training officer should identify an assistant to help administer first aid if necessary. Also first aid supplies should be on hand, plus the knowledge of how to activate the emergency medical system is a must.

Should an injury occur, the training officer must first stop any physical activity. The training officer can't supervise a class and attend to a training injury simultaneously. Administer first aid and summon medical assistance if indicated. The training officer should complete a training injury report form or some other suitable means of documenting the facts of the injury. This documents the cause and the facts. It demonstrates an open, caring attitude with regard to training safety, one that would shed a favorable light upon a training officer in the event of litigation.

 The ninth component is that of **instructor training and certification**. Simply put, training officers should limit teaching to areas in which they have expertise, experience, and credentials. While this sounds like common sense and not worthy of mention, there is plenty of documentation detailing cases where "trainers" taught topics in which they lacked proper training and credentials. The consequences ranged from agency embarrassment to litigation.

In addition to initially becoming "certified" in a topic area, training officers must maintain certification when required and stay abreast of new knowledge, equipment, and techniques in the particular field of expertise. Training officers should provide documentation of credentials to their agency, training commission, or other authoritative body with responsibility for training supervision. Finally all professional trainers should maintain affiliation in some professional association that fosters training and education in the topic area. That affiliation provides the forum for continuing growth and provides a network of peers and resources for the training officer.

 The final or tenth area is that of a **safety audit or review**. The key here is to have an objective, detached, third-person review of the training program. This can be done by committee, peer review, a fellow instructor, or a member of a POST Commission. This person observes and evaluates training programs as to safety. Recommendations are made in writing and is an excellent means of establishing a safety "credential" for a given program.

Additionally, course evaluations can solicit feedback relating to training safety. Improvements can be made based on this feedback and, if the responses rate the program as safe, this is another tremendous "credential" or "report card" establishing the program as "safe" in the event of future litigation.

Training officers have a tremendous responsibility in a law enforcement agency. It is most rewarding to see the fruits of the trainers' labors when a technique or skill taught saves a life or makes a case. Yet, for professional survival training officers must conduct the business of training in a manner designed to effectively deliver the material to be taught in a realistic manner and yet do so with the utmost concern for safety.

While one may never achieve the zero training injury goal, by applying the ten components of training safety presented here, training officers can reduce the likelihood of injury. Further, if training officers have followed these principles, fully documenting them and an injury occurs, they will not be regarded as uncaring and neglectful. Rather, they will be viewed as having demonstrated a sincere concern for the safety and well-being of their students. That is all anyone can ask.

Michael J. Carpenter

Mr. Michael J. Carpenter has worked in the field of law enforcement for almost twenty years with a municipal police department, state police agency, and as a state-wide police training specialist. As a retired sergeant, he has first-hand experience in dealing with the variety of issues that face a supervisor.

In addition to years of practical supervisory experience, Mr. Carpenter has presented supervisory/management training programs to police officers at seminars and in college classrooms, and has written numerous articles for law enforcement publications. He holds a Master's Degree in Criminal Justice and a Master's Degree in Teaching, and works as a police training consultant.

Chapter 6

The New Supervisor

by Michael J. Carpenter

Congratulations are in order to the police officer who gets promoted to the rank of sergeant. However, about the time that the last set of chevrons is sewn onto the uniform sleeves, many newly promoted sergeants start feeling a little . . . funny. This "funny" feeling is usually a combination of being nervous, happy, anxious, worried, and excited . . . all at the same time. Every new sergeant wonders how well they will handle this new role. Do "it" right and being a supervisor can be fun. Do "it" wrong and being a supervisor can be a nightmare.

In addition to carrying three extra stripes on their sleeves, new sergeants face a major transition in their lives. Sergeants are no longer employees; they are supervisors. They are no longer "grunts"; they are the "boss." They have more to worry about than themselves. They have to worry about "the shift." The bad news is that this is a major adjustment for most police officers, but the good news is that every other sergeant has gone through this transition . . . and survived!

Skills for Successful Supervisors

Most police officers are promoted to the rank of sergeant because they demonstrated both the technical skills and knowledge to perform as a police officer *and* the potential to be a good supervisor. There is an assumption that a good police officer will develop into a good supervisor. However, new sergeants cannot completely rely on the skills and knowledge of a police officer to solve the many problems they will face.

Each new sergeant develops a particular style that is built in part on personality, in part on individual work habits, in part on the influence of previous supervisors, and in part on trial and error. There is no "absolute right" or "absolute wrong" solution for many of the situations that new sergeants face. However, there are certain guidelines that successful supervisors follow in working with their people, and more important, in getting their people to work for them.

Learn as much as possible about subordinates. A big part of supervision is motivating, directing, and learning how to work through and with police officers. New sergeants should learn enough about each officer to be reasonably sure how each will react under different conditions, learn when to ask questions, learn when to talk and when to listen, and learn how to push the right buttons to get the best possible performance from each officer.

Learn how to make decisions. Effective sergeants *must* make decisions. Supervisors earn respect through *action*. Inaction and indecision lead to a void in the supervisory chain that will rapidly strip away respect, power, and authority. Becoming an effective supervisor requires the ability to make timely decisions based on available facts and circumstances. (Sometimes decisions must be made on *available* facts, not *all* the facts.) The worst decision to make is not to make a decision.

Learn how to give orders. Effective sergeants seldom need to give a direct command to their police officers. Research shows that workers have higher respect for a boss, and will cooperate more willingly, if "requests" are made rather than "orders." Generally speaking, a request carries the same weight and authority as an order, but gives the impression that workers have some freedom in decisions.

"Participatory management" is a recent buzz word in management circles, but all it really means is that employees will work harder when they have a chance, or a perceived chance, to participate in the decision making process. There is nothing wrong with saying, ". . . will you try . . ." or " . . . won't you please . . . " or " . . . can I count on you?"

Learn how to praise and reprimand. There is an easy rule for new supervisors to remember: Praise subordinates frequently in public and reprimand subordinates infrequently in private. One of the most popular management books of the 1980's was *The One Minute Manager*, written by Kenneth H. Blanchard and Spencer Johnson that deals very well with praising and reprimanding, and should be *must* reading for every supervisor.

 Learn to avoid mediocrity. Sooner or later, every sergeant faces the problem of dealing with a police officer who is either disruptive, fails to perform adequately, or demonstrates some other form of inappropriate behavior. Avoiding personnel problems is the sign of a poor supervisor. There may be many reasons for inefficiency on the part of a subordinate, but there is seldom an excuse for a supervisor who fails to deal with unsatisfactory performance promptly and effectively.

Although no one gives 100% all the time, new sergeants should set high standards in what they expect from their people. Mediocre supervisors usually *expect and get* mediocre work from their officers. Mediocre supervisors usually have mediocre subordinates and supervisors with high expectations usually have subordinates with high expectations.[1]

Take Care of Management, Subordinates, and Yourself

New sergeants have to shift mental gears. They must think differently because they no longer live in the "I World." The "I World" is for police officers who drive to work each day saying, "What do *I* need to do to keep the sergeant off *my* back?" "How many tickets do *I* need this month?" "Do *I* really need to write a report for this complaint?" "How can *I* cover *my* backside?"

New sergeants must leave the "I World" because they have to take care of three separate groups of people:

☐ their subordinates

☐ their superiors

☐ themselves

All of these groups are equally important and all demand a certain amount of time and attention. Ignore or mistreat any of these groups and new sergeants will immediately start their supervisory careers with one strike against them.

The police officers new sergeants are responsible for are *very* important. The most valuable tool that new supervisors can possess is "people skills." How well a sergeant gets along with the shift, how much they respect those new stripes, how much they *want* to work, depends on how they are treated as *people*, not as *workers*. If new sergeants don't have people skills, they need to get some quick! Police officers can make new sergeants look *very good* or *very bad.*

Communication with subordinates is critical for the success of new supervisors. This involves three different skills:

☐   talking

☐   listening

☐   getting feedback

Effective communication is perhaps the quickest and easiest way of showing the officers that their new boss cares. It is the sergeants' responsibility to build long-lasting and strong relationships with their subordinates. The first step is to show them that the boss is receptive by being willing and able to communicate. New sergeants must take the first step . . . and second and third step if necessary to develop strong relationships.

Sometimes new stripes inflate egos. New sergeants have been known to have "heavy stripes." They expect people to step aside when they walk into a room. "I'm never going to be like *that* when I get promoted . . . that'll never happen to me!" Don't bet on it! New sergeants can guard against this "power trip" with a strong dose of humility. Start by asking questions. This will not take away authority or power.

A new promotion means that a new supervisor has a lot to learn, especially if it involves a transfer to a new location, onto a new shift, or getting a new assignment. By asking questions, sergeants can find out their strengths (use them) and their weaknesses (work on them). They may also find out their employees strengths (use them) and weaknesses (retrain or work around them). No one is good at everything.

Good supervisors should learn enough about their subordinates to find out who is *weak* in a particular area, but supervisors should *not* use this weakness against them; should *not* hold it like an ace up a sleeve; and should *not* ridicule or belittle them. This will guarantee an enemy for life, and no one, especially a new sergeant can afford that!

If new sergeants use their strengths and their employees strengths, they will be successful. If they plan to improve their weaknesses and their employees weaknesses, they will also be successful.

The number one priority of new sergeants should be to build and maintain strong, positive, and productive relationships with each employee. Put this on top of the list! New super-visors cannot succeed if their employees aren't behind them. Police officers will not stand behind a sergeant they don't respect. Respect cannot be bought, but it can be earned!

 New sergeants must also work with management. The most important rule to remember is, be loyal to the boss. There may be disagreements between management and supervisors with a particular policy or a decision, but supervisors must show loyalty when explaining it to the officers. If sergeants show a negative attitude when explaining a new policy, the officers will show a negative attitude when, or if, they carry it out.

Unless the lieutenant demands immediate changes, new sergeants should not try any "new broom" techniques. Until this transition becomes comfortable, new supervisors should make every effort to keep things running as normal as possible while starting to build strong relationships with each subordinate. Buy some time until the lieutenant can give a better understanding of expectations. Changes can always be made later, but successful changes will only be made if solid relationships are built early.

Keep in mind that a boss needs good supervisors as much as good supervisors need a good boss. Management's job is to get things done, and management knows that good supervisors are the key to getting things done. New sergeants must remember to treat the boss fairly, and never embarrass them either intentionally or accidentally. One very important rule about bosses: They want to know what is going on, and they do *not* like surprises. Keep them informed.

New sergeants have to learn how to satisfy both their boss and their subordinates. As a supervisor, it is important to keep the boss happy. The transition to being a successful supervisor will be very difficult without the support of management. However, sergeants need to protect their subordinates also. Part of being a supervisor is being a buffer between two very important groups of people.

Part of the new role involves making the police officer's job *easier*, not harder. Sergeants should keep the "negatives" to a minimum, expect some mistakes, stand up for the officers if false accusations are made, praise subordinates in front of others, BUT don't let employees ruin a good working relationship with the boss.

 New sergeants must learn to help themselves. This begins by learning to work with others. By sharing time, resources, and ideas, new sergeants will become valuable and respected. Good supervisors work with subordinates to improve their skills, work with management to make them look good, and work with fellow supervisors in solving their problems. Smart supervisors won't expect anything back, but some time in the future they will need *and get* help from these people.

Good supervisors should be realistic about themselves and others. They don't make excuses about mistakes; they state the facts, accept the blame, and *learn* from their mistakes. Bosses "expect" mistakes, especially from new sergeants. They may not like mistakes or want mistakes, but they accept them.

Also, smart sergeants will "expect" mistakes from their subordinates. Police officers who don't make mistakes don't do anything! Smart sergeants will take positive corrective action so mistakes are not repeated, but they won't "destroy" their subordinates by embarrassing them, name calling, using negative body language, or ignoring a "weakness." Intentionally ridiculing or belittling a subordinate will make an enemy for life.

New sergeants should set goals for themselves, both short-term and long-term. How can they get better? Where will they be in five or ten years? Effective supervision needs constant attention, and effective supervisors are continually trying to improve themselves.

If a police department cannot or will not spend the money or time on supervisory training, then smart supervisors will spend their own money and invest their own time. There are many seminars, videos, paperback books, or college courses available to improve the skills of supervisors. Successful supervisors aren't afraid to invest in themselves. If new supervisors do not progress, they will regress.

Common Mistakes of New Supervisors

New supervisors are suddenly responsible for the activities and performance of others. The role of sergeants is less defined, there is more room for discretion, and there isn't always going to be an absolute right or absolute wrong answer.

Sometimes new sergeants try too hard and sometimes they don't try hard enough. New sergeants will make mistakes and should plan on them! Smart supervisors learn from their mistakes, analyze them, dissect them, reconstruct them, then . . . DO NOT REPEAT THEM!

Invariably, new sergeants make mistakes; whether through a lack of preparation, lack of training, or lack of common sense. There is often a pattern to the types of mistakes made by new supervisors. Some of the most common mistakes new supervisors make include:

- ❏ making changes immediately after promotion

- ❏ failing to develop people skills

- ❏ trying to be one of the guys

- ❏ failing to delegate

- ❏ being inconsistent in handling subordinates

- ❏ not talking to or listening to subordinates

- ❏ failing to motivate their people

- ❏ not keeping their boss informed

- ❏ making serious administrative errors by not getting enough information from their boss about their expectations

- ❏ failing to effectively use time

With proper training, a desire to treat people fair, and a good dose of common sense, new sergeants can avoid these mistakes during their adjustment and transition to wearing the new stripes. New supervisors can avoid many problems by remembering what **S-U-P-E-R-V-I-S-I-O-N** stands for. A successful supervisor:

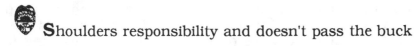 **S**houlders responsibility and doesn't pass the buck

Understands people . . . is fair but firm as a boss

Plans on improving themselves and their subordinates

Enforces all regulations . . . sets a good example

 Respects subordinates . . . builds the team up, doesn't tear down

 Visualizes problems . . . plans and anticipates

 Inspires confidence . . . learns to lead and develops morale

 Sells ideas . . . gets cooperation from subordinates in implementing change

 Instructs clearly . . . realizes that some mistakes are caused by their own poor communication skills

 Originates ideas . . . isn't afraid to be creative or try new ideas

 Notices performance . . . gives credit where due

Contributed by: *George Terry, Office of Management and Control*

Conclusion

There is no magic formula to becoming a good supervisor. There is no 800-number to call, there is no cassette to learn supervisory skills in 10 days or get your money back, and there is no magic potion to get a "quick-fix" cure over the weekend. Learning to be a good supervisor involves a combination of experience, common sense, and a willingness to learn. It is a learning process that must continually be worked on.

New supervisors have been compared to new parents . . . neither think they're really ready, they're never quite sure what the job is about, and they're never sure how good they're going to be . . . but if new sergeants (or new parents) aren't afraid to ask for help, are flexible, and are willing to accept new challenges . . . they do fine!

Footnotes

[1] William VanDersal, *The Successful Supervisor* (New York: Harper and Row, 1982), 39-51.

Dr. James T. Chandler

Dr. James T. Chandler is an individual contractor in the areas of training, seminar presentation, writing, speaking, and personnel management consultation. His primary focus is on human relations in law enforcement and corrections. He also conducts assessments for child and family service organizations.

Dr. Chandler achieved his Bachelor's and Master's Degrees in Psychology at Wayne State University in Detroit, Michigan, and his Ph.D. in Program Design in Community Mental Health at Holy Cross College in Merrill, Wisconsin. He is certified by the National Academy of Certified Clinical Mental Health Counselors.

Dr. Chandler's occupational history is quite long and involved. His last full-time assignment was as Chief State Police Psychologist for the Illinois Department of State Police, where he inaugurated and directed the Office of Psychological Services.

"Doc" is a retired Commander in the United States Naval Reserve, where he is a Surface Warfare Officer.

Chapter 7

The Psychology of Supervision

by Dr. James T. Chandler

For purposes of this chapter, let us assume all supervisors to be depicted have had the necessary supervisory/management courses, and comprehend all the necessary theories, approaches, and "buzzwords."

Thus, these individuals have the ability to drop the names of current organizational behavior and management gurus with aplomb. You can find the latest supervisory texts on their shelves. Yet, why do we know they can still be lousy supervisors?

In this chapter, we focus on the ability of supervisors to analyze, predict, and control their behavior and that of their subordinates with the use of practical psychology. Without this knowledge and ability, successful supervisory experience becomes less likely.

This author's Thesaurus defines supervision as "the function or duty of watching or guarding for the sake of proper direction or control." However, without adequate knowledge of the psychology of supervision, "watching or guarding" can amount to paranoia, and misguided "direction or control" can lead to administrative chaos.

"Paranoid" supervisors spend much of their time watching for negatives, and this approach is often contagious. Subordinates "pass it on," and the focus of the organization turns to seeking weaknesses, rather than strengths.

The whole organization soon becomes a "paranoid palace." So many people are posted to the battlements to look for "danger" that few are left to carry out vital projects. Work also suffers because paranoid supervisors cannot delegate.

Their approach to supervision is, "You'll have to prove yourself first, and then I'll give you a free hand." However, these supervisors are psychologically incapable of trusting anyone.

Other supervisors have a need, perhaps as a result of personality traits, to seek change for change's sake. They are easily bored with routine, and are prone to jump to fads. Every time they return from a conference, a new program is rushed into place. Each new and popularly-acclaimed management book is worshiped in turn.

However, such supervisors do not allow programs to remain in place long enough to become effective, and subordinates begin to subtly or directly challenge any new program. "Direction and control" have thus deteriorated into misdirection and lack of control.

What's the point of depicting these misguided supervisors? Well, unless you are familiar with the concept of the paranoid personality, how are you to correct the problem? Would you recognize this behavior in yourself, or could the psychological concept of denial interfere with your self-evaluation?

Would you know, for example, to concentrate on empathy training with paranoid individuals? Are you aware this would cause them to focus more on how they hurt others, and less on how others are hurting them? For that matter, are you familiar with the most successful ways to conduct empathy training?

The point is that there is benefit in obtaining practical knowledge of, and training in, psychology, especially the psychology of supervision. Do not make the mistake of thinking supervisory psychology is "just good common sense." We are too often the victims of our past, ineffectively modeling our behavior after supervisors from very different settings and eras.

What do you confidently know about your own personality? Are you a "tough-minded" individual working with primarily "tender-minded" subordinates? What does psychology predict as to the odds of you changing your approach, or of them altering theirs? Just what is possible in this situation? Will you simply be reactive, or take a proactive stance by planning a psychologically-based strategy?

Proper supervision implies gentle pressure, relentlessly applied. Supervisors who are overly-relentless usually fail to achieve a gentle touch. Conversely, too-gentle supervisors lack the ability to be relentless when this approach is necessary. Somewhere in between these extremes lies success. The ability to spout good organizational development theory does nothing to overcome maladaptive personality traits.

How do we evaluate and train supervisors to achieve this balanced approach? Certainly not by the mechanical application of some current management guru's popular approach. What fits your psychology – your view of the world – just may not fit the group or individual psychology of your subordinates.

It is not enough to say, "I'm the boss, and they'll just have to conform." If the golden days of this approach ever existed, they are long-gone now. As a retired naval officer, the writer is not even sure that approach is still valid in today's military services.

While the supervisor is not required to coddle subordinates, an understanding of their viewpoint, psyche, and motivation is necessary for success in today's world.

However, all-too-many supervisory training courses focus on paperwork, organizational charts, or highly structured approaches. There is often a mechanical application of devices developed by psy-

chologists (e.g., personality or supervisory inventories), without sufficient training to evaluate or apply them properly.

"Feely-touchy" approaches, "let it all hang out" group discussions, and other team-building approaches leading to negative results
in law enforcement agencies have been conducted by those who failed
to properly assess the psychological readiness and ability of the average law enforcement officer to accept them.

I am not suggesting successful supervisors obtain a Master's Degree in Clinical Psychology. I am concerned, however, that we in law
enforcement carry out less than 20 percent of our supervisory training
in the specific area containing most of our problems: a lack of practical knowledge of human psychology.

For example, more than 80 percent of local law enforcement
field time is devoted to helping citizens, which usually falls into:

- ❑ Dispute management (family, landlord-tenant, business)
- ❑ Victim management/citizen assistance
- ❑ Response to the mentally ill or handicapped
- ❑ Response to situations involving angry individuals.

Are supervisory problems resulting from these citizen contacts
likely to result from the improper application of a law, or from a lack
of knowledge of rules and regulations? No, it is usually that while an
enforcement action was carried out within the letter of the law by an
officer, his or her psychological approach needlessly escalated the situation.

The author recently reviewed an outline of lesson plans for a
police academy. In this 400-hour course, a total of two hours were devoted to responding to the mentally ill and handicapped, while the
same amount of time was given to enforcement of a seat belt law. Does
that tell you something?

How much time do we spend, for example, on demanding
common courtesy both on the street and within the department? For
that matter, how much specific training is conducted to promote
courteous behavior by supervisors toward subordinates? Do we really
understand the power of the psychological concept of role modeling?

Adequate knowledge of the psychology of courtesy (positive empathy) by a supervisor could do much to reduce the amount of
administrative time spent in answering those, "He treated me like a
dog," complaints.

Knowledge of psychology also allows supervisors to know the
difference between what should be, and what can be. For example, you
may feel participant management in law enforcement is the way to go.
As a retired naval officer and law enforcement psychologist, I would
warn against the fallacy of thinking participant management techniques will (or even should) be universally useful in a semi-military,
crisis-oriented setting.

What makes theoretical and logical sense to managers or supervisors can be erroneous in terms of the current group psychology of a department. For example, some believe the law enforcement profession would be better served if it dropped the semi-military approach.

They propose that a simple changing of position designations (like Chief to Director), the dropping of military-like titles (e.g., Sergeant to Mister), the elimination of uniforms, or the elimination of command levels in a law enforcement agency are valid solutions to law enforcement management difficulties.

The psychology of most police departments would predict the Chief would still be "Chief" to a street officer, whether renamed "Director," "Mister," or even "Big Ed." We also know many officers entered the profession primarily because it *is* semi-military, and would feel a loss without some military flavor.

It is naive to fail to recognize the psychological reality that organizations *must* have a means to recognize achievement and authority, and that individuals are not, and seldom can be, equal. Even in liberal academic circles, such titles as "Doctor," "Dean," "Chancellor," "President," and "Professor" are used to show achievement, status, and authority.

In the participative style, each person is involved in matters affecting him or her, and the organization "cares" about personal needs. In terms of the psychology of the situation, the participative style can certainly lead to increased motivation and communication and can encourage team approaches.

Psychology also would warn, because of a resultant broader distribution of views, that inaction, vacillation, and confusion may occur with this approach. Participative management takes time. Thus, emergency situations and quick-response modes may not be adaptable (in the psychological sense) to the participative management approach.

The law enforcement supervisor must be clear on areas where a strict, autocratic, military model is necessary for the psychological comfort of subordinates. With the autocratic approach, decisions are made quickly and uniformity is insured. Would a tactical response team buy a participative management approach? We should hope not.

There is no "quick fix" or "miracle pill" in the management and supervision of people possessing a variety of personalities and experiences. The supervisor can learn to assess each subordinate's psychological approach to life, and predict the best approach to that individual to achieve acceptance of new approaches.

The author finds individuals can be categorized into at least nine personality types – psychological approaches to life. How, then, can a supervisor state, "I treat all my people equally." With a knowledge of psychology, we can treat individuals fairly, but hardly "equally." For that matter, how can one theoretical management approach fit the needs of all subordinates?

Supervisors who learn proper human relations skills not only function more effectively, but accomplish tasks in a shorter time. While a successful supervisor must learn to "read" each subordinate, a more introverted supervisor must learn a different approach than an extroverted one.

"Accurate empathy," for example, is difficult to achieve by the inner-directed individual. However, with the proper training program, a reasonable degree of empathic ability can be achieved in even the highly introverted supervisor.

The ability to be warm to subordinates without giving in to over-protection is a problem with the outer-directed supervisor. Being kind-hearted for these personality types is easy, but possessiveness is often their supervisory downfall.

"Non-possessive warmth" requires a reasonable degree of personal distance be maintained between supervisor and subordinate. With a proper training program, a reasonable degree of "warmth at a healthy distance" can be achieved in even the highly extroverted supervisor.

All good supervisors are positive models, and they honestly portray "genuineness." "Do as I say, and not as I do" is not their approach. However, the law enforcement environment too often leads to a lack of genuineness (e.g., "the cop face" or "proper military bearing") which does much to insure genuineness is hard to achieve. Knowledge of the psychology of body language is thus essential to good supervision.

Adequate skill in two-way communication is another requirement for the successful supervisor. However, if the message is, "I send well, and I receive well, so it must be your problem," the state of "valid communications" can not be achieved. In law enforcement, while the author agrees we should train our people to be confident, we should not train to the point of achieving foolish cockiness.

Have you had practical training in the psychology of motivation? Are you aware that most efforts to improve the job environment (so-called hygiene factors) are only pain relievers? Do you know true motivation factors involve changes in job content (so-called reward producers)?

Good supervisors understand the psychology of motivation and leadership. Their subordinates are not treated as a means of production, but as people. Instead of assigning all tasks, the good supervisor understands the psychology of the situation requires that most tasks be initiated by the workers themselves.

In summary, when this writer uses the term "psychology of supervision," it includes much more than the usual organizational or management psychology approaches. It includes knowledge and skills about clinical, group, and personality psychology in addition.

Why not train supervisors to "diagnose" and "treat" human behavior? We train law enforcement officers to become EMT's without becoming concerned they will practice brain surgery. Law enforcement supervisors can be educated and trained in the analysis of the personality of subordinates without running the risk of them becoming "junior shrinks." With that knowledge, the best method of working with a subordinate individual can be achieved.

Thomas Christenberry

Mr. Thomas Christenberry is currently a Supervisory Special Agent (SSA), assigned to the Education/Communications Arts Unit at the FBI Academy in Quantico, Virginia.

SSA Christenberry entered on duty with the FBI in January 1978. He was assigned to the Minneapolis and New York Field Divisions prior to his current assignment at the FBI Academy.

SSA Christenberry teaches a course entitled, "Mass Media and the Police" at the FBI Academy. In addition, he is the host of TV show entitled "Viewpoints from the FBI Academy" which is shown on the Law Enforcement Television Network (LETN) once a month.

SSA Christenberry earned a Bachelor of Arts degree in Social Studies from Purdue University in West Lafayette, IN and a Master of Science degree in Educational Administration from Butler University in Indianapolis, IN.

Chapter 8

Dealing With the Media

by Thomas Christenberry

Historical Perspective

"Congress shall make no law respecting an establishment of religion, or prohibiting the free exercise thereof; or abridging the freedom of speech or of the press; or the right of the people peaceably to assemble, and to petition the government for redress of grievances."[1]

The First Amendment to the United States Constitution, ratified in 1791, is simple and direct. Congress (government) can't enact legislation "abridging the freedom of speech or of the press." These simple words are clear, but for society, which includes politicians, judges, law enforcement officers, citizens, and even the press, the meaning can be difficult to understand.

This chapter is designed to help the law enforcement supervisor understand freedom of the press and how to deal successfully with the media. To deal with the press, we must first look at where the press views its birth, the First Amendment to the U.S. Constitution. This chapter will also offer suggestions on how to deal successfully with the media.

Historically, the U.S. Constitution, ratified in 1787, was written by our founding fathers to organize its Colony-States into a unified government of the people. This was not an easy proposition. The War of Independence had separated the colonists into two groups: those loyal to the crown of England and those loyal to the emerging America. The early media, "Printers, publishers, and editors were important influences in preparing the public for revolution and in maintaining the fighting spirit during the War of Independence."[2]

Prior to the ratification of the Constitution in 1789, the press, along with intellectuals, philosophers, and social reformers, tended to associate with the Anti-Federalist faction.[3] This might point to the early liberal indoctrination of the press.

The Federalists wanted to govern the new nation with a mandate from the people. They wanted a strong central government elected by the people. The Anti-Federalists basically feared a strong central government because of the crown tradition. They saw the possibility of abuse from a strong central government. The press, which had helped fuel the revolution with print, would become the "watchdog" of this new emerging government.

The writers of the Constitution, men like Thomas Jefferson, James Madison, and James Monroe, saw the importance of free speech and free press. These concepts were incorporated into the First Amendment of the U.S. Constitution. Few have debated what the First Amendment said, "Congress shall make no law . . . abridging the freedom of speech or of the press . . . ;" they have debated over what freedom means. Certainly, the founding fathers didn't anticipate what society would be like in the last decade of the 20th century.

As America grew and suffered the pains of maturity throughout the 19th century and the first half of the 20th century, the press went through its growing pains too. In every major historical event from the War of 1812 to the rapid expansion of the West, the rise of sectionalism, the Civil War in 1865, the Industrial Revolution, World Wars I and II, and Roosevelt's "New Deal," the press played a significant role.

Prior to 1920 and the radio, the print journalist had a monopoly on disseminating information. Radio changed the ways in which information was reported. Radio became broadcast journalism. Citizens could not only read about the news, but now they could also hear about it.

In 1950, television entered the broadcast journalism field, and this electronic medium greatly affected how information was communicated to the people. Remember, that the proponents of free speech and free press had stated 200 years earlier that for citizens to make an informed decision in self-government, they must have access to information. Hence, the role of the press is to provide that information. Have you ever heard the phrase, "The people have a right to know."

Larry Sabato's book, *Feeding Frenzy: How Attack Journalism Has Transformed American Politics*, looked to the period 1966-1974 as a period of "watchdog" journalism. Sabato said, "Reporters scrutinized and checked the behavior of political elites by undertaking independent investigations into statements made by public officials."[4]

During this period, law enforcement agencies came under the media microscope. The media had explored the Vietnam War Effort. They had to cover civil rights marches in the South, and in 1968, the Democratic National Convention in Chicago, Illinois. Television brought the scenes of law enforcement tactics and force into view for all Americans to see.

The violence and the law enforcement reaction, and in some cases overreaction, were displayed on the television set. Reporters, like Dan Rather and others, were becoming personalities because of their coverage of the war, the protests, and the riots. Who was at fault? In this period of time which Sabato called the "watchdog" period, law enforcement agencies began to really look internally at the problems and how to correct them.

Law enforcement agencies began to restructure their training programs. What were the goals of the agency? What did it take to be a law enforcement officer? Law enforcement agencies developed extensive job descriptions for the law enforcement officer. Instructional objectives were written to meet the needs of the job description, and training academies were enhanced to meet the educational requirements.

The role of the law enforcement supervisor was identified as a critical part of the law enforcement agency. One element of law enforcement supervision is dealing with the media. What can you, the supervisor, do to survive the media? There are two important criteria when discussing media survival:

☐ you must have a reason for being involved with the media

☐ you must be prepared

Criteria: Dealing With the Media

What do we mean by having a reason for being involved with the media? The law enforcement supervisor must ask the following questions. Why is the media talking to me? What do I have that the media needs? The mere fact that you are a law enforcement supervisor answers both questions.

To understand why, it's important to know that law enforcement is news. Newspapers, televisions, and the radio on a daily basis carry stories about law enforcement work. The rapist that has attacked several young women, the gangs that have been involved with numerous drive-by shootings, the fourteen-car accident on a fog-covered interstate, the law enforcement officer killed in the line of duty, the failure of a law enforcement agency to hire qualified women and minorities, and the law enforcement officer who ran into a burning building to rescue two young children are all news items. Why?

These incidents are timely, controversial, impact the community, and are about human nature. They constitute news. People want to know! The media is the vehicle by which the information is communicated.

As with the news items mentioned above, why would you, the supervisor, want or have a reason to deal with the media? Let's say the community is concerned about a rapist prowling the neighborhood. Law enforcement must tell the community about the steps being taken to apprehend this individual. This is a good reason to deal with the media. The accident on a fog-covered interstate highway; citizens will want and need to know about the incident.

Have you ever wondered why there are so many traffic reports on the radio and even the television? Many law enforcement officers have gained instant stardom for being the "eye in the sky." This is a good reason to deal with the media.

Let's take the law enforcement officer killed in the line of duty. In May 1991, a well-liked and respected Midwest law enforcement officer was killed while pursuing a stolen car. The funeral was enormous, with hundreds local, state, and federal law enforcement officers from several states attending. The funeral procession was carried by all the local stations. The media brought the death of the law enforcement officer and the funeral procession into everybody's home that day. The citizens of the community needed to be involved with this tragic incident. This is a good reason to deal with the media.

The law enforcement agency has resisted change and continues not to hire women and minorities, or if they do hire from these groups, they are not promoted in the ranks of the agency. This is controversy; it impacts the community. The media also communicates the inequality of the agency to the home of the citizens. This is a good reason to deal with the media.

In New York City, there was a large billboard on one of the major arteries crossing the city that portrayed a white law enforcement officer carrying a small black child out of a burning building. The caption read, "Cops Care." There is a good reason to deal with the media.

The situations described above fall into two categories. The first is the "public's right to know," in which the media has played an important role and the second is, law enforcement's need to promote its own good image.

In recent years, the "public's right to know" has been a banner call of the media. It is unknown whether the media has somehow elevated itself to a special plateau of privilege or is acting purely as the general public's representative.

The First Amendment to the U.S. Constitution doesn't address or guarantee the "public's right to know." The Supreme Court, however, has decided several court cases which have outlined the media's access to news as it relates to law enforcement.

One such case was *Branzburg v. Hayes* in 1972.[5] The Court ruled that "News gathering is not without its First Amendment protections."[6] The Court went on to rule that the media does not have a constitutional right under the First Amendment to demand that news be provided to them. The Court, in addition, added that the media, "newsmen have no constitutional right to access to the scenes of crime or disaster when the general public is excluded."[7]

The second category for dealing with the media involves promoting the good image of the agency. Law enforcement has traditionally not promoted itself to the public through media encoun-ters. But the media can be an effective tool for law enforcement.

Several years ago, the oil tanker Exxon Valdez ran aground in Alaska. The leaking oil caused tremendous damages to the environment and to the way of life for people living in that region. Exxon Corporation had to accept responsibility for the actions of the ship's Captain and the damage caused by the leaking oil. Exxon sent its top executives to Alaska almost immediately to deal with the crisis and to deal with the media.

Exxon Corporation, in the time of severe crisis, had to explain to Alaskans and to the rest of the world what had happened and how Exxon would take care of the damage. Exxon was doing damage control. Exxon had to put forth the positive image of the company. The best way to do this was to deal with the media. It cost Exxon millions of dollars to correct the damage caused by their ship, but in the long run, the corporation survived, and people are still buying Exxon products.

Law enforcement can learn a valuable lesson from the Exxon disaster. Even in bad times, a law enforcement agency must always promote a positive image. The media can be an effective tool during tough times, but let us not forget the good times. Good times provide an excellent opportunity to promote the law enforcement agency.

Earlier, the question was posed, "What can you, the supervisor, do to survive the media?" Two important criteria were mentioned: one, you must have a reason for dealing with the media and, two, you must prepare. Let's address preparation. A coach wouldn't take his or her team into the championship game without preparation. A general wouldn't lead his or her men into a battle without a plan of action. A law enforcement supervisor should not deal with the media without preparing for it.

How do you prepare for the media? The media wants information from you, the law enforcement supervisor. Why? Ask yourself, "Why me and not someone else?" The answer is that you are the media representative for the agency or you are the supervisor of the law enforcement officers involved with the case.

Next, what can the media be told about a given situation? The best sources of information are your peers, and possibly, the investigator involved with the particular case. Talk to those individuals and determine what you can disseminate to the media. A good technique is to develop as many questions as possible about the media interest. Probably your fellow law enforcement officers will ask most of the media's questions. After you all determine the questions, then figure out the answers. Answer the questions several different ways, always staying consistent with agency guidelines.

If the law enforcement supervisor doesn't have a reason for dealing with the media and isn't prepared for dealing with the media, then the law enforcement supervisor is susceptible to the various media traps.

Media Traps

As we have discussed, having a reason for dealing with the media and preparing for the media are two essential criteria for being involved with the media. What happens when those two essential criteria are not there? The answer is that you lack control, an extremely important factor when dealing with the media. You can't control the media and the questions they ask, but you can control yourself. Lacking control makes you susceptible to the following media traps: "dead air," "big word," "off-the topic," "editorial," "commercial," "post-conclusion," "interruptions," and "distractions."

"Dead Air" occurs when the reporter stops talking and the guest doesn't talk either. Whose responsibility is it to fill the dead air? Most people would feel that it is the responsibility of the interviewer or the host of the TV or radio show. Sometimes the host asks a question and the guest responds with only a short answer. The host might take the opportunity to let the guest sit and sweat.

Prepared guests, ones with a reason for dealing with the media, should use the opportunity to "bridge" back to their original message. In any media encounter, the guest should bring with them several 30-40 second spot messages that they have memorized. These messages should focus on why they are there and on positive attributes of the law enforcement agency. "Bridging" effectively returns the focus of the interview to what the law enforcement supervisor wants to discuss. This technique can often turn a negative situation into a positive one.

The second trap is the **"Big Word."** Law enforcement supervisors often feel that not knowing something is somehow wrong or a sign of ignorance; it is neither. Supervisors can't be expected to know everything. Actually, it may be a sign of good judgment for a supervisor to admit when something isn't known. The media will use words, terms, or expressions that are unfamiliar. If you find a word, term, or expression unfamiliar, ask for an explanation.

Ignorance comes out more if you try to bluff your way through an explanation. For example, during a recent training exercise, a police chief was asked, "Chief, it has been said that your new young recruits coming out of the academy have a very cavalier attitude toward the public trust; is it true?" The chief responded, "Yes, they do, and in fact, we teach that at the academy." The chief was obviously confused about the meaning of "cavalier." Webster's Ninth New Collegiate Dictionary defines "cavalier" as "marked by or given to offhand dismissal of important matters."[8] When you don't know ask! As a general rule, the media doesn't try to trick you, but if it happens, you are at their mercy.

The **"Off-the-Topic"** trap is another to watch for when dealing with the media. Remember to have a reason for dealing with the media and be prepared. The media or press will often try to change the topic of discussion. The media has an agenda that they want to cover, and sometimes they can hide the agenda from you, the law enforcement supervisor.

The important lesson here is that you should discuss the prearranged topics for which you have prepared. Stick to those topics! Use the "bridge" technique to bring the media back on track.

The trap is that as you venture into unprepared topics, the reporter can get a piece of information that you didn't want to discuss. To avoid this trap, you might respond, "That topic (or question) is important, but I'm not in a position to discuss it at this time."

A good example of the successful handling of the "off-the-topic" trap occurred in 1987, when then Vice-President George Bush appeared on the CBS Evening News with Dan Rather. The appearance was live and unedited with Rather in the CBS studio in New York and Bush in his office. Before the interview, CBS aired a long segment on Bush's alleged involvement in the Iran-Contra Affair.

Vice-President Bush went on the offense and stated that CBS had misled him as to the purpose of the interview. Bush stated that he thought he was there to talk about why he wanted to be President and why a large percentage of Americans wanted him to be President. Bush used the "bridge" technique to get back to his prepared message. This technique can work for law enforcement supervisors too.

Have you ever watched a TV anchor make an opening statement about the upcoming news story or interview? This opening statement can be the **"Editorial"** trap. The opening statement, or "lead," usually indicates the tone or focus of the news story or interview.

After running the news story or the interview the TV anchor can't help but make a closing statement or editorial comment about what just happened. This editorial comment can reflect the opinion of the anchor or of the news agency. If the opening statement or the editorial conclusion is incorrect or misleading, the law enforcement supervisor must correct the error or ambiguity.

Letting the information stand without comment says that the information might be accurate. Remember, many people watch or listen to what is being said, and their perception is important. In media, the perception of what is read, heard, and seen can mean more than the facts.

What happens when you appear on a television talk show or a radio call-in show and the studio breaks for a commercial? There is a tendency to relax because you think you are off the air. This is the **"Commercial"** trap. You can avoid this trap by following a simple rule (solution): the camera is always "on" and the microphone is always "live."

Think of the situation in which a well-known person has made a comment or done something in public that the media has caught on camera or tape. For example, President Reagan made a joke on his five-minute weekly radio show about "beginning to bomb Russia in five minutes," hardly a statement he wanted broadcast.

Media outlets put out tapes, called "Tapes of Wrath," that contain example after example of mistakes made by well-known people and media people who forgot that the camera is always on and the microphone is always live.

Finally, don't say or do anything that you are not prepared to read about in the newspapers, hear on radio, or see on television.

The **"Post-Conclusion"** trap is similar to the previous trap. This trap can occur during an electronic (television and radio) or a print (newspaper, magazine, etc.) interview. The reporter has finished the interview. It is time to leave. Don't say or do anything that you were not prepared to do when the interview was live. You take your chances with off-the-record comments.

Roger Ailes, media adviser to U.S. Presidents, said in his book, *You Are The Message*, that the only words that are truly off-the-record are those never spoken.9 Remember the rules, the camera is always "on" and the microphone is always "live."

During an interview, with the electronic or print media, you may find yourself being constantly interrupted by the media. This is the next media trap, **"Interruptions."** This trap is difficult to identify because people always interrupt other people.

The press or media usually has a list of questions that they want to ask the law enforcement supervisor. They have their own agenda that they convey with their questions. For example, many times throughout an interview a reporter will interrupt the guest, perhaps because the guest's answer is too long for the air time or the reporter just wants to move to another topic.

However, law enforcement supervisors must insist on completing their answers to the original questions. The supervisor can be at fault if his or her answer is "long-winded" and does not fit into the time allowed. The media does have time limits; radio and television hosts usually have only a specified amount of time to talk with you. It is a good idea to determine the time limits before the discussion begins.

How do you handle the interruption if you know you are right? Use a hand gesture or your voice to say, "Excuse me, please let me finish my answer." This shifts control back to you and away from the interviewer. You can escalate this technique to the degree of control you want. You may want to note that "interruption" and "off-the-topic" traps can constitute the media's attempt to confuse you and get that quotable quote, often at your expense.

 The final trap is **"Distraction."** Distractions can be deliberate, but often, are just the usual activities surrounding the media. With the exception of the print journalist with a notepad or radio reporter with a tape recorder, the distractions surrounding a television interview, TV studio interview, or radio booth interview, can be overwhelming.

Your focus must be on the media person. The television studio can be a most confusing and busy place. There will be many technicians (camera, sound, lighting, make-up, and directors) running around the studio.

A law enforcement supervisor related a story about appearing on a local television talk show. The law enforcement supervisor was in the guest seat, and his lapel microphone went dead. The camera moved in for a close-up head shot while a long, silver mechanical arm moved in and removed the dead microphone and replaced it with a live microphone. The law enforcement supervisor stated that he watched the whole thing happen with his head down and following with the mechanical arm. This posture didn't look good on television.

Remember to avoid the distractions as much as possible and pay attention to the media person. Distractions combined with other traps can lead to misstatements and confusion on your part.

Summation

To deal with the media, the police supervisor must have an understanding of the background of journalists. What makes reporters do what they do? This chapter, hopefully, gave you some insight into the media and what you can do to deal with them effectively. The more media encounters you have as a law enforcement supervisor, the better you will become. There is no substitute for experience when it comes to "Dealing With the Media."

Acknowledgments

In early 1981, the FBI Academy's Education/Communication Arts Unit began on a program of executive media training to the law enforcement community. The Academy used the expertise from the private sector and specifically the Royal Canadian Mounted Police to formulate its program.

The FBI media training program has evolved with tremendous input from thousands of law enforcement executives and officers who have participated in the program. It should be noted that significant contributions from former and current members of the Education/Communication Arts Unit at the FBI Academy have helped develop this program. This chapter, "Dealing With the Media," has encompassed the expertise of many in the field of law enforcement training.

Footnotes

[1] Jones 1991, 1.

[2] Emery & Emery 1978, 65.

[3] Emery & Emery 1978.

[4] Larry Sabato, *Feeding Frenzy: How Attack Journalism Has Transformed American Politics*, 1991, 26.

5 *Branzburg v. Hayes* in 1972 (Higginbotham, 1989).

6 408 U.S. 707, 1972.

7 408 U.S. 684, 1972.

8 Webster's Ninth New Collegiate Dictionary, 1986, 217.

9 Roger Ailes, *You Are The Message*, 1988.

Robert C. Crouse

Mr. Robert C. Crouse holds a B.S. in Anthropology, and a B.S. in Psychology from Grand Valley State University in Allendale, MI. He also holds an M.S. in Criminal Justice from Michigan State University.

Mr. Crouse's police experience includes the Grand Valley State College Campus Police, Ottawa County Sheriff's Deputy, and an East Lansing (MI) Police Officer. Prior to taking a position at the Southern Police Institute, he was Director of Public Safety Programs at Sauk Valley College in Dixon, Illinois.

Chapter 9

Performance Appraisal: The Key to High Performance

by Robert C. Crouse

Performance appraisals provide supervisors the opportunity to develop a proactive managerial activity essential to creating an environment within the workplace that fosters high performance work habits in all personnel. Performance appraisals unlock the potential of employees, encourages employees to engage in task driven job performance, and develops work habits which cause an increase in individual and group performance. Performance appraisals offer supervisors a method of communicating specific recommendations to employees in a progressive format which helps ensure compliance with predetermined job task and work behavior criteria.

What Should a Supervisor Know About Performance Appraisals?

Performance appraisals should be a constant activity of the supervisor.

Performance appraisals must accurately reflect the job tasks that actually are being performed by the employees evaluated.

Performance appraisals should be based on performance standards jointly established between the employee and the supervisor.

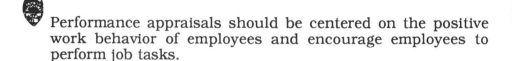 Performance appraisals should be centered on the positive work behavior of employees and encourage employees to perform job tasks.

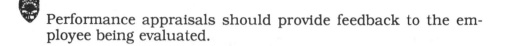 Performance appraisals should provide feedback to the employee being evaluated.

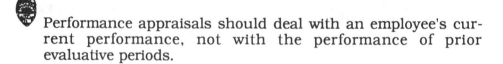 Performance appraisals should deal with an employee's current performance, not with the performance of prior evaluative periods.

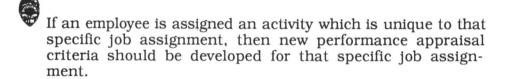 If an employee is assigned an activity which is unique to that specific job assignment, then new performance appraisal criteria should be developed for that specific job assignment.

Creating an Environment for Interactive Performance Appraisals

Employees play a significant role in their own performance appraisals, because to be effective performance appraisals must be accepted by those being evaluated. When given the opportunity to have input into their own performance appraisals, the supervisor and the employee being evaluated must consider the process to be fair.

Feedback should be offered by the supervisor on an on-going basis. Poor performance results should never be a shock to the poorly performing employee and superior performance should be noted and commended on as it is demonstrated. These activities together create an approach to performance appraisals which are highly interactive.

A primary responsibility of the supervisor is the creation of communication channels where two-way, unobstructed exchange of information, questions, and ideas can take place. Even the newest employee should be viewed as a source for ideas which can be developed into performance criteria. All personnel must be shown that it is in their own best interest to seek answers to questions involving their own performance.

Finally, it is in the best interest of the supervisor to communicate information to personnel which directly impacts the work unit's overall performance. Supervisors discover that constant attention to employees' performance will keep the work unit performing at an above standard level.

Interactive performance appraisals are a significant component required for building an environment within which high performance work units can form. Interactive performance appraisals grant supervisors the opportunity to guide personnel to higher levels of performance. Effective interactive performance appraisals are prerequisites to empowering employees, building high performance teams, and encouraging employees to perform at higher levels.

Constant Attention to Performance Appraisals

Law enforcement agencies, as most units of government, evaluate performance of personnel periodically. These evaluative periods are often yearly or quarterly. Supervisors make a serious error in assuming evaluations may be made only periodically and should be dealt with only when the supervisors are required to complete them as required organizationally.

Performance appraisals driven by organizational requirements may not meet the needs of the supervisors who are in the process of developing high performing personnel. Performance appraisals done only to meet a requirement of the organization fail to encourage interaction between the supervisors and employees on an on-going basis. Supervisors who only concern themselves with performance evaluations when they are required by the agency may find it difficult to deal with individual officers.

Performance appraisals should be seen as tools to assist supervisors in gaining commitments from personnel to perform to a mutually agreed standard. This standard is set by the supervisor and the employee, and must take into account the employee's training, job experience, ability to manage their own time, ability to identify and complete job tasks, and to a significant degree, the ability to self evaluate performance. The employee with a greater degree of reliance on the supervisor requires much more evaluated feedback than the employee who can identify job tasks requiring attention and properly complete those tasks.

Performance appraisals should be seen as tools to assist employees to focus on their work efforts, career development efforts, and the collective efforts of the work unit. The supervisor who evaluates an employee's work effort on an on-going basis is in a better position to provide prompt, responsive, and accurate feedback.

Positive appraisals, which often are understated, can be documented as events unfold. Negative appraisals can be documented and corrective actions recommended early. When the periodic evaluations are due, the supervisor who has been constantly appraising performance has formal evaluative material on each employee. The evaluative information has a higher probability of containing information responsive to the needs of the employee, the work unit, and the organization.

Focused Communication

Performance appraisals should be seen as tools to increase communication between the supervisor and the employees within the work unit. Communication can be enhanced when performance appraisals are effectively used to open communications within the work unit.

Interactive performance appraisals facilitate job related communication between the supervisor and the members of the supervisor's work unit. Focused communication is required in interactive performance appraisals to ensure that two way communication lines remain open and that the supervisor deals with job task performance. The supervisor who is able to focus on the job tasks and encourages positive work behaviors will be identified by employees as an effective leader.

Gaining effective communication linkage with personnel requires that the supervisor develop trusting relationships within the work unit. Trust building may well be the most difficult and energy consuming process that a supervisor must master. Trust will exist only when the employee and the supervisor both feel free to be open and candid with one another. Trust is earned, not granted by the position or rank of a supervisor. Trust cannot be rushed, because it is earned with a series of small successes.

Focused communication is reliant on the employee's understanding of the job task associated with a particular work activity. Focused communication deals with job criteria established in the position description of a particular position.

Once the job tasks are clearly communicated, the supervisor can begin to evaluate the work methods used by employees in the work unit and how they are used in completing the task. An analysis of the work methods used by several employees completing the same task will grant the supervisor a clear understanding of the work requirements needed to complete the job task.

Communication becomes "focused" when a supervisor is able to discuss the job task and its associated work methods with employees and stay on topic. By appraising the work methods and specific job tasks, the supervisor is able to present feedback to the employee on that employee's performance.

Performance Appraisals Should Not be Confused With Discipline

The maintaining of effective organizational discipline is an activity which can consume a significant portion of a supervisor's work energy. Caution should be used to ensure discipline issues are not confused with job task performance issues.

When an employee being evaluated has had disciplinary action enforced during the *current evaluative period*, it may be appropriate to address changes in performance with direct linkage to the disciplinary action during a performance appraisal session. Beyond establishing a direct linkage, discipline should be viewed as a separate supervisory function.

Accredited police agencies have discipline policies which include provisions for "positive discipline" (rewards) as well as "negative discipline" (organizational sanctions). Only when a direct linkage can be established between the rewards or the sanctions, and the individual job task performance, should the discipline be made part of a formal performance appraisal.

The supervisor in an accredited agency may find that the requirements for rewarding the employee will involve a form of performance appraisal. The supervisor is documenting how, while performing specific job tasks, the employee excelled beyond the normal expectations to the degree that an honor is owed the employee.

Past Performance Should Not Be a Factor in Performance Appraisal

Past performance which occurred during a prior performance appraisal period should not be brought into the current performance appraisal. It is very inappropriate to document past performance, discuss past performance, or site examples of past performance which took place outside the current evaluative period, during a performance appraisal. The employee being appraised would feel that the past performance is now unduly impacting the supervisor's current evaluation of the employee's performance.

Data Driven Performance Evaluation

Data provides information to the supervisor as it relates to the work activities of specific personnel. Data provides the supervisor with a "snap shot" of an employee's performance in terms of numbers. This information is normally based on numbers of arrest by category, assigned and non-assigned work time, miles patrolled, and data of a similar character. There is nothing wrong with using this type of data to form a data driven appraisal. When properly used, data provides a supervisor with a clear picture of part of the work activity of personnel. Data measures types of activities in terms of volume.

Performance appraisals driven by data and nothing else do not provide anything more than a "snap shot." Using only data as a basis for a performance appraisal means that the supervisor is looking only at numbers.

Granted, when a road patrol officer on a specific shift writes 12 moving traffic violations per month and the rest of that shift averages 21 violations per month, there is clearly a problem with the performance of the individual writing 12. Data can provide the supervisor with a reference point upon which to base a judgment on acceptable levels of activity. However, anyone who has been assigned to road patrol can tell you that basing performance appraisals on data only, will result in increased activity in the area the data is collected.

In terms of motivating personnel you gain increased numbers when you focus on data. However, how have you affected motivation? Have you increased performance by building a high performing work unit, or have you increased work activity to increase data? It is important to understand that on a short-term basis, any supervisor can increase activity by "baby-sitting" personnel and forcing them to engage in work activities that the supervisor prefers they complete.

Criteria Development

The criteria used to evaluate personnel must be based upon the employee's position description. It is possible that a position description may not reflect the job tasks that are being performed by the employee. The employee may perform job tasks beyond what the job description states.

An employee assigned to a community policing work unit, a special weapons and tactics work unit, youth gangs, or any of a number of specialized units will not appropriately fit under a general heading. In fact, a major portion of the overall evaluative period may be occupied with duties not covered under the general heading which they, in theory, fall.

Specialized work units require specialized criteria upon which the members are to be evaluated. In order to develop a fair evaluative tool on which the formal performance appraisal will be written, criteria must be developed which indicates the typical job tasks performed in those specialized job assignments. This can be a complicated and time consuming task. The process should include direct input from the members of the specialized unit, including supervisors and commanders.

The criteria developed will provide the basis for a clear understanding of specialized roles within the agency. Community Policing Officers, for an example, would be able to explain the CPO's role. Performance appraisals would then be based on the degree to which the employee was able to meet the goals and objectives developed for that role.

The criteria would be used for the development of an internal position description used for the recruitment of personnel as CPO's. The criteria would be used during the selection process for CPO's to screen out those individuals who do not appear to understand, who do not have the required commitment to the special role, or who do not possess the requisite skills and knowledge required for the position.

The Process of Performance Appraisals

Supervisors must:

» gather data on the employee being evaluated;

» review any notes made during the current evaluative period with regard to the employee's performance;

» write a formal performance appraisal in the format used by the agency;

» schedule an appropriate time to meet privately with the employee in a controlled environment;

» present a copy of the performance evaluation to the employee during the private meeting and review it point by point;

» allow time for the employee to fully review and discuss the performance appraisal document;

» offer the employee the option to respond to the formal document in writing, have the employee sign the original copy, and send the signed document to the supervisor; and

» review key points, suggestions for career development, and work methods to assist the employee to meet objectives outlined in the performance appraisal, as often as possible, until the objectives are met.

When these eight steps are followed, the supervisor can document the procedure followed for each performance appraisal. Only a small segment of the process is data driven, and the process requires the supervisor to keep notes on current review and informal appraisals made throughout the appraisal period. The supervisor who uses the same process to evaluate everyone in the work unit will be viewed as a fair and impartial evaluator by the personnel evaluated.

Gathering Data for a Performance Appraisal

The degree to which a supervisor uses data in a performance appraisal may depend on what the administration focuses on and considers important. Some units will require a greater reliance on data. For example, officers assigned to a traffic unit will have a greater weight attached to the number of traffic citations issued than a road patrol officer. The supervisor must determine what is important activity and what activity is less important. The supervisor must clearly communicate what data will be most important to the members of the work unit so that they know where to focus their efforts.

Reviewing Appraisal Notes

The supervisor should be appraising performance at least weekly, if not daily, on every employee in the work unit. An appraisal log should be maintained to list milestones throughout the evaluative period. Without such a log, the supervisor will have difficulty pulling the required information together that will form the basis for the performance appraisal.

Milestones will be appropriate for more documentation than a log provides in some situations. These milestones should be noted in memorandum form with a copy for the employee and a copy for the supervisor. Normally this information will be maintained on the positive accomplishments of the employee. Remember performance appraisals are not discipline.

Writing the Formal Performance Appraisal

The formal written performance appraisal document should be developed based on the raw data collected which deals with quantity measures; number of arrests by category for example. More important, the formal performance appraisal should be based on the employee's work activity from throughout the entire evaluative period. That information comes from the appraisal log and, if any have been issued, from the appraisal memorandums.

Attention should be paid to the objectives established in the prior performance appraisal, which the employee agreed to meet during the current appraisal period. Remember that you should never make reference to prior performance that occurred in another appraisal period.

The formal document should include objectives that the employee will agree are appropriate and that the employee can reasonably meet during the course of the next performance appraisal period. These objectives should be developed by the supervisor and the employee jointly. The appropriate time for their development is during the current evaluative period, through constant performance appraisals of the employee. These objectives should be recorded in appraisal memorandums.

Schedule the Performance Review Meeting

The performance review meeting is a formal meeting between the supervisor and the employee being evaluated. Critical to a successful performance review is where you can meet, in private, for thirty to forty-five minutes without being interrupted. The room should contain furniture that allows the supervisor to sit facing the employee so that both parties have an unobstructed eye-level view of each other.

The review would be more personal without a desk or table between the supervisor and the employee being reviewed. Telephone calls should not interrupt the review session. Forward calls to another telephone, locate a room without a telephone, or unplug the telephone to assure that there are no interruptions.

Copy of the Performance Appraisal for the Employee Being Appraised

A copy of the performance appraisal should be handed to the employee being evaluated. The appraisal should be read to the employee by the supervisor as the employee follows along by reading the provided copy. Where appropriate, the supervisor should ask if there are any questions, or offer a rationale on specific points.

Allow Time for the Employee to Respond

The supervisor should not race through the performance appraisal document. The employee should have time to ask questions about the outcome of the performance review document. The supervisor will find it helpful to have developed a rationale for every point being made in the formal appraisal so that the supervisor is prepared to respond to the employee's questions or concerns. Allow the employee to present points that differ or support the statements made in the formal document.

Signing the Formal Performance Appraisal Document

The employee must sign the formal performance appraisal. If the employee desires to write a response to the appraisal document, allow the employee the time to formalize the response and to commit the response to writing.

Reviewing the Outcomes of the Formal Performance Appraisal

The supervisor's obligation to the employee does not end with a signed performance appraisal. The employee has agreed with the performance appraisal and has jointly established objectives which will be met during the next performance appraisal period. The supervisor must facilitate the employee's effort to meet, or if possible, exceed those objectives.

When those objectives include specialized training, the supervisor is obligated to help the employee gain that training. When those objectives include improvement of report writing, for example, the supervisor is obligated to help the employee produce better reports. The supervisor is obligated to give constant feedback that is focused on job tasks, or work behavior, to improve the employee's skills and abilities.

Summary

Performance appraisals can build trust between a supervisor and the employees that make up that work unit. Supervisors who engage constant performance appraisals have an enhanced ability to evaluate the employee over the whole evaluative period. These supervisors engage in focused communication that deals with the performance of job tasks and the work methods employed by the personnel which make up the work unit.

The use of appraisal logs and appraisal memorandums provide information required to construct a quality performance appraisal, while granting the employee constant feedback on job performance. Granting personnel the ability to freely express themselves with regard to performance appraisals, in writing and orally, helps maintain trust within the work unit.

Chapter 10

Planning

by Gorden E. Eden, Jr.

No well-trained law enforcement officer would enter a dark and unfamiliar building occupied by five armed people without having a plan. This entry plan would include: the floor plan of the building; exits and entry points; whether the people had weapons; criminal history on each individual; what equipment will be required; the background and training of each law enforcement officer on the entry team; and the alternatives to resolve the situation without risking the lives of the entry team. Yet, law enforcement managers, at all levels, fail to prepare in a similar manner for the day-to-day or future operation of the department. Some managers are not comfortable with the planning/decision-making process which can make a crooked road straight.

Planning, organizing, leading, and controlling are the functions of management, and planning is the most critical. Planning is the first function of management as it establishes goals, objectives, policies, and procedures needed to achieve the purposes of an organization. This broad statement concerning planning implies that planning prepares an organization and its members for the future (proactive).

Today's law enforcement managers have been forced into a situation of providing greater amounts of service with fewer resources. Thorough planning provides the framework for the resources of an organization. These resources include people, equipment, and money. Planning will provide for organizational structuring and the controlling activities to guide and direct employees.

Planning is best defined as: *the process of defining an organization's objectives and how it will achieve them.* Managers plan every working day when they must decide:

 what is to be done (goal or objective),

when it is to be done (time frame),

how it is to be done (activities),

where it is to be done (location), and

who is to do it (people required).

Top level managers are concerned with long range plans. Long range plans project where the organization will be in five years. This will include long range goals and objectives, and the major policies required to keep the organization on track.

The middle manager's responsibilities are focused on the implementation of activities to achieve the "where" and the "when" of the plan. The first-line manager has the responsibility of scheduling employees, deciding what work must be done and developing procedures to keep the plan on track.

Types of Plans

In the law enforcement organization, managers must have a strategic plan. A **strategic plan** involves the entire organization and the preparation of this plan requires multi-level involvement and cooperation. Strategic plans prepare the organization for growth and expansion, and forecast where the organization will be in two, three, or five years. This type of planning requires vision on the part of those who participate in this planning process. Depending on the size of an organization and the managerial style of top management, the first-line manager may have a critical role in all types of planning.

Strategic planning begins with an organizational mission statement. The mission statement is clear about why the organization exists. Peter Drucker, a leading management consultant, suggests that we must understand and define, "What is our organizational purpose?" Managers must look to the people they serve for this answer. Ask yourself this question, "What does the public expect from our department?" Look at the organization from their perspective, and know for a fact what they think, believe, and perceive as law enforcement duties.

Predicting future trends is an important part of strategic planning. While the future is difficult to predict, managers must look at future events which can impact the organization and the community. Any strategic plan must include an assessment to determine projected activities and events, and the impact of these on human resources and equipment. Law enforcement managers can increase their knowledge in these areas by reading professional business publications.

Do strategic plans change? Yes, as no strategic plan is etched in stone. Strategic plans are revised as the conditions which effect it change. However, managers should and must keep focused on the mission statement.

The next type of plan is the **tactical plan**. Tactical plans are usually directed at the divisional level. Middle management transforms strategic plans into more specific and directed objectives. Tactical plans describe what the division must do, how to do it, and who will be assigned the responsibility to complete the task.

Tactical plans are concerned with a shorter time frame and are focused on specific divisional or work unit activities. Most tactical plans are associated with an annual budget and as a result of the budget cycle, they are usually one year in length. Tactical plans are directed at attaining strategical objectives.

Types of Operational Plans

Operational plans are the first-line manager's tools to accomplish their job duties and responsibilities. These plans include standing and single use plans.

Standing plans cover the routine or recurring situations that are not a challenge to management once the situation is under control. Standing plans include policies, standard operating procedures, rules, and regulations.

A **policy** provides managers and employees with a broad guideline to follow when dealing with critical events. A policy provides the framework for decision making. A policy guides managers by pointing them in a common direction. However, a policy does not tell managers how to do it, where to do it, or what to do.

A **procedure** is an explicit set of actions, often, sequential, that are required to achieve a desired result. Procedures exist for preparing for duty, handling routine complaints, preparing correspondence, submitting time sheets, preparing a budget, and how calls for service will be handled.

A **rule** is a specific control mechanism for dealing with people, employees, and conduct. Rules are, "do and do not" statements for which people are held accountable, regardless of the situation. Rules are stricter than policies and do not allow for individual decision making.

In most cases, procedures and rules are the results of management's attempts to organizationally correct the behavior of one or two individuals rather than address the individuals. The end result of procedures and rules is that they stifle the creativity of the workforce. Employees are locked into a specific course of action where there is no situational flexibility or means for adjustment.

Single-use plans are for non-recurring activities which include budgets, programs, special events, and projects.

The Planning Process

A manager plans each minute of every working day. Work schedules must be made to establish the allocation of resources based on the demand for service. If the manager fails in the planning process, chaos will prevail and services will not be delivered or provided. First-line managers will use the informal planning process a majority of the time. **Informal planning** is defined as *a process of intuitively deciding on objectives and activities needed to achieve those objectives without rigorous and systematic investigation.* [1]

The competent and efficient first-line manager will use the theories and practices of formal planning to develop effective informal planning abilities.

First-line managers are often the first to recognize a potential problem or situation which may require a formal plan of action. Therefore, the first-line manager must be familiar with the formal planning process. **Formal planning** is *the process of using a systematic criteria and rigorous investigation to establish objectives, decide on activities, and formally document organizational expectations.* [2]

The first step in the planning process is the recognition of the need for a plan. The manager is aware or made aware of a situation, problem, or potential situation that requires attention. The manager then must authenticate or verify this warning through the collection of data and information. One question which should be asked is, "Do the risks appear serious enough if no action is taken?" If the response is, "Yes," then ask, "what is the desired end result?" This series of critical questions will assist the manager with writing a goal statement. A goal is a realistic statement of an ambition or desire. If the ambition (goal) is to vacation in Hawaii (end result), there must be a plan for the trip. All of this information must be analyzed prior to the establishing of objectives.

Objectives are road maps with routes marked to the end results of plans. Managers and staff will use the objectives as guides throughout the plan. Therefore, the objectives must be clear, concise, and defined. An objective of the Hawaiian vacation may be to visit three islands in six days. Once the objectives have been established, the planner must examine the many alternative courses of action.

There are many ways to solve or resolve a situation or potential problem. Therefore the manager must be innovative in developing alternatives. In some cases, the manager is wise to seek the assistance of others, including those who will be responsible for implementing or following the plan.

Some techniques used to develop alternatives include brainstorming and conferences. Avoid idea killing statements such as, "we tried before," "the boss won't go for it," "where are we going to get the money?" or "it will never work."

Encourage all employees to be innovative. In getting the job done, managers must mentally start at the finish and work backward. The clearer the end result, the more effective the plan.

The next step in the planning process is to examine the internal and external environment. The internal factors which can impact the planning process may include the availability of resources and resistance to change. External elements often include the procurement of funds, the economy, political timing, and the social climate.

However, the veteran planner will not allow these issues to block a plan. The only way to approach these issues in the internal and external environment is with a comprehensive plan with well defined and defendable goals and objectives.

The neglected plan is when the divisions or work units develop their own goals. A good management team gives those responsible with plan implementation the opportunity to develop appropriate goals and objectives based on the information provided. A comparison is then made of the lower level and organizational goals for compatibility. This review process will assist all levels of management in closing any gaps which may have an adverse impact on the plan or the organization.

Once these issues have been resolved, managers will have a plan that meets the needs of society, the organization, and the employees. The plan is ready for presentation to those concerned, and the course of action is defendable and well defined. The plan is then ready for implementation and evaluation.

The manager must have a feedback mechanism to monitor the progress of attaining the objectives. The initial objectives serve as a standard for measuring progress toward the stated goal. Initial objectives may need to be re-evaluated and adjusted as the plan matures.

Common Barriers to Effective

Successful managers have learned that a critical component of the planning process is identifying, predicting, and overcoming planning barriers. The majority of these barriers are internal, and in all likelihood are other managers.

Managers must work hard to develop effective planning skills. This skill must be practiced enough that it becomes routine. When managers are not comfortable with planning, there is a greater tendency to lack commitment to the planning process. All of this can be summarized into one barrier: the lack of planning experience.

Misinformation can destroy the first phases of planning. Managers must evaluate information sources for credibility. Inaccurate or incomplete information will create havoc and confusion with the planning process. Successful managers will obtain as much information as possible, using as many sources as possible, and involve others in the planning process.

Summary

Most plans do not get carried out exactly as designed because of changing circumstances. However, studies show that organizations that do plan tend to be more successful than those that do not plan.

First-line managers must realize that their plans have an impact on subordinates, peers, middle and top management, and on the public. Therefore, planning must be effective and careful consideration must be taken when examining the tactics and strategies of plan implementation.

Footnotes

1 & 2   David H. Holt, Management, Principle and Practices, second edition (Englewood Cliffs, NJ: Prentice-Hall, 1990).

Anout the Author

Mr. Gorden E. Eden, Jr. is Bureau Chief in the Training and Recruiting Division of the New Mexico Department of Public Safety in Santa Fe. He is in charge of research, development, scheduling, and instructing advanced and specialized training programs.
Mr. Eden is part-time Director of Genesis Management Systems, Ltd. in Albuquerque, a company that researches grants in the

areas of substance abuse in the workplace and preventive programs for youths at risk. He is also an Adjunct Faculty Member of Northwestern University in Evanston, Illinois.

Mr. Eden has a Bachelor of Science degree in Business Administration from the University of Phoenix, Albuquerque Campus.

Ginny Field

Ms. Ginny Field, a Communications Instructor at the FBI Academy in Quantico, Virginia, teaches "Executive Writing," "Effective Writing," and "Instructor Development" to law enforcement officers from around the nation and world. She has a B.A. from the University of Richmond and an M.A. in Professional Writing and Editing from George Mason University in Virginia.

Chapter 11

Supervisory Editing

by Ginny Field

Introduction

Supervisors can save their time and energy and help improve their employees' morale simply by following a few guidelines for editing their subordinates' writing. Editing someone else's writing can be tricky, because people tend to view their writing as an extension of themselves.

Supervisors can unwittingly anger and even degrade their subordinates either by improperly editing their writing or not helping them change and learn the "right" way to write. This chapter lays out guidelines for supervisory editing by first discussing what to avoid and then covering what to do.

What to Avoid

Few supervisors receive formal training in editing their subordinate's writing. Yet editing or approving what others write often takes a major portion of their time.

When promoted to a supervisory position, some people will mimic how their supervisors edited or approved their writing. Unfortunately, they may forget how they felt as the subordinate trying to figure out what their supervisors wanted. Thus, they continue to violate the three major taboos of supervisory editing:

 not communicating what they want or expect from the subordinate

 editing for the sake of editing

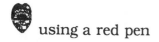 using a red pen

Not Communicating What They Want or Expect

Anyone who has worked for a boss who says, "This is not right – fix it," but who doesn't say how to fix it or what is "right," can empathize with subordinates who never seem to be able to write the way their supervisors want. They learn the hard way, by trial and error – and lots of time, stress, and negative feelings – how to write to gain their supervisor's approval.

Supervisors cannot depend on their subordinates to read their minds or automatically know what they expect in ways of writing. They cannot assume subordinates will "get it right" the first time unless they tell the writers what "right" is.

If supervisors do expect perfection without direction, they will create much resentment and anger among their subordinates that could spill over into other aspects of the subordinate's work. Resentful subordinates rarely lead in productivity and often take valuable time by causing problems that need a supervisor's attention.

Supervisors who expect their subordinates to write using a specific style or format or set of phrases must first tell or, better yet, show those subordinates what they want. They should give their subordinates good examples to follow. If they have no examples, they should talk with their subordinates, either individually or as a group, and clearly explain exactly what they expect.

At times, supervisors may not be able to verbalize what they want until after they receive a document that fails to fulfill their expectations. If this occurs, they need to edit the document to make it conform to their desired format or style. Then they need to make the time to sit with the writer and explain the changes, taking care to clarify their expectations for future documents.

Editing for the Sake of Editing

Some supervisors feel that they must earn their pay by changing something, anything, on the documents they have to approve. So, instead of changing content or style to improve the document, they change words or phrases according to their personal preferences or whim of the moment. Such editing rarely clarifies the meaning or purpose of the document; thus, it does nothing but increase the vanity or control of the supervisor and the negative feelings of the subordinate.

Supervisors need to remember that their subordinates will not always write the way the supervisors would have written – different people use different words and phrases and, therefore, say things differently.

While the supervisors may feel that their way is best, if the document conveys the correct meaning and does so clearly, the supervisors should let it stand without unnecessary "corrections." They'll not only save their time and the writer's time, they'll give their subordinates a boost in ego that could result in a more productive, or at least a happier, employee.

Using a Red Pen

While this may seem a minor or even petty point to bring up here, red can have profound psychological effects on writers. Although red may make changes the most visible to writers (or typists), it also tends to anger people. It may remind writers of school – often in a negative rather than positive way.

Red pens remind people of their grammar school teachers who constantly pointed out their mistakes in using the many boring rules of punctuation and grammar they were supposed to embrace. How many people find such a memory inspiring or empowering?

Even if red reminds a few people of a positive school experience, red also connotes power and control. Subordinates can view its use as another form of a supervisor trying to control rather than lead them.

Using a less threatening yet still easily seen color, such as green or blue, often alleviates the defensiveness or anger subordinates can feel just by seeing red on their writing.

What To Do

If supervisors should avoid what was done to them and what they perhaps do now, what can they do to help their subordinates when they edit their subordinates' work?

Writing is such a personal thing to people – if someone attacks their writing, they, in effect, attack the writer. Thus, supervisors must take care to emphasize the constructive nature of their editing, ensuring that the writer understands that the changes make the writing clearer (rather than "better," though that should be true too).

One method that helps supervisors defuse immediate defensiveness from the writer and helps writers understand the constructive nature of the supervisor's editing is the

☐ Praise

☐ Question

☐ Polish

or the PQP Method.

Praise

Writers, regardless of what they say about their writing, want others to like what they write and think it close to perfect. Any change tends to threaten their self-concept, unless they suggest the change themselves or the change stems from a skill they lack.

If a supervisor wants to discuss with a subordinate what the subordinate wrote, the subordinate comes to the meeting already nervous and, perhaps, defensive. Supervisors can defuse this "fight or flight" syndrome by beginning the meeting with praise for what the writer did well.

General praise like, "This looks great," won't work. It tends to sound insincere, and writers forget it as soon as they hear the "but" that inevitably follows.

However, if supervisors take the time to really search through a document to find specific good things to praise about the writing, they will earn it back by spending less time with an argumentative or defensive employee who tries to explain away all errors.

Writers may not expect immediate praise, but they certainly hope for and want it. So, supervisors will benefit by giving it to them.

Supervisors can praise specifics about sentence and paragraph structure, wording, organization and flow, punctuation and grammar, information content, reader awareness, style, conciseness, and format and structure. Anything is better than nothing.

Supervisors can make more impact by learning what is important to their subordinates and, if it applies, praising that part of the writing. For example, some people may know they are weak in grammar, but feel proud of the care they take with format and organization. Praising their format and organization, if warranted, can help them justify that pride.

Question

The next step in PQP involves asking writers questions about ambiguities or areas the supervisors simply did not understand. A question somehow threatens less, especially if coined in terms of "I" instead of "you." For example, "I didn't understand what this meant" takes more responsibility away from the writer than, "You didn't make this clear." Through questioning, supervisors can point out many areas of concern: lack of information, too much information, not getting to the point or making the wrong point, lack of organization, inappropriate style or tone, no awareness of the readers' needs, unusual formatting or structure, and even poor mechanics.

Making suggestions in the form of questions, such as "I wonder if another paragraph on this topic would help clarify what you mean," also works better than a blanket statement like, "you really need to put another paragraph in here to clarify this."

Often, supervisors will find that questions will help the writer discover problem areas and suggest solutions themselves. Even if writers don't come up with solutions the supervisors wanted to suggest, at this point, supervisors can jump into a brainstorming mode and offer their solutions as though they just came to mind.

Polish

Finally, after starting with praise and then asking questions, supervisors can begin offering specific suggestions on how to improve any remaining problems. Again, couching their suggestions in first person, such as "I think you can make this clearer by . . . " will probably accomplish more than second person commands, such as "you have to change this to . . ." Areas conducive to polishing include changing specific words or phrases, reorganizing sentences within paragraphs, restructuring paragraphs, correcting grammar and punctuation, meeting the readers' needs, making the point, and including or excluding specific information.

Summary

Many supervisors may read this and think PQP a nice theoretical solution to supervisory editing, but an impractical one due to their time constraints. Besides, subordinates have to do what they say – won't asking questions and using first person with suggestions make them seem like weak leaders? Perhaps the best way to answer these legitimate concerns is to point out the benefits of using this method.

No matter what position they hold, people like to be treated with respect. A strong request will always work better than an outright order. Supervisors should save orders about writing only for those who show they need them.

More important, while using PQP may initially take more time than supervisors think they have, it definitely saves them more time in the long run. Subordinates handled in this way leave their supervisor's office with ego intact, feeling good about both themselves and their supervisors. They will more likely want to please their supervisors and try to write more in line with their supervisors' thinking the next time they write.

Supervisors who spend a great deal of their valuable time editing their subordinates' work instead of helping the subordinates edit their own work often find themselves in a vicious, hard-to-break cycle. If they make the time to help their subordinates from the start, they will ultimately save time by permanently reducing the problem rather than perpetuating it.

David M. Grossi

Mr. David M. Grossi is Senior Instructor with the Calibre Press, Inc. Street Survival® Seminars and has lectured to thousands of federal, state, and local police officers on the topic of Officer Survival. He is a retired Lieutenant with the Irondequoit (NY) Police Department.

Mr. Grossi holds a Bachelor's degree in Police Administration from the State University of New York and is an FBI National Academy graduate. He has also testified as an expert witness in State and Federal Court in both criminal and civil matters on the issues of deadly force and police policy and procedure.

Chapter 12

The Supervisor's Role in Officer Survival Training

by David M. Grossi

Introduction

To properly address the supervisor's role in officer survival, we first have to discuss how and when this whole issue of officer survival really came about. The "Officer Survival Movement" really began almost two decades ago when Captain Pierce R. Brooks, retired from the Los Angeles Police Department, wrote the book, *Officer Down, Code Three*. From the book evolved the training film of the same name and the Officer Survival Movement was born.

Some old-time cops might remember Sergeant Pierce Brooks as the homicide detective in charge of the tragic Onion Field Case in Bakersfield, California, and Joseph Wambaugh fame. However, Brooks is also considered to be the father of the Officer Survival Movement. In fact, before Brooks wrote the now-immortal text, most officer survival concepts centered on the notion that, "There's a bullet out there with your name on it, son, and there ain't a damn thing you or anybody else can do about it. When your number's up . . . it's up!" (I heard that exact same line way back in February 1969 upon my arrival "in-country" and assignment to a recon/ambush unit in Pleiku, South Vietnam.)

Now we know that all that macho, John Wayne, "leave it all to chance" crap just isn't true. Brooks' concept was almost revolutionary – you really can exercise some control over your own safety on the street by using proper tactics. Chuck Remsberg further illustrated and re-enforced that fact with the *Street Survival* and *Tactical Edge* books. Also Calibre Press, Street Survival® Seminars continue to demonstrate this issue twenty-seven times a year around the country.

Who Is Responsible for Training?

For years, the responsibility for instructing officer safety and survival tactics has always fallen on the shoulders of academy instructors. If recruits are lucky, maybe they receive about eight hours of basic academy curriculum in building search tactics and felony car stops, unless an innovative firearms' staff implements officer survival topics into their in-service programs.

Most departments, even the progressive ones that offer frequent and relevant in-service training, never reinforce realistic officer survival tactics on a regular basis. The once-a-year tactical course that augments range training is what most street cops relate to when they are asked the question, "What kind of officer survival training does your department offer?" And 90% of officer survival training, if it does exist, only center around street tactics . . . physical survival. The concept of emotional or legal survival is virtually non-existent.

Realistically, is this enough? Is it sufficient to leave officer survival concepts, theories, and tactics to the academy staff or department instructors? Most competent trainers say "no."

Officer survival concepts have to be ingrained into the everyday thinking of today's street cop. To just talk about officer survival in today's society and only mean physical survival is doing our men and women "in blue" a tremendous injustice and disservice.

Officer survival today must include not only physical (street) survival, but also psychological (emotional) survival and legal (liability) survival. Any competent in-service training program has to contain these aforementioned officer survival theories and concepts that we, as trainers, should be instilling into the minds of our recruits and veteran officers.

In our officer survival training, we must include concepts dealing with approach, tactical thinking, threat assessment, anticipating the unexpected, the survival mindset, and tactical withdrawal. Even topics such as pursuit driving, firearms, defensive tactics, batons, chemical and electronic options, as well as those dry, mundane issues such as report writing must be approached and instructed with a legal survival mindset.

To just talk about officer survival from the concept of the trainer's responsibility is approaching it from a very myopic point of view. First and second-line supervisors need to preach these concepts in their everyday management duties.

Part of being a manager or supervisor means assuming responsibility for subordinates in every aspect of their official duties. It has been said that officer survival is everyone's business and it has never been more true than today. Anyone who has followed the trial of the four LAPD officers (California v. Powell, et al.) surely has realized by now that legal survival can be just as important as physical survival.

Officer survival is truly everyone's responsibility, not just the training staff. And that's what this chapter will discuss . . . the role of the supervisor (first and second-line command staff) in officer survival training.

The Role of the Supervisor

Law enforcement management and supervision books and courses have always been replete with such subjects as vicarious liability, discipline, ethics, performance evaluations, budgeting, manpower planning and staffing, and other corollary issues that go hand-in-hand with hiring, firing, and inspection. And that's good, because these issues are necessary. In fact, the accompanying chapters in this book contain some very important topics that address these issues. But for a long time, the role of the supervisor in officer survival has been downplayed or even overlooked altogether, and this role is a very important one.

I had the experience of overseeing and participating in an academy class several years ago as a critiquer on officer survival concepts. My job was really to evaluate how our cadre of instructors was handling their individual group sessions during role-play scenarios.

In my capacity as a command officer, I began to see and understand how my visible presence interacted with the class itself. The recruits had been inundated with the officer survival mindset for several days during their blocks of instruction on vehicle stop tactics, building searches, domestic disputes, etc. But now with the "brass" there watching, it became evident that this stuff wasn't just the usual "scare tactic" crap planned by the training staff just to see who could cause the first anal evacuation in the class. It had to be pretty important if the "Lou" was watching and taking names.

It was also very revealing, not only from the perspective of the recruits, but also from the perspective of the instructors themselves. After returning to the department, I used this obvious reaction to my presence at the academy to suggest to my superiors that a planned program of officer survival topics be implemented for every watch commander to incorporate into their roll call training.

Any supervisor knows that time management is important and budgeting time is critical for today's law enforcement professional. So when asked to justify this little tangential venture into the field of roll call training, I had to do a good selling job to the Chief.

Roll call training is important in our agency, but it is also many times a luxury. Frequently, calls of a non-emergency nature are stacked up at the end of the shift to keep overtime costs down and emergency jobs that come in during roll call have to be answered Code-3. In fact during the hot summer months, roll calls may not even be conducted beyond the first 3-4 minutes of assigning cars, beats or zones, and "special attentions." So the idea of delaying calls even longer to extend roll call was obviously not a really popular one. "It had better be important, Lieutenant."

My intentions were to use the roll call format as a classroom for officer survival topics. The Chief bought it, within the usual area of constraints, such as cost, time out of service, etc. I was allowed to budget 10 minutes of each day's roll call, or if manpower constraints prohibited that, then at least once each tour of duty, to discuss officer survival topics.

Some topics discussed included Approach to Danger in Domestic Disputes, Danger Cues in Vehicle Stops (out-of-state rentals, trunk locks missing, or just calling for "wants and warrants" before lights are activated), Contact and Cover (when back-ups were available), and Silent Alarm Response (parking the vehicle two houses down). Little "survival" reminders were also discussed after each roll call rather than a simple, "And hey, let's be care out there," a la *Hill Street Blues*. Sometimes when the lesson plans were 30 minutes long, the topics were extended over two or three day. Our hopes were to make officer survival not just something to practice during firearms training, but something to think about in the officers' everyday, "routine" calls for service.

Now, you're probably thinking that ol' Dave here has lost it, right? But think about it. Death notifications have caused a great many psychological reactions among recipients. Is this any safer than a call of a full-blown EDP (emotionally disturbed person)? DOA notifies can, and in many cases have, caused short-term dangerous EDP's.

EMS assists quite often involve drug overdoses. Ever start your day with a PCP freak? And "barking dog" calls have led to a great many in-progress burglary arrests, and I'm speaking from personal experience here. We even used a short segment from the Calibre Press, *Surviving Edged Weapons* video tape for a mini-class on Edged Weapon First Aid. But the roll call training didn't just stop with physical survival tactics.

The academy sent down a training program/video tape on Sudden Infant Death Syndrome (SIDS). We also prepared and distributed a short roll call training presentation on Critical Incident Stress so officers could understand that their reactions (if they did occur) were normal.

Again, when the police academy produced an in-service training program/tape on defensive/pursuit driving, we followed it up with a short lesson plan on the legal issues of pursuits, and the effects of siren hype and adrenaline dump during chases. It wasn't hard getting our watch commanders to understand that officer survival training can and should be a year round program.

During my last three years on the job, I was a field training officer watch commander, which means that my shift had the rookies who were coming right out of the academy for their fourteen weeks of field training. I also had two FTO sergeants working for me. The FTO Evaluation Form measured, among other categories, "Officer Safety." It was very rewarding to see the ratings climb after our roll call training sessions began to include officer survival issues.

As an added advantage, we found out that many of our "brass" were closet instructors too. This made each of them, without exception, see how important their roll calls could be. Rather than simply reading the previous sixteen hour crime run-down and assigning which officer to which car or partner, their roll calls now became classes on tactics, situational analysis, and critiques of different jobs. Later, when our department was undergoing the New York State Accreditation Review, and the evaluators looked at "department provided training," the charts for each officer looked very impressive; another added benefit.

Young, impressionable officers tend to follow the leads of their senior officers and supervisors. I have seen many young officers take on the command style of their long since retired commanders after they themselves were awarded their stripes or bars. Preaching and following good officer survival concepts will be an asset to those command officers who just happen to find themselves at the scene of a high risk incident on the street. They can also be secure in the knowledge that they're "leading by example" principles might rub off on their subordinates.

Conclusion

Many years ago, I worked for a lieutenant who personified what the ideal command officer should be. He was impeccable in his appearance, fair in his decisions, and tough in his standards. When asked what was most remembered about him, his subordinates would very often say, "His men would follow him into Hell." I truly admired that man.

Years later, when I was promoted to lieutenant myself, I patterned a portion of my command style around "ol' Lou." I envied the fact that "Lou" commanded the loyalty of all his men. Then I finally figured out why. It was because, while all his men *said* that they'd follow him into Hell, I realized that "Lou" *would never ask them to go.*

In his own way, he preached the modern day tenets of officer survival. Years before Pierce Brooks put his ideas into words, "ol' Lou" was applying them on the street and in a squad room in upstate New York.

"Ol' Lou" is gone now, and I'm three years retired from active duty. But shortly before I sat down to draft this small piece on *The Supervisor's Role in Officer Survival Training,* I overheard a young cop talking to his fiancee. The scene was a PBA Social and I was attending with my wife. This young cop, on the job about five years, was pointing out certain people to his future bride. I heard him utter these words, "I'd follow that man into Hell," and I instinctively turned and looked for "ol' Lou." The young cop was pointing to *me.*

If this was my contribution to officer survival as a supervisor, then maybe I made a difference. Every command officer in their own way, has to be an officer survival instructor. Our subordinates need it, they desire it, and they truly deserve it.

Craig V. Hasting

Mr. Craig V. Hasting, Deputy Inspector of Police, is a 27 year veteran of the Milwaukee (WI) Police Department. He is a graduate from the University of Wisconsin-Milwaukee with a B.S. in Criminal Justice and an M.A. in Political Science. He is also an Adjunct Faculty Member at Milwaukee Area Technical College and a Special Presenter at many other area colleges.

Mr. Hasting is an active member of many professional associations including: Law Enforcement Training Officers Association of Wisconsin; International Personnel Management Association; and American Society of Law Enforcement Trainers.

Chapter 13

Motivation and Morale: The Supervisor's Challenge

by Craig V. Hasting

"In the early years of this century, supervisors ruled by combining force and fear." [1]
— Jack Horn

Most studies confirm several major reasons why people become law enforcement officers: Good pension, excellent opportunity for advancement, job security, good life and health insurance programs, fairly decent salary, and an overwhelming desire to help people. All these positives are reinforced throughout recruit training. Knowledge of the job is absorbed. Skills ranging from communicating to first aid are learned and practiced.

Acquiring and maintaining a positive attitude is soon understood to be a cornerstone of the training program. Attitude is everything! Graduation represents a successful culmination – the transition of citizens to law enforcement officers, resulting in able, willing police officers who are sensitive to the needs of the community they are sworn to protect.

Why law enforcement officers do what they do has been an intriguing study for many non-law enforcement *experts* who fashion *models* for real law enforcement to implement. Developing profiles based on personal traits, knowledge, or skills appear to work best when recruiting and selecting applicants. Even standard pre-employment questions — why do you want to be a law enforcement officer? — have fairly standard responses. Much less clearer, however, is the question – once employed, why do officers continue to perform (behave) as they do or don't do? And finally, can supervisors have a positive effect on the behavior of their officers?

Remember when . . .?

To try to understand the complex issues involved in human behavior and to set the stage for your subsequent behavior as a supervisor a little review is appropriate.

Do you remember those first several years you were on the job? Naturally, you joined the police force because you wanted to be of service to your community; to change things; to make a difference. The next thing you know you are working nights and thinking something is definitely wrong with this picture. When every sane person is sleeping, you are walking in some deserted alley accompanied only by stray dogs, cats, and rats. You get up to go to work when your family is going to bed. You go to bed when your family is going to work or school. And how about the sweltering heat, freezing temperatures, or occasional snow storm that greets your freshly shaven or perfumed face as you step out the door for the midnight to 8:00 a.m. shift. Why on earth are you doing this?

Do you remember working hard to be a professional police officer and to live up to the law enforcement code of ethics, only to see the rest of the system break down around you? To realize you must bear the awesome responsibility to enforce all laws equitably, fairly, and without regard to race, sex, religion, national origin, or lifestyle only to find out that everybody else, including fellow officers, have their own viewpoint on who should be arrested and why. So much for discretion.

Do you remember how you lost most of your civilian friends, to be replaced only with other cops? Only they could understand the seven hours and fifty-five minutes of routine and the five minutes of life and death. Only 'my partner' could appreciate life on the street. And while on the subject of appreciation, no one seems to recognize your supreme efforts to save the world; not the community; not even your boss. Certainly not the media whose existence rests on selling bad news. Just screw up on a slow news day to find out!

Do you remember how careful you were while searching and arresting suspects so as not to have a case overturned later in court? The fear you felt should you actually have to use deadly force? Working with the knowledge that your every action (or inaction) would be reviewed months, maybe even years later, and lead to dismissal of charges against the suspect, or the issuance of charges against you?

Do you remember the culture shock when you first realized that working the street was nothing like what you had seen on *Hill Street Blues*? And yet you go to work, work hard, work smart, and behave as a professional law enforcement officer. Why?

Why would a reasonable police officer perform tasks that most intelligent people don't want to do, but that almost every citizen seems to know how to do better? What would motivate people to perform their proscribed duties in a manner befitting a professional law enforcement officer?

Do you have the answer? If yes, in all likelihood, you are a police officer. If not, you are probably a supervisor. That is precisely the problem. Supervisors frequently forget what motivated them; what the incentives were that spurred their actions. Consequently, they are unable to identify with the needs, wants, goals, and objectives of their officers.

Further, these supervisors are unable to effectively motivate their officers to perform toward achieving personal goals while meeting organizational goals. Lastly, these supervisors will never resolve the primary function of supervision: Get the job done and keep the group together. Faced with this administrative dilemma, too many supervisors resort to a leadership style that can only be characterized as force plus fear.

As a result, supervisors lose sight of the very needs that served as their own incentives. The frustrations, fears, and apprehensions stemming from ambiguous organizational goals, non-participatory management styles, inequitable performance reviews, and ambivalent supervision are all set aside, forgotten. The simple truth is that a new supervisor has created a new set of goals to attain and they don't include the officers. This only confirms what most street-wise officers know already: To be the boss, you do what is good for the boss and forget what is good for the officers.

Boss Versus Leader

Paul Hershey and Kenneth H. Blanchard developed "The Leader Effectiveness and Adaptability Description (LEAD)" testing instrument designed to measure an individual's self-perception of three aspects of leadership behavior: Style, style range, and style adaptability.[2] After several years of administering this test to newly promoted first line supervisors, I found that the results have never failed to surprise the participants.[3]

Remember, most supervisors really believe that they not only care about their subordinates, but are understanding of their needs. They also perceive themselves as anything but a dictator with a telling style of leadership. The results say otherwise. Indeed, a majority of the class falls squarely in the telling style of leadership. The leader is decidedly concerned with getting the job done – high task behavior and little or no attention is paid to the socio-emotional needs of the individual or group (relationship behavior). Test results further disclose that most supervisors are not very flexible in their use of other styles, irrespective of the situation or problem.

Another revealing aspect of this test is the failure of supervisors to employ a leadership style dependent on the maturity of the subordinate. A subordinate who is both able (job content) and willing (attitude), is likely to respond better to a participatory or delegating style of leadership. You can plainly see the problem: A leader who continuously relies on "a telling style of leadership" may be successful in the short run, or even in a few selected situations, but will ultimately be less effective when the maturity of the subordinate is considered.

An emergency situation such as a car accident with injured people may appear to be an ideal situation for a supervisor to revert to "a telling style of leadership." If the officers on the scene are trained, know what to do, and are doing it, is it proper to step in and take charge? You are the boss, right? You have the authority to do that, but what will it cost?

Motivation

"Motivation involves the application of incentives which encourage a certain positive pattern of behavior and attitude, and contributes to the accomplishment of organizational goals."[4]
— N.F. Iannone

"Motivation is the willingness to do something and is conditioned by an ability to satisfy some need for the individual."[5]
— Whisenand and Rush

A while ago, as a supervisor, I received the following telephone call from an officer: "Captain, I won't be coming in to work today." What's the problem? "I'm having trouble with my eyes." I'm sorry to hear that, anything serious? "No, I just can't see coming to work today."

This kind of conversation makes you stop and think about Iannone and Whisenand. Has this individual lost (maybe temporarily misplaced) the willingness to perform? He no longer acknowledges the presence of any incentives for him to accomplish. He is unwilling to expand any further energy toward a need that either has been satisfied, does not have value, or is no longer attainable.

Clearly, controlling and directing this subordinate's behavior goes well beyond the supervisor's reliance on policies, procedures, and rules. Understanding individual needs in the context of the work environment is central to the ability of the supervisor to motivate the subordinate.

In the February 1980 issue of the *FBI Law Enforcement Bulletin,* "Management Control Through Motivation," Special Agent Donald C. Witham presented a review of motivation.[6] Witham explains the most common tasks of management are planning, organizing, directing, staffing, and controlling. Further, he suggests controlling is the least understood management tool and, as a result, is underutilized.

A historical review of motivational theory and processes are presented to enhance police supervisors' capacity to get the job done and to be able to control a subordinate's behavior. A key element of this approach is the supervisors' recognition of the goal of having subordinates control their own behavior. Central to this issue is the creation and implementation of a system of rewards for superior performance.

In a creative approach to Abraham Maslow's hierarchy of needs, Witham developed a hierarchy most police officers can readily identify with. Recall that Maslow's needs are incremental in nature, goal oriented, and each level must be achieved before proceeding to the next level.

At the base of the pyramid, rather than physiological needs of food, water, and air, Witham suggests the basic need is pay. At the next level, rather than safety needs such as physical and emotional stability, there are seniority plans, union representation, grievance procedures, and pension plans. Both include social needs at the next level.

Maslow suggests social needs of affiliation and love. Witham proposes the need is to be part of informal work groups, sports, car pools, and picnics. Choir practice? At the fourth level, Maslow suggests ego and self-esteem needs that Witham defines as titles and status symbols. Your own office with a telephone? Both pyramids are capped off with self-actualization, "To become what one is capable of being."

Peter Drucker has stated, "People act as they are being rewarded or punished."[7] As indicated earlier, supervisors certainly can motivate through fear, force, and punishment. The challenge, then, is to know the needs of your subordinates to facilitate how and when to reward.

One last thought on knowing and understanding human needs as a means to control through motivation. Human behavior can be both emotional and rational. Victor Vroom's expectancy theory of motivation suggests that people will act in a particular manner based on how certain they are of a reward and to what degree that reward has value to them.[8] The prospect of an extra day off would in most instances be a valued reward, but has absolutely no value to the officer who is required to appear in court that day – probably as a result of the original good police work that earned the officer the day in the first place!

These are not experimental or 'rocket scientist' concepts. Volunteer adult leaders in the Boy Scouts of America have been instructed this information in knowing and understanding the characteristics and needs of youth since 1917.[9]

Morale

Up to this point, we have discussed motivation from two distinct perspectives. One perspective emphasized the existence of a hierarchy of needs supervisors must be cognizant. The second perspective stresses the mandate supervisors have to use this knowledge to motivate subordinates to achieve organizational goals. Both perspectives have a central theme: To achieve a point at which subordinates assume self-control, lessening the requirement of management to rely on traditional means of fear, force, or negative discipline to motivate.

A third perspective is the role of the supervisor in creating a healthy environment within which work is to be performed. Frederick Herzberg suggested a two-factor theory to the study of human needs.[10] The first, or good factors, are job related and correspond to the third and fourth levels of Maslow's hierarchy of needs. Herzberg's second factor identifies what people feel are bad feelings toward their jobs. These include the environment in which the work is performed. In comparison to Maslow, these "hygiene" factors are the first and second level of needs. For example, what is the reply of a recently retired police officer to the question, "Do you miss the job?" Inevitably, the response is, "I miss the guys, but I don't miss the work."

It is important for the supervisor to understand that the work environment can have a significant influence on work performance. A good leader frequently is described as one who has the ability to maintain a high level of discipline, morale, and espirit de corps. Getting the job done and meeting subordinates' needs, largely through instilling self-control mechanisms, can be closely associated with motivation.

A separate but interconnected issue stems from the environment in which the subordinate works. In this respect, morale becomes an important consideration for supervisors to address. Iannone defines morale as "a state of mind reflecting the degree to which an individual has confidence in the members of his or her group and in the organization, beliefs in its objectives, and desires to accomplish them."[11]

Morale of the individual or group of individuals can fluctuate up or down as a consequence of events occurring in the work place. Supervisory acts of partiality, unfairness, or uneven discipline are a few examples of working conditions which may result in low morale.

David M. Mozee distinguishes between motivation and morale, stating motivation is more of an individual and personal force. Morale is a "feeling of a state of mind that is expressed in pride in the police agency, devotion to duty, cooperation with others, and loyalty." He laments that so many supervisors have failed to recall their days on the street; absent today is a sense of pride in individual work and in the organization.[12]

Summary: The Challenge

For managers and supervisors to become effective leaders, there is a clear mandate to understand how motivation and morale impact on individual officers. Traditional management functions of planning, organizing, staffing, directing, reporting, and budgeting must include the single most critical factor in any organization: The human element, the employee. Reliance on fear, force, or rank will no longer be acceptable or tolerated. Police officers, by the nature of the job, operate within a series of complex and changing conditions.   Clearly, supervisors also must be able and willing to respond to the needs of the followers.

Finally, supervisors who forget where they came from will only become the nemesis of their subordinates and their performance (the job will not get done), and the creator of an environment that fosters low or poor morale (keeping the group together).

Footnotes

[1] Jack Horn, *Supervisors Factomatic* (Englewood Cliffs, NJ: 1986).

[2] Paul Hersey and Kenneth H. Blanchard, "So You Want To Know Your Leadership Style," *The Leader Effectiveness and Adaptability Description, Training and Development Journal* (February 1974).   Also see Hersey and Blanchard, *Management of Organizational Behavior* (Englewood, CA: Prentice-Hall, 5th Edition, 1988).

[3] Northwestern University Traffic Institute, *Supervision of Police Personnel* (Evanston, IL: Instructional Course Designed For Newly Promoter First Line Supervision, 1986 to present).

[4] Nathan F. Iannone, *Supervision of Police Personnel* (Englewood, CA: Prentice-Hall, 4th Edition, 1987).

[5] Paul M. Whisenand and George E. Rush, *Supervising Police Personnel* (Englewood, CA: Prentice-Hall, 1988).

[6] Donald C. Witham, "Management Control Through Motivation," *FBI Law Enforcement Bulletin* (February 1980).

[7] Peter F. Drucker,*The Practice of Management* (Harper and Row 1954).

[8] James A.F. Stoner and R. Edward Freeman, *Management* (Englewood, CA: Prentice-Hall, 4th Edition, 1989).

[9] Boy Scouts of America, "Woodbadge," *Adult Leader Advanced Training Manual* (Irving, TX: 1991).

[10] Stoner, IBID

[11] Iannone, IBID

[12] David M. Mosee, "Motivation of Police Personnel — A Different Approach," *Law and Order* (May 1989).

Bryce D. Kolpack

Mr. Bryce D. Kolpack has worked for the Appleton Police Department since March of 1979, serving as a patrol officer, Patrol Supervisory Sergeant, SOU Supervisory Sergeant, Resource Development Unit Lieutenant, Operations Bureau Captain, and finally Operations Bureau Deputy Chief. Prior to that, he was a dispatcher for the Merced County Sheriff's Department and a patrol officer with the City of Merced, California.

Mr. Kolpack is a contributing editor for Law Enforcement Technology magazine and has had numerous articles published for Law Enforcement Technology, The ASLET Journal, and other journals primarily in the area of management and personnel practices.

Mr. Kolpack holds an Associate degree in Criminal Justice from Merced Junior College and a Bachelor's in Management from Cardinal Stritch College in Milwaukee, Wisconsin. He is a graduate of the 164th class of the FBI Academy in March 1991.

Chapter 14

Professional Networking

by Bryce D. Kolpack

Within the last forty years, America left the Industrial Age and entered the Information Age. We now live in a world where ideas shape, sustain, and challenge us. The critical base that will sustain future development is communications – both interpersonal and commercial. Examples of the recent changes in physical communication technology include:

☐ low-cost, self-directed phone service,

☐ development of the personal computer and modem communication

☐ Formation of computer bulletin board systems

Law enforcement administration has shared in this evolution. Criminal justice agencies have adapted communication technology to management techniques. Old methods of gathering vital management data are being surpassed by technological wonders that couldn't have been imagined a century or even a decade ago.

We have moved from call boxes on street corners to car radios. The technology has continued to expand to include mobile computer terminals that can be configured to have fingerprint identifying capacity.

Even as law enforcement uses new technology and innovative management techniques, the common refrain of, "We have a problem. What's the best solution?" remains.

We may try to create new or unique solutions for our problems and assume that no other law enforcement agency has ever experienced this type of dilemma. Unfortunately, law enforcement agencies exist in limited, independent, and remote environments. These circumstances often lead to restricted thoughts and ideas of how to fix the dilemmas facing us today.

It is a rare occasion when a local problem is so unique that someone else hasn't already met a similar situation. It is quite probable that other law enforcement agencies have discovered a specific solution to an unanticipated problem. The critical, missing element is finding out which agencies have found an appropriate resolution which will help with the our local problem.

When a law enforcement supervisor has a management problem, a connection could be made with someone who has the necessary resources or information to assist. The first contact will often lead to other law enforcement managers who can provide additional insights. This type of communication is called "networking."

Networking is as old as the development of language and tools. Stone Age cooperation led to the development of social groups beyond the family circle. But modern networks are also an example of a new paradigm. Multiple solutions and alternatives are identified through informal interactions with knowledgeable peers. Multiple viewpoints of a specific problem will often provide new insights that haven't been considered before. Moreover, the consensus of multiple experts regarding a singular issue strengthens the agreement of the solution.

Networks are collectives of peers, friends of friends, organizations of peers with mutual interests, coalitions of organizations, and alliances of all sorts. In the book, *Megatrends*, John Naisbitt identified networking as a movement which will be replacing hierarchical, bureaucratic systems as a means of organizing people into effective work groups.

A good example of the power of networks occurred over 300 years ago. Before the American Revolution, "Committees of Correspondence" were loosely organized within small communities. Homespun philosophies and economic theories were transmitted through letters that were shared with many local neighbors. News sheets and pamphlets were carried from village to village as a means of sharing mutual information.

A professional network could be defined as an independent group of peers who share values, interests, or occupations. Then, through an informal exchange of concepts, thoughts and ideas, friends are able to learn from one another.

The conditions of personal trust and respect for another individual provide the basis for intense communication that would not be possible within a formal relationship. The underlying constant must be professionalism — a commitment to integrity and to the underlying law enforcement mission of "serve and protect."

Primary communications theory identifies networking connections as nodes or links. Nodes are the source or recipient of a particular piece of information — the end points. Links are the carriers which information uses to travel between nodes.

In human networks, an individual might be a link or a node. On one occasion, an individual might have the specific knowledge needed to help with a problem. At another time, that individual might act as a conduit to bring two parties together who have a joint interest.

Generally, networks will have a few participants, acting as primary nodes, who create many links to other nodes. Most of the informal network members tend to act as secondary connections, dispensing specific information to those who need it.

If one contact is unable to provide the specific information needed, they will probably refer the individual to a more knowledgeable expert. There are countless combinations of members within even a relatively small professional group.

The predictable advantages of information sharing could include:

Problem Solving — Discovering successful solutions to mutual problems. It can also provide details on those occasions when proposed solutions were *not* effective.

Creating Agency Programs — It is much easier to adapt an existing, functioning program than to create something from scratch. Learning from the mistakes of others will provide a means to implement new strategies within a community in an effective manner.

Public Relations — Networking is a two-way street. While interacting with local sources, law enforcement managers can communicate positive information to local contacts.

Expanding Personal Knowledge — "Knowledge is Power!" As law enforcement supervisors use their contacts to expand agency operations, they will gain additional experience and wisdom.

Job Opportunities — In private business, the majority of positions are filled through personal contacts. Public agencies may operate under different criteria, but the myriad contacts established through networking will provide a means for an ambitious professional to advance.

There are many different methods and opportunities to establish new, effective relationships. The important point is that a new supervisor needs to *recognize* such opportunities. When a contact is established, the professional law enforcement manager must find an effective means of noting and stabilizing the new contact.

Examples of the type of opportunities for networking:

 Individual Social Encounters — Conversations, meetings, phone calls, and conferences. The majority of information connections begin at a personal level. These are opportunities to reaffirm or redefine shared values. We also will use these events to establish or realign relationships, to develop new information, and to have social fun.

It is human nature to seek out common interests with a new acquaintance. An unexpected conversation may often lead to pointed discussions and personal insights into mutual problems. That preliminary discussion may later prompt a thought or an idea which falls within your own personal sphere of interest.

A scheduled meeting may have a specific *content* (the agenda), but the *structure* of the encounter also will generate knowledge. The specific time blocks of an organized schedule will usually allow chances for free form discussions. By creating an opportunity for interaction, outside normal channels, the social meeting will often provide all participants with additional experiences.

Professional conferences may provide the ultimate in networking opportunities. Such seminars bring professional associates together who share mutual interests and will often provide participants with phone numbers and mailing lists.

 Document Analysis — Letters, memos, reports, articles, and books. Most law enforcement managers tolerate paperwork as a necessary part of the job. They also make the assumption that external materials that are circulated through the agency will have little or no future impact on their personal job.

However, magazine articles, professional newsletters, and other documents may provide valuable contacts with other professionals. They have completed basic research on issues of mutual concern. Quite often, the authors of such documents will be very willing to share their findings, or they may direct your inquiry to others who have encountered similar situations.

Effective supervisors who want to stay abreast of professional developments will manage to read appropriate documents. By skimming some material, making copies of others, or purchasing original manuscripts, the supervisor will have necessary details available at a later time.

If supervisors are responsible for the preparation of letters, memos, and internal reports, they will have to consider all aspects of a problem situation. Seeking the input of others will assist effective supervisors. This will provide a broad perspective to a document.

Similarly, knowledgeable supervisors will keep those documents that help them in shaping future opinions and practices. Connecting with the original author can give the supervisor a different viewpoint on critical issues.

 Group Interactions — Professional associations, social groups, and community organizations. These interactions will include active and inactive contacts that are layered through experiences, friendships, and needs. The relationships will reflect shared values, goals, and objectives. Network bonds will be subjective rather than objective. This fact supports the common observation about the invisible relationships between network members. The specific principles that guide our personal and professional lives will often be reflected in our external relationships.

By nature, law enforcement officers tend to gather into professional groups. Such collegial organizations may mirror peer groups (work associations), special interests (crime investigators) or work assignments (police chief). These provide a natural, well recognized network which supports the formal members through services and contact lists.

Law enforcement managers may decide to abstain from formal contact with community organizations, but they are missing a rare opportunity. Necessary business relationships created the informal networks that eventually led to such associations as the Rotary or Kiwanis clubs.

Generally, self-reliant business people who are involved in aiding the community also participate in the creative sharing of related problems. In addition to the community service aspects, invaluable information and contacts can be developed through participation in such clubs.

 Electronic Communications — Computer networks– internal and external, free-standing computers interlinked through common electronic protocols. Without question, the best conduit for information sharing in the 21st century will occur through participation in Electronic Bulletin Boards (BBS).

In Wisconsin, the Attorney General's office is sponsoring the development of a system accessible by a toll-free telephone number. It will allow all state law enforcement agencies to communicate regarding common problems and shared interests.

Additionally, there are national systems available through major groups, such as Police Executive Research

Forum and International Association of Chiefs of Police. Some individual departments have developed internal electronic bulletin board systems which also can be accessed by other agencies. Supervisors, who are computer literate, will have a major advantage in knowing how to use the available information and message posting of an electronic system.

Action Steps to Professional Networking:

Actively Seek New Contacts — Do not wait for people to approach you. Join professional groups and make friends with peers in other local agencies. Respond quickly to any inquires made of you or your agency. Don't be afraid to share new programs with others. Don't be afraid to ask a personal friend for further contacts that can be of assistance. Use your friend's name as a reference. This will put the new source more at ease.

   When attending a large social event, make a point of introducing yourself to others. If a training conference includes a meal, try to sit down with people you have not met before. While discussing topics of mutual interest, you may find that your new acquaintance has information that you had not known before.

Look Outside Law Enforcement — Make friends with managers and supervisors in local industries, especially those who work in similar capacities. Participate in local service organizations.

   Join classes, at local educational institutions, on topics that are useful for personal growth (Business management, computer applications, foreign languages). The instructors may be a rich source of information. They can also be a conduit to additional research or experts in the educational field.

Exchange Names and Numbers — Use business cards when making contacts. This is a good way to remember who can be of future assistance. Dry gluing business cards to 3 X 5 note-cards provides extra room to write additional material. Make note of special interests, current programs, or activities that may be of use to you later.

Make Lists — Most managers receive phone message forms. Don't just throw them away! Keep track of prior contacts through an informal list that will provide a future resource. It is a normal practice for most formal organizations to distribute membership lists. Compile the lists into a three-ring binder for future reference.

 Read — In addition to law enforcement journals, an active supervisor will seek recent books and publications that aren't directly related to law enforcement work. Look for materials which will help you do your job. Skimming through all types of written material may trigger creative ideas, provide insights to problems, or provide the base for future action.

Multi-publication reading will not only improve personal knowledge, but it also exposes the manager to new concepts which can assist the agency. Authors of management books and articles will often refer to successful programs that can provide the reader with possible contacts.

 Identify and Contact Local Power Sources — The "good ol' boy network" has provided a clear but limited historical version of how well networks work. Unfortunately, they were used to reach limited goals. There are occasions when accomplishing agency goals may require additional "leverage." An effective supervisor will know who in the community has the knowledge and local cooperation to complete projects.

The networking process changes all those who participate by expanding their horizons. Through an increased matrix of relationships, our personal and professional lives can be enhanced. It is the intertwined information connections that sustain us.

Masterful supervisors must make the effort to develop a professional network that will help them meet their individual goals. The key ingredient is the willingness of the new manager to proactively communicate openly.

Edward N. Kondracki

Mr. Edward N. Kondracki is the Chief of Police for the City of La Crosse, Wisconsin, which has a 110-person police force. He is also a twenty-eight year veteran of the Milwaukee Police Department. During that time, he performed in all facets of law enforcement including patrol, investigation, administration, and training. He retired as an Inspector of Police, commanding the Office of Management, Analysis and Planning, assigned directly to the Chief of Police. During his last three years with the Milwaukee Police Department, he developed many of its Community/Problem Oriented Policing implementation strategies. He was responsible for having the Community/Problem Oriented Policing concepts adopted as the corporate philosophy of the department.

Mr. Kondracki is a graduate of Marquette University with a B.A. in Criminology and a graduate of the Northwestern University Police Management Program. He is co-author of A Practitioner's Field Guide to Problem Solving and is a faculty member of Northwestern University.

Chapter 15

Problem Solving Policing

by Edward N. Kondracki

A great deal of interest in recent years has evolved around a new philosophy of policing. The philosophy of Community/Problem Oriented Policing (CPOP) has evoked both skepticism and optimism among various community and police circles. For some it is viewed as a program which, in light of increasing crime rates, is long overdue and should be implemented immediately. For others, it represents mere rhetoric or a band-aid approach to more serious problems requiring greater attention.

In its broadest context, problem oriented policing is a comprehensive plan for solving problems, shaping the police agency, influencing personnel decisions, and organizational practices and procedures. Thus, problem oriented policing not only pushes policing beyond its current status, but calls for a major change in the direction of those efforts.

The philosophy goes beyond arrests as sole means to address problems. Strategies that address the underlying causes of crime or which impact on quality of life issues are developed with community input.

In Newport News, Virginia, where the objective was to introduce the concept to an entire police department, it was clear from the outset that more specific guidance would be required. A department task force met the need by creating a four-step process that officers were subsequently trained to use for a wide-range of problem solving:

 Scanning — which was designed to identify the problem;

 Analysis — which called for learning about the causes, scope, and effects of the problem;

 Response — which encompassed actions taken to alleviate

the problem; and

 Assessment — which reminded officers of the need to determine if the response worked.[1]

This systematic problem solving process has since been proven to be successful for addressing those many problems encountered by police. The process, which I will describe in more detail later, confronts street supervisors with a special challenge. That challenge being tapping the creative knowledge of those line officers with whom they have daily contact.

Traditional police agencies arranged around a quasi-military organization and management styles seldom take the time to empower their line officers to engage in problem solving. By encouraging line officers to interact with the public and by coaching them in problem solving, the line supervisor can enrich the work environment and increase productivity.

Call it total quality management, or participative management, the key here is employee involvement. Most police recruits will tell you that they selected a law enforcement career because they like working with people and want to make a difference. Here then lies the challenge, allowing police officers to work with people while solving problems and at the same time, meeting the many demands of the day to day calls for service.

Structured problem solving increases the reliance on the knowledge and creative approaches of line officers to analyze problems and develop solutions.

Creative problem solving requires no additional expense to police agencies, but rather taps new resources. The effectiveness of agency-wide problem solving can be judged by the extent to which the process taps additional resources in three major areas:

☐ line personnel

☐ the community

☐ other agencies both public and private

The line supervisor plays a pivotal role in bringing these new resources to impact on problems. The true problem solving agency will have a department-wide commitment to CPOP.

In such an agency, liaisons will have been established which provide contact persons in both the community and other agencies. Where such liaisons do not exist, it is incumbent upon line supervisors to establish such contacts.

The community can offer both technical and, in some cases, monetary support to police initiated problem solving efforts. Block clubs, citizen watch groups, and other volunteers are increasingly showing their support to police/community partnerships.

The community should be the first source for problem identification. When problems identified by the community are acted upon, citizens' support is a natural follow-up. Line supervisors should recognize and foster such interaction by attending community and neighborhood meetings.

The supervisor's role is to listen to community concerns and to seek solutions. The search for solutions should not be limited to what the police can do alone, but toward an effective combined approach. In other words, "We need not be limited by own limitations."

Other agencies both public and private offer a vast and to some extent untapped resource. Municipal agencies may be responsible for conditions which are contributing to a community problem or which can help to solve the problem.

The police serving as a trigger agency is often in the best position to recognize these contributing factors. They are, after all, the only governmental agency that makes "house calls" 24-hours a day. The key to the success of using other agencies is knowing who to contact and precisely what the role and limitations of other agencies are.

Line officers are critical to problem solving since they possess both the knowledge and often potential solutions to the underlying causes of crime and disorder. The supervisor as a coach or group leader must encourage line officers to provide feedback. Officers need to know that their input is considered important and that it will be acted upon.

By demonstrating the effectiveness of systematic problem solving, supervisors can lead their personnel through problems and toward the development of solutions. Without problem solving as its foundation, community policing and similar efforts make little sense.

The Process

The following discussion of the actual problem solving process is derived from a combination of the processes described by Professor Herman Goldstein in his book *Problem Oriented Policing.*[1] "The Community Patrol Officer Program," *Problem Solving Guide,*[2] was also used along with the author's personal experience dealing with law enforcement agencies across the country.

The actual problem solving process should be modeled to suit the needs of each police agency. The S.A.R.A. Model (Scanning, Analysis, Response, and Assessment) described by Professor Herman Goldstein has been proven to be successful for many police departments. This simple four-step process is most effective when accompanied by an uninhibited search for knowledge.

Scanning — This step involves discovering and identifying the problem. It is of the utmost importance to avoid mistaking a symptom of the problem for the actual problem. Repeat calls for service as an example, may indicate a deeper problem which when resolved will not only solve the problem, but reduce calls for service at the same time.

Problems which require police service, but which are not violations of the law, represent the bulk of police business. These problems are therefore legitimate targets for police problem solving.

Learning About Problems — The search should include:

- [ ] personal observations; looking beyond symptoms
- [ ] talking and listening to other officers
- [ ] reviewing all police reports
- [ ] newspapers
- [ ] interviews of people in the area
- [ ] political leaders
- [ ] civic groups

Learn More About the Problem — Two or more incidents may represent a problem. Evaluate indicators and recognize symptoms versus problems, i.e., is a theft really a lost wallet, etc.

Verify the Problem — Does the community perceive the problem as a problem? Avoid labelling problems from a purely police perspective.

Make Sure You Have Identified the Problem — It may be difficult to separate problems from symptoms. Is a series of shootings an indication of turf wars, lack of gun laws, drug problems, or do they have other causes?

Take Interim Action — When discovering and identifying problems it is *always* essential to take interim action. Interim action should address the immediate causes of concern to the community. The community needs to know that such action is being taken even though a long term response is still being developed.

Analysis — This step is directed at determining each aspect of a problem. This critical stage will determine the effectiveness of a tailored response. Most police/community problems can be separated into the three components of actors, actions, and reactions.

 Actors — When analyzing problems, it is important to identify the various actors involved. Actors include offenders, victims, and third parties. Consider all actors and their relationship to the problem. This includes their relationship to one another, to the problem, along with its causes and results.

 Actions — The actions contributing to a problem must be viewed in their entire physical and social context. Consideration should include physical settings, social context, sequence of events, and results of such events. Fear and isolation may well be the result of loitering in a social and physical setting which results in personal intimidation.

 Responses or Reactions — The present responses or reactions of institutions and the community must be considered. Is the problem being ignored by existing institutions? How do the neighborhood and community feel about the problem and are they willing to do something about it?

 Response — What will be the goal or goals of your action plan to address the problem? What do you hope to accomplish by addressing the problem? The success of this step is dependent on an accurate analysis of the problem as described in step two.

 Objectives — In designing a response to a community problem, several objectives must be kept in mind;

☐ The strategy chosen must go beyond the incident and address the underlying problem. Intermediate actions address incidents; solutions address problems.

☐ The strategy should be aimed at providing a long lasting solution to the problem.

☐ The solution should provide a substantial improvement for the residents of the community, reducing both harm to them and fear of future harm.

☐ The strategy should also be aimed at reducing police workload by eliminating the problem.

Types of Solutions

Types of Solutions — Solutions for police problem solving should not be limited to arrests. Arrests alone do not always address incidents or circumstances that are viewed as problems by the community. The planned response can be aimed at any of the following solutions:

☐ Eliminate the problem; while this may well be the best solution, it is not always possible.

☐ Reduce the frequency of incidents arising from the problem.

☐ Reduce the harm to the public from such incidents.

☐ Improve the public's perception of police handling of the problem. Frequently the public is not aware of the current handling of problems. Public information may solve a perception that problems are not being addressed or that they are not as large as originally perceived.

☐ Clarify responsibility for the problem. If the problem is properly the responsibility of another agency, the public needs to know this. The other agency should be alerted to the proper handling of such problems.

Developing A Strategy To Solve the Problem

Developing A Strategy To Solve the Problem — Proper problem analysis allows us to address strategies by altering specific behavior which has been identified as a component of the problem.

Altering the current effect of actors, actions, and reactions as they contribute to the problem is a key aspect of developing an effective response. Enforcement, requests for compliance, education, or providing alternatives to harmful behavior may be effective in altering the current activities of the actors.

The surveys of victims and third parties are a valuable tool in determining current responses by these individuals. Survey instruments are relatively new to law enforcement and are proving successful for many agencies in both identifying problems and in developing responses.

The physical setting, social context, and sequence of events are all areas in which conduct can be altered to change the end results of events.

Types of Strategies — The following types of strategies have been proven to be successful in addressing a wide variety of problems:

❐ Identify high risk offenders, locations, or victims and targeting them for special attention.

❐ Support existing relationships of social control as a means of influencing and controlling the behavior of persons responsible for creating problems.

❐ Organize and assist the community to get directly involved in solving their problems.

❐ Address directly social and economic conditions that may be contributing to problem behavior.

❐ Coordinate the police response with responses of other governmental agencies or urge other agencies to alter their responses.

Communicating With the Public — Communicating with the public is an area too frequently overlooked in police problem solving. Public fear can often be reduced by proper communication. The following communication techniques are among those which have been proven to be successful for police agencies when included as an aspect of an overall response to a variety of police problems.

❐ Educate the public about the seriousness of a problem.

❐ Reduce exaggerated fears about perceived problems.

❐ Convey accurate information to the public to help them comply with the law or to resolve problems themselves.

❐ Warn potential victims about their vulnerability and advise them about ways to protect themselves.

❐ Warn potential offenders that their behavior will be

monitored and warn them about the consequences of that behavior

The aforementioned steps in developing responses to police problems should be helpful when considering solutions. It is extremely important to consider getting help in developing such solutions. Other unit members, other police personnel, public and private agencies, community organizations, and individual citizens should be considered as sources of help when developing problem solutions.

Obstacles both internal and external must be evaluated when developing solutions and means to overcome such obstacles should be developed. Enough cannot be said about the importance of an overall project director to oversee both development of an action plan and to its proper implementation.

The project director should be responsible for developing a time table for gaining concurrence from other department and unit members for the response to be used. The project director should be responsible for communicating with other department members and for coordinating department resources necessary to implement the plan. The line supervisor, patrol sergeant, or patrol lieutenant is often the best choice for a project director.

 Assessment — Evaluating the effectiveness of the response is an essential part of the problem solving process. Without evaluation, we can never be sure if the strategy we have implemented is having the desired effect or indeed any effect on the problem at all.

The proper evaluations of police responses require that measures of effectiveness be developed. Effectiveness measures should determine if the solution is actually being implemented and if so, do the initial results indicate a need to modify the plan of action.

Effectiveness measures should be developed to ascertain the effect of the strategy on the goals of the plan. As an example, if the goal is to reduce drug sales and the strategy involves arrest and/or the closing of drug houses, have drug sales in fact been reduced?

Looking at the effect of the strategy on the dimensions of the problem is helpful. Have the actors, victims, and third parties been affected so that their responses and reactions have been modified to meet the goal of the planned response?

⮝ The following are some appropriate measures for determining the effectiveness of the plan:

☐ your personal observations while on patrol,

☐ talk to other police officers who work in the area,

☐ review police department records,

☐ conduct crime analysis,

☐ talk to representatives of other governmental agencies,

☐ talk to representatives of local civic organizations, and

☐ talk to the people who live and work on the beat.

Conclusion

Over the course of the past decade, the very role of law enforcement has changed from a responsive to a proactive mode. For the line supervisor, this change offers both challenge and opportunity.

The challenge lies in bringing together the collective resources of the community, line personnel, and other agencies both public and private to address problems.

The opportunity is that of advancing law enforcement toward the ideals of a true profession. Slowly but surely the police are emerging as the trigger agency to address community problems.

Line supervisors can enrich their careers along with that of line patrol officers by providing the opportunity to make a difference. The creative supervisor will look beyond calls for service seeking an understanding of their causes and long-term solutions.

The leader with a purpose will be followed. The problem solving process offers a structured approach for line supervisors who pursue the purpose of making their communities a better place to live.

Footnotes

[1] Herman Goldstein, *Problem Oriented Policing* (Mc Graw Hill Inc., 1990), 65.

[2] Community Patrol Officer Program, *Problem Solving Guide* (The Vera Institute of Justice and the New York City Police Department, September 1988).

Dr. Frank J. MacHovec

Dr. Frank J. MacHovec is a licensed psychologist and clinical supervisor of behavioral services at two Virginia adolescent corrections facilities. He is also a licensed private investigator and member of the American Society of Law Enforcement Trainers (ASLET) and the American Society for Industrial Security (ASIS).

Dr. MacHovec's chapter for this book is based on twenty years training of law enforcement and mental health professionals, most recently at the 1992 and 1993 ASLET conferences.

Dr. MacHovec is adjunct associate professor of psychiatry and behavioral medicine at the University of Virginia, and past President of the Virginia Association for Marriage and Family Therapy. He has written numerous articles in professional journals and eight books in mental health and law enforcement, one of which is Interview and Interrogation published by Charles C. Thomas.

Chapter 16

Counseling Skills for Supervisors

by Dr. Frank J. MacHovec

Supervisors are faced with the need to personally counsel those who report to them despite suggesting they consult others, such as a trusted family member, clergy, or professional therapist. Despite this effort there are times supervisors are in a counseling function and some knowledge of counseling skills is helpful. To help others requires *self awareness* to neutralize personal bias and "clean up your act" and *understanding others*, a basic knowledge of human nature.

Self Awareness

Socrates, the ancient Greek philosopher, is credited with saying, "Know thyself." He considered self awareness the first step to understanding others. It is more easily said than done. The poet, Carl Sandburg wrote, "Life is like peeling an onion – we peel off one layer at a time and sometimes we weep." Knowing the truth about yourself can be embarrassing, even painful. But "no pain no gain" applies to improving mental health just as it does to physical health.

Tinted Glasses

Forces within you from the moment you were conceived to this very moment exert a powerful effect on your perception, how you seeothers and what you think of them. How you see life and people shapes your personality and influences your behavior. When based on hurt feelings, anger, or resentment, they interfere with normal development and are obstacles to objectivity. It is as though you are wearing tinted glasses.

Sometimes you see what you want to see, what you've been

conditioned to see, not what's there. Some of us see the truth, some see part of the truth, and some never see the truth. It is as though "we can't see the forest for the trees."

Following is a list of roadblocks to clear perception. Reflect on each of them. Knowing them will ensure that you are not misled in conversation and that you don't prejudge others.

Genetic predispositions. What you inherited at conception such as sex, race, intelligence, fine motor skills, predispositions to height, weight, body build, and resistance to disease. People who are markedly taller, shorter, more obese or slender, or less intelligent are sometimes treated differently. Much sexual harassment occurs when women or gays are a minority in the work place. Being born and raised in a racial majority or minority can influence perception of yourself and others who look or seem different.

National, ethnic, and cultural differences. Israel Zangwill described the United States as "the Great Melting Pot." The flip side is that people who "talk or dress funny" are likely to be ridiculed.

Religion. A Constitutional right protected by law and "a personal matter." Courts rule that crime in the name of religion is not exempt from prosecution. Extremist religion can be destructive and divisive on the job if used to discriminate, belittle, or to show preference.

City, state, and regional pride. There are significant differences in regions (Grits, anyone?), sports and teams, holidays and history. Sometimes your behavior toward people "out of town" may not be the same as for local people.

Sex. Sexual harassment is more common than most people (especially men) have realized. Extreme feminism, male chauvinism, or gay rights advocates are sexist if they attempt to exclude others not like them.

Sexual experience. For many people, the first sexual experience was awkward, embarrassing, and may have conditioned us to distrust or fear the same or the opposite sex.

School experience. Your first day at school and the days that followed were a dramatic change from the safe nest at home. You had to share with strangers in a strange new place and be supervised by a grown-up you didn't know.

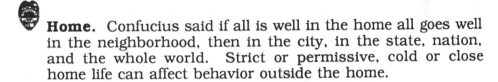 **Home.** Confucius said if all is well in the home all goes well in the neighborhood, then in the city, in the state, nation, and the whole world. Strict or permissive, cold or close home life can affect behavior outside the home.

Family and friends. Your "birth order" (only, first, middle, eldest), number and sex of brothers and sisters, whether both mother and father were present, grandparenting, number, age, and sex of childhood playmates all have an effect on your behavior. Ralph Waldo Emerson once said: "Show me your friends and I'll show you your true self."

Social status and standing. Generally, the higher your social standing the more removed you are from stressors of lower status, but the more is expected of you as "a pillar of the community." Example: Minister's and judge's sons and daughters are noticed more, especially if they get into trouble.

Physical health. "If you feel good you do good" is an old saying with much truth. If sickly as a child, you may tend to withdraw from others or still feel inferior. Or you may overdo to make up the difference. If always healthy, you may also overdo to "win" approval.

Occupation. Your occupation can influence behavior. Police officers tend to be more skeptical about human behavior because they are exposed to criminal behavior. Sometimes offenders from good families and "should know better."

Military experience. Severe stress of combat is a very powerful force. Even peacetime military service can condition behavior. The rigorous training far from home and civilian life to the use of weapons that prepare you to take life if necessary can distance you from feelings.

Marriage. Living with a person for most of your life is a dramatic change from unmarried life. Partners must adapt to one another and this has positive and negative aspects.

Children. People fall in love, marry, have children, and "live happily ever after." That's the "Hollywood ideal." There are unexpected or unwanted pregnancies, children with physical or mental problems, chronic or sudden illnesses that stress home and marriage. Children offer greater opportunity to share a loving relationship that overflows into daily life, with friends and fellow workers.

Money. Poverty robs people of dignity as well as food and property. Being "dirt poor" is not a happy or healthy way to live. Money is a force for good or evil. There can be heated disagreements over its use and management. Scrooge in Dickens' Christmas Carol is an example of how money management affects personality.

Trauma or loss. Catastrophe, crisis, sudden loss of a loved one or job can occur at any time; if severe and sudden, the greater its effect on personality and behavior. If not processed well, if it's avoided or blocked, it can continue for a life time, reflected in everyday behavior.

Listening Skills

A major obstacle to effective communication is also the simplest: just listening. Good communicators are *attentive listeners*, active, alert, and aware. They show it with *following behavior*, cues or signals that you *are* listening. They are nonverbal and verbal, such as nodding the head, a gesture, smile, or an occasional "uh huh" or "I see." Effective listening is to *hear what is said* not *what you want to hear*. The ARC Method is a three-step approach to effective listening:

- ☐ **A** = Active listening
- ☐ **R** = Reflecting in your own words what's said
- ☐ **C** = Clarification, when the interviewee confirms your rephrasing

The goal of active listening is not to exchange opinions, debate, or question the other person, but rather to *hear what is being said*, free of your own bias, without tinted glasses. The second step, reflection, is often missed or misused. It is best done neutral wording such as "I hear you saying" or "do you mean" or "are you saying." It is *most important* to avoid sounding sarcastic or belittling. Reflection must sound natural, not phony or manipulative. Clarification gives the other person the opportunity to correct or revise what was said, to more clearly state the message. Practice the ARC Method with friends and family in normal conversation. It will in time become automatic.

Defense Mechanisms

Under stress or threat (real or imagined) when we cannot control a situation we often use *defense mechanisms.* Most of the time we are not consciously aware we use them. They block awareness of realities that might hurt us. Usually they are obvious to others, not to us, but it *is* possible to recognize them. You can then choose to discard them if they prevent you from interacting positively with others. They can be strong or weak. Some overlap. A defense can be positive or negative depending on the situation. Study the list. Which do you *use*? Which should you *lose*?

≫ **Displacement** is dumping strong emotions onto something or someone not the direct cause of the problem, usually someone in an inferior or vulnerable position. Example: Boss gives you hard time, you dump on husband or wife, he or she dumps on kid, kid kicks dog, cat gets chased, mice death rate skyrockets!

≫ **Symbolization, identification** can be positive (*idealization,* hero worship and role models you admire or try to emulate) or negative (*devaluation, stereotyping, scapegoating,* targeting someone to blame to overcome your own inferiority feelings. Example: Jews in Nazi Germany.

≫ **Projection** is criticizing in others your own innermost thoughts or feelings, motives or wishes. Example: You peep out the window criticizing teenagers noisily having fun. You'd like to be young again and join in!

≫ **Isolation,** to "nit pick" or exaggerate a minor point. Example: You recommend against promotion of an employee you saw in a bar over the weekend, or you witnessed one incident when he or she had a heated argument with someone.

≫ **Somatization.** Physical symptoms due to psychological stress (*psychosomatic disorders*). Examples: Headaches, diarrhea, stomach problems, other aches or pains that occur only when the boss is there or an especially bothersome report is due.

⫸ **Denial-avoidance** is an inability to recognize or deal with a problem. Denial is total blocking ("I didn't do it!"). Avoidance is evading scrutiny by distraction such as changing the subject or refusing to discuss the matter further.

⫸ **Withdrawal** can be physical (walking away) or mental (going blank), direct (aware refusal) or indirect (passive aggressive), to avoid a painful reality. Example: The "Elephant Man" who physically avoided people and personal relationships because he feared rejection.

⫸ **Rationalization** is making excuses. Robert Louis Stevenson wrote: "I've heard many excuses but not one good reason." Example: The classical sexual rejection: "I have a headache!"

⫸ **Compensation** is coping with something negative by concentrating elsewhere usually on what we do well. Example: Napoleon, of short stature, became an audacious military commander, "Tall in the saddle."

⫸ **Reaction formation** or **paradox**, opposite behavior to what you really think and feel. Example: Little Johnny likes Sweet Sue so he teases her more than the other girls.

⫸ **Intellectualization**, a wordy, brainy, usually boring smoke screen or tangent to avoid dealing with reality. *Generalization* and *oversimplification* are forms of intellectualization.
Example: Doctor Drye over-explains medications and diagnosis to distance himself personally and emotionally from his patients.

⫸ **Regression** is to return to an earlier usually childish behavior to avoid dealing with a present problem. Example: Temper tantrums, jealousy, calling in sick when you're well (playing hooky), sexual harassment (teasing), affairs (playing).

⫸ **Humor** can be positive (an icebreaker, team builder) to overcome distance and show caring or affection or negative (to avoid or attack), a pointed verbal sword with which to deflect attack or to aggressively stab and jab. Example: Supervisor ridicules women officers' appearance in uniform (negative). Supervisor deliberately dresses *himself* improperly to demonstrate proper attire (positive).

 Repression is an unconscious (you're not consciously aware of it) complete *block* of awareness or memory of an event. Example: Child physical or sexual abuse that is not remembered until years later — if then.

 Suppression is willful blocking of awareness, conscious avoidance. Example: Scarlett O'Hara, hurt and frustrated, says: "I'm not going to think about it now. I'll think about it tomorrow."

 Dissociation is a break from reality or conscious awareness, usually under severe stress, into blank-mind withdrawal or fantasy. Example: A small child severely abused goes blank or becomes someone else, another personality, to survive (multiple personality disorder).

 Sublimation is diverting unattainable or improper impulses or ideas into socially appropriate channels. Example: Sam Satyr, high school student with the strongest sex drive in history, plays on the baseball and football teams, runs miles every day, and swims on weekends. If he didn't, every girl within 50 miles would be pregnant!

 Substitution is to replace someone or something for a lost loved one or object. Examples: Spouse dies, you date someone much like him or her. Car dies, you replace it with the same make and model. Pet dies, you replace it with same breed and color.

 Acting out is impulsive over-reaction, excessive, extreme venting, usually inappropriate. Example: Your car won't start so you get your shotgun and shoot it. Rejected by your lover you sit at a bar, drink a bottle of beer then throw it threw a window.

 Undoing is placating, over-apologizing, to "undo" previous behavior. Example: "Survival guilt" of persons who lived through a catastrophe feeling they must make up for not dying.

Understanding Others

Personality

It is useful to know something about personality to better understand human nature and help others. There are three major theories:

- ☐ psychoanalysis
- ☐ behaviorism
- ☐ humanism

Psychoanalysis is the theory originated by Sigmund Freud. Its major concepts are the:

- ☐ unconscious
- ☐ ego states
- ☐ life phases

Freud taught the mind is like an iceberg, only the small part above the surface is known to us, the **conscious mind.** Most of our mental processes are hidden below the surface, the **unconscious mind**, accessible only with effort. Painful memories, mental unfinished business, are stored there.
There are three co-existent **ego states:**

- ☐ **id**, the primitive self
- ☐ **ego,** the conscious self
- ☐ **superego**, the conscious or internalized parent

We all pass through the same **life phases:**

- ☐ **oral phase** at birth (sucking)
- ☐ **anal phase** at about two years of age (toileting)
- ☐ **genital phase**, teens through adulthood

Bottom line: Most of what we think and do is influenced by factors and forces not known to or acceptable to us.

Behaviorism is the personality theory founded by John Watson, a psychologist, and further advanced by B.F. Skinner. It is a reaction to the insight and instinct emphasis of Freud and his concept of the unconscious. Watson charged there is no scientific proof for Freud's ideas.

Behaviorists see basic motivation in animals and humans as pursuing pleasure and avoiding pain. They see most behavior as learned and not innate or instinctive. In 1925 Watson wrote: "Give me a dozen healthy infants and I'll take any one at random and train him to become a doctor, lawyer, artist, merchant, Indian Chief and yes, even beggerman and thief, regardless of his abilities and race of ancestors." Bottom line: Much behavior is learned from others and ourselves by trial and error, reward and punishment.

 Humanism. Psychoanalysis and behaviorism view human nature as predetermined, either by instinct (Freud) or conditioning (Watson). In this sense they are deterministic. Because they search for simple causes they are reductionistic. Some psychologists found this approach too rigid and narrow, ignoring creativity and unique human achievements.

Great art and music exceed simple explanations. *Humanistic* psychologists believe there is more to human nature than learning or instinct. Bottom line: There is potential in everyone to transcend the past and present and realize a higher self.

Needs

Abraham Maslow formulated a hierarchy of needs that are universal. We pass through these need levels from infancy to adulthood, from basic survival to self actualization.

 Survival Needs are food, air, warmth, and shelter, to be dry, warm, fed, and held close. Example: Tender, loving care of an infant.

 Safety and Security, the need to be physically safe, protected from danger. Example: Relaxing by the fireplace with a good book; living and working in a safe, secure environment.

 Emotional Support, the "apron strings" dependency of early childhood. Examples: Feeling good knowing you have backup on a security post; getting advice from someone you trust; holding the hand of a dying person.

 Self Esteem, the need to belong, to feel accepted, approved, to have recognition and status. Examples: Teen gangs; fraternal organizations; a team working closely together.

 Self Actualization, the need to realize your own unique individuality, fulfillment, creative achievement, to become the best, the real you. Examples: Solving a tough case or security problem all by yourself; a happy marriage or close relationship in which you feel more fulfilled, complete than you would have been alone (1 + 1 = 3).

In a crisis situation, a natural catastrophe or violent crime situation, victims and witnesses will slide down the need levels in direct proportion to the severity of stress. In the most severe situation, people will be reduced to the lowest need levels, survival and safety. Here, a blanket, cup of soup, and a safe, quiet place, perhaps even a hug, are more effective than verbal reassurance.

Verbal Tactics

When faced with a person with a problem, there are many ways to respond. Saying the right thing in the right way at the right time is the key to effective counseling. Here are 18 ways to respond to others:

 Silence. Tactical use of pauses, "artistic repose"

 Time and Timing. Pacing, tracking, matched to need

 Direct Confrontation. "Hard line" or "tough love" approach

 Indirect Confrontation. "Soft sell" or "Columbo method" such as "I wonder if . . . could it be . . . if it were me . . ."

 Questioning. Quickly to outflank defenses, slowly to encourage deeper reflection

 Support/Rescue. "Pat on the back" reassurance, approval

 Explore Alternatives. To see choices and reward their decision-making

 Here and Now Focus. Only on the present moment or situation ("What are you thinking/feeling right now?")

There and Then Focus. Only on past events ("When's the last time it happened? Before that? When did it start?")

Underlying Reason(s). Probing for deeper unknown causes beyond/before the present problem situation

Clarify by stopping, repeat question, rephrase. Cools feelings, lessens anxiety, deepens understanding

Self-Disclosure, sharing your own thoughts, feelings, and behaviors in similar situations. Be Judicious!

Humor lowers defenses, builds trust but *must* be natural not hostile, to ridicule or belittle (timing important)

Role Play. Improvised hypothetical or real-life situations

Behavior Focus. "See, you're doing it now . . ."

Body Language Focus on posture, gestures, face, etc.

Verbal Behavior Focus, on what is said, quoting verbatim

Rules or Contract. Enforce ground rules or agreement

Use this list to find your communications style. On a separate sheet make three columns and list those you usually, sometimes or rarely/never use. This *is* your verbal interaction style. Try them all and build up your verbal skills.

And so . . .

If you are in a counseling situation, know your shortcomings and don't "play doctor." Refer to a mental health professional if you're in over your head. But in the many non-therapy situations where advice and support are needed, read, study, practice, and use the material here and — good luck!

Dr. Edward H. Mazur

Dr. Edward H. Mazur is professor of Behavioral Sciences in the City Colleges of Chicago Inter-Governmental Executive Development Program. He is also the vice-president of Mazur & Associates Training and Development.

For the last twenty-five years, Dr. Mazur has worked with a variety of local state, federal, and international public safety and security agencies. Recently, he has collaborated with officers of the Chicago Police Department (including the last five superintendents who were among his students), Cook County Adult Probation, and the NorthEast Multi-Regional Mobile Assist Training Unit.

Dr. Mazur holds Bachelor's and Master's degrees from the University of Illinois and a Ph.D. from the University of Chicago.

Chapter 17

Keys to Survival for Law Enforcement Managers

by Dr. Edward H. Mazur

How many law enforcement officers willingly stand behind their supervisors? Probably many fewer than any of us will honestly admit. The difficulty all supervisors, managers, and leaders face is how to effectively lead others to meet the goals of their organizations. This is very difficult work. Supervisors, managers, and leaders probably spend half their time at work struggling with this problem and the accompanying concerns caused by ineffective supervision and leadership.

Supervisors, managers, and leaders are made; not born. They can be provided with the necessary tools to survive the unique challenges of their jobs. The proper application of these tools can result in the production of excellent workplace supervisors, managers, and leaders.

The role expectations, focus, and ingredients for law enforcement supervisory and leadership success is undergoing continuous, rapid, and far reaching changes as the year 2001 nears. This chapter examines the changing nature of leadership and describes thirteen qualities needed to achieve success in law enforcement services.

In 1968, I was a young, idealistic, "wet behind the ears" assistant professor of social and behavioral sciences hired to teach sociology and psychology to probationary and veteran officers of the Chicago Police Department. Subsequently, I have worked with law enforcement personnel from more than 150 urban, rural, suburban, state, federal, and international agencies.

At the outset of my career, I frequently told my officer/students that leadership is an influence process. The act of leadership occurs when the leader succeeds in influencing the behavior of another person. Leadership style, the pattern of behaviors used by the leader when trying to influence the behavior of others, is identified frequently by two extremes – autocratic and democratic.

Extensive research, data, and observations over the past two decades have created a more comprehensive understanding of the qualities of leadership that are necessary for organizations to achieve their objectives. Successful leadership styles vary considerably from situation to situation. Instead of thinking of leadership style as an either/or continuum, it is more beneficial to think of leadership as situational. Directive and supportive leader behaviors are not either/or leadership styles.

Current research, field observation, and experience support the contention that there is no single best leadership style. To survive as a successful leader – we must be able to adapt our style to fit the situation. A number of variables influence which leadership style will be appropriate to each situation including time, job demands, organizational climate, and superiors, associates (peers), and subordinates' skills and expectations.

The increased diversity of the law enforcement workforce, the impact of the media (especially electronic), the demographic complexities of American society, individual and societal changing values, and national state and local public policies have all come together to challenge the leadership abilities of law enforcement leaders. Simply put – it is much more difficult to be an effective leader in the 1990's than it was in the 1970's.

In each of the law enforcement agencies that I have consulted with in the past decade, the workforce has become dramatically more diverse. In response to this diversity, the role of the leader has become more complex, challenging, frustrating, and rewarding.

Today, there are many more women in the workforce. Most men have not worked for a female manager or have not had the experience of supervising a multicultural workforce. Since in many jurisdictions there is no forced retirement at approximately age 60, the age range of the workforce will be even greater in the near future. A workforce of adults ranging from age twenty-one to eighty could be a real possibility. The difference in wants, needs, and values of such a divergent workforce places unique demands on the contemporary leader.

Court decisions, federal, state, and local legislation, government regulations, unions, and the increased use of modern technologies all combine to add scope, ambiguity, and newfound pressures to the role of "leader." The law enforcement leaders of 2001 will need to understand the new attitudes, needs, behaviors, and mindsets of the subordinates in their organizations.

Historically, law enforcement agencies have lagged in responding to non-traditional ideas for effectively using their human resources. Contemporary leaders will need to be technically proficient and adept at using interpersonal skills, and be able to conceptualize how their jurisdictions relate to other jurisdictions, agencies, and institutions. These leaders will need to accept that genuine recognition for jobs well-done, combined with decision making powers for subordinates on how their jobs are done, will be among the foremost management and leadership concepts they must incorporate into their survival kits.

The search for effective leadership is an ongoing dilemma that confronts all law enforcement agencies and their personnel. By effective leadership, I refer to leadership that is able to distinguish that which is the right and proper activity or policy to promulgate. Conversely, efficient leadership is leadership that accomplishes the task or objective in the proper manner, but it may not be correct.

We are continuously seeking answers to the ever perplexing question, "Can our organizations train a supervisor or manager to become a leader?" The often asked follow-up query to this is, "Can a person develop leadership abilities?" I submit that law enforcement managers must become leaders if they are to be successful.

On a daily basis, law enforcement practitioners are confronted with the necessity and challenge of developing leaders within their jurisdictions. Individuals, organizations, institutions, and even nations are making serious, conscious, and concerted efforts at developing effective leadership for the twenty-first century.

This chapter discusses thirteen qualities of effective supervision and leadership. All leaders at one time or another are either more or less effective in the process of influencing the activities of others in their efforts toward achieving a goal in any given situation.

The more effective leaders are comfortable with these thirteen qualities and characteristics. They are skillful at using them in the proper time, place, and with diverse populations, be they within their own organizations or in the larger public and private community.

There are clear differences between supervisors, managers, and leaders, but they are beyond the scope of this chapter. However, there are enough commonalities so that the three terms can be used interchangeably in the context of our discussion.

Law enforcement supervisors are integral factors in human resource management. Historically, the term "supervisor" covered those who have direct-line responsibility for the management of other employees. The National Labor Relations Act defines a supervisor as:

"Any individual having authority, in the interest of the employer, to hire, transfer, suspend, lay off, recall, promote, discharge, assign, reward or discipline other employees, or responsibility to direct them, or to adjust their grievances, or effectively to recommend such action, if in connection with the foregoing the exercise of such authority is not of a merely routing or clerical nature, but requires the use of independent judgment."

Most supervisors in the public and private sectors do not exercise all of the above responsibilities. However, all supervisors exercise some of them.

The primary difference between supervisors and managers is that supervisors deal with the day-in, day-out problems of handling people and production on the workforce front line. Managers are generally several steps removed from the so-called "firing line." In law enforcement sectors they manage other sworn and civilian supervisors, assistants, managers, corporals, sergeants, lieutenants, captains, deputies, assistants, and so forth.

Both supervisors and managers share some responsibilities including dealing with people, handling people problems, meetings goals, and keeping things moving. Unlike most supervisors, managers are concerned with activities that include long-term strategic planning, finance, marketing supplies, and productivity rather than directly impacting on the production of services.

Law enforcement supervisors are concerned almost exclusively with the challenges of people directly engaged in the delivery of services. They deal with people and people problems. To survive in the modern workplace, the law enforcement supervisor must visualize their roles as that of human resource managers. They must be managers of the workplace, keepers of procedures and rules, trainers of employees, workforce advocates, representatives of the organization, maintainers of safe and productive workplaces, and out-in-front leaders.

Leadership originates and resides within each law enforcement manager and relies as much on philosophy and values as it does on learned skills. During my twenty-two years as a criminal justice educator and trainer I have observed the importance of the following thirteen key leadership qualities:

 The first supervisory survival and leadership quality is **knowing your followers**. Supervisors have to help those who work for them to grow and prosper. To do this the leader must be sensitive to the needs of employees and recognize that there are certain human relations skills that need to be practiced. Effective supervisors get to know those whom they desire to lead. They do not spend their time closeted in their office (bunkers) surrounded by a circle of parasites who practice groupthink.

Effective leaders comprehend, emphathize, and if need be, disagree with the hopes, fears, values, biases, dreams, nightmares, aspirations, and disappointments of their personnel. These leaders manage by wandering around. They have mastered turning "win/lose" into "win/win" scenarios by demonstrating how the interests of the followers will be served best by aligning with the goals of the leader and the organization.

 The second quality is **leading by example**. Supervisors and leaders recognize the inherent skepticism that abounds among their employees. Differences arise between line and staff, between "street and desk officers," between those who wish to "serve" and those who wish to "protect," between those with decades of experience and little training and/or education and those with limited experience and significant amounts of training and/or education.

The effective leader understands the positive geometric potentials of diversity and uses role modeling. These leaders accept the concept of, "You can do anything I can do." Thus, "If you see me come in late, leave early, stay in my office, and not communicate with others, I expect you to do the same." Effective leaders set high standards and expect their people to live by the same standards that they do.

The third quality of supervisory survival and effective leadership is **courage**. Law enforcement personnel strongly believe that leaders should "have the courage of their convictions." They appreciate and expect their "bosses" to take a stand. Observation, interviews, and data all support the idea that personnel will follow those who believe strongly in their decisions and are equitable in creating them.

Employees want their leaders to set a fair and reasonable discipline line, and then maintain it for all employees. They want to be lead onto higher ground. Effective leaders stand on principle, yet they listen, understand, and empathize. Thinking must be ethical and based upon concepts of equity. A strong belief system is necessary to meet the countless number of challenges from within organizations and from the outside communities that are a daily encounter for the law enforcement leader.

Effective leaders maintain a strong belief and seemingly inordinate amount of conviction in their own physical, emotional, intellectual, and spiritual standards and values. The resulting intensity enables leaders to focus and direct all their creative energies when challenged by problems, difficulties, and opportunities of a technical, interpersonal, or conceptual nature.

General George C. Patton claimed that, "Courage is fear holding on another minute." Effective leaders are holding on. These individuals have a "breakfast of champions" and venture forth with stamina and faith that causes others to follow.

Visualization is the fourth quality necessary for supervisory survival and effective leadership. Those individuals who rise to the top in the law enforcement professions are those who have the ability to visualize the "big" picture. They "see" events, personalities, and issues from a multiplicity of perspectives.

They are curious people. They have the fortitude to be willing to challenge tradition. At times, this may seem unwise or even impossible in law enforcement organizations. However, the times are changing. To succeed in 2001, law enforcement leaders must become comfortable with managing change.

Leaders are not reluctant or fearful of being idealistic. Rather, they are eager to develop, create, and draw out the best that their personnel have to give their departments, their profession, themselves.

Visualized leaders have clearly defined their personal and organizational goals and objectives. They have the ability and patience to assist others in expanding their own thinking and imaginations. They are able to align the goals and objectives of line and staff with the overall mission.

The ability to **master change** is the fifth quality needed for supervisory survival and effective leadership. Leaders move and impel people and events in directions that are beneficial to all. The current emphasis on community oriented policing and the bottom-up empowerment makes this ability highly desirable.

Leaders not only have the ability and perseverance to create change, but they also relish, take-on, grapple with, and succeed during the highly stressful times that accompany change. Leaders welcome change. They have acquired the knowledge from the past and have trained themselves to be mentally equipped to let the past go when it is no longer useful to achieving individual and organizational goals.

The accomplished law enforcement leader does not burden their organizations and personnel with tired ideas, shopworn prejudices, habits, or processes. Even when these leaders do not personally delight in change, the effective leader seeks out the novel opportunities that accompany change. These individuals have institutionalized the so-called serenity prayer: "God, grant me the serenity to accept the things that I cannot change, courage to change the things I can, and wisdom to know the difference."

Persistent realism is the sixth quality of the effective supervisor and leader. This trait enables goals to be established that are realistic and capable of being followed through to completion. Even under diverse pressures, both from within their organizations and from without, effective supervisors and leaders remain committed to their realistic goals. These individuals have the ability to differentiate between real and imaginary obstacles and to acknowledge that both are powerful and unique forces.

Leaders recognize that current challenges are essential

to goal achievement in the future. Most dramas have several acts and effective leaders are willing to forego immediate satisfaction for future and long-term gain. Training, development, and philosophy have equipped these leaders with tenacity and endurance. Although, the strategies and positive and negative barriers to goal achievement are constantly reassessed, leaders are able to maneuver the effects of distractions that may hinder the completion of their tasks.

These effective leaders are skillful at assisting their personnel in surmounting both work and non-work related obstacles. The ability to convince staff that patience is a desirable and positive characteristic is by no means a small accomplishment in a profession where the emphasis has been placed on "taking charge."

 A **sense of humor** is the seventh leadership quality that is needed to survive and be effective. Over time, pompous asses will not succeed as leaders, managers, or supervisors.

The constant challenges of dealing with bureaucracy, unions, media, and diverse communities are no matter to be taken lightly. Yet, leaders who are positive role models have the ability to maintain a healthy and proper sense of humor. These leaders have the ability to be amused by and even laugh at themselves and some of their actions.

Frequently, leaders with a sense of humor are also enthusiastic, spontaneous, and have the ability to express and communicate their feelings. This contributes to trust, openness, and the camaraderie that is found within successful work teams and organizations. When the everyday stresses (those that may be planned for as opposed to emergencies) become problematic, the leader's sense of humor serves as a vehicle to give everyone a necessary, albeit brief, emotional release. The *sense of humor* tool enables the completion of at hand tasks with both balance and clarity of direction.

Effective supervisors and leaders are **risk takers**. This eighth quality is an integral part of the subject under discussion. Survivalists assess, evaluate, plan, and embark on a course of action. They are not "bulls in a china shop." They have the capacity to be initiators while others await safer situations, assured results, and permission from elsewhere.

Leaders are inclined to assume a risk because they have considered and weighed the alternatives. They are cognizant that being overly cautious and indecisive are "robbers" of opportunities and success.

Leaders recognize that they do not always emerge victorious. They understand the meaning of failure and how to build future successes. They have mastered the ability to put the overwhelming majority of challenges and problems into "win/win" contexts. They understand human nature and are able to act accordingly.

The ninth quality of supervisory survival and effective leadership is the ability to **set high standards and to accentuate the positive**. From a philosophical standpoint, effective leaders are optimistic and they have the ability to transfer this quality to others.

They have a high degree of trust in themselves and others. They keep things under control in order to lead. They produce reports to their superiors, their peers, and their subordinates on time.

They maintain their equipment. They honor the necessary precautions for individual and group safety and security – all without neglecting their employees and the goals and mission of the organization.

They accept the concept of employee empowerment. Long before the impact of W. Edward Deming and *Total Quality Management*, these leaders recognized and acted upon the premise that the smartest organizations put people first. These leaders are obsessed with making full use of their personnel.

These leaders reward empowerment. They train people how to empower and be empowered. They recognize that there is no such thing as an insignificant amount of empowerment. Any significant increase in empowerment is important to their organization's well being and the achievement of the mission.

The empowering of others to act is especially important in the law enforcement professions where often the lowest ranking individuals have the greatest amount of discretion. Conversely, the upper levels of supervision and management are the most circumscribed.

Leaders must recognize that all behavior has consequences, and they have the obligation with the input of those affected to see that these consequences are meaningful and will produce the desired results. Within this context, leaders are constantly taking and creating the actions needed to reinforce employee self-worth and the value of the various constituencies that are involved and affected by the decision making process.

Effective supervisors and leaders **make decisions**. This

tenth quality is augmented by the fact that leaders have strongly held beliefs. They are focused, and they clearly identify and believe in their mission. This enables their followers to recognize the leader's commitment on a daily basis.

Leaders acknowledge and recognize that not to decide is in effect to decide by fate, circumstance, and time. Leaders would rather take a chance of making an incorrect decision than to make no decision at all. In law enforcement there is truly a minority of decisions that are so critical that there is either no or limited opportunity for corrective action.

Indecision wastes precious resources including time, talent, finances, energy and motivation, and opportunity. If leaders are incapable of making a decision, then they will forfeit control of the future and be placed in danger of extinction.

 The eleventh quality is the **wise acceptance and use of power**. Effective leaders understand power. They recognize the positive and negative aspects and limitations of power. They do not shrink from employing power, nor seek it out unnecessarily. Rather, power is applied as applicable.

Leaders recognize that there are different kinds of power and power bases, and they have the ability to select the proper power mode to solve the challenge or problem. They skillfully use their power to direct others to assist them in achieving their fullest potential.

Leaders are those individuals who take responsibility for themselves, their actions, and the results of their actions. Power is not an end in itself, but a means to an end. Power is a by-product of understanding and mastering the services aspect of the law enforcement profession.

 Honesty is the twelfth quality of supervisory survival and effective leadership. When leaders make promises to their constituencies they earnestly seek to keep the promises. Honesty becomes the foundation for trust.

In order to gain the support of the rank and file, of the supervisory and management team, and of the larger community, the leader must be viewed as honest, credible, and capable. The leader is seen as focused, available, fair, and as a good listener – not just an individual who hears, but one who actually listens.

Credibility must be earned and many have learned how fragile this commodity can be at times. The important foundations of honesty and credibility must be serviced through regular and ongoing maintenance.

 Commitment is the final quality for supervisory survival and effective leadership. Without commitment all else becomes meaningless. Leaders have a zeal and a *joie de vivre* that serves as a magnet and attracts others to their sides.

The committed leader creates an atmosphere that exudes confidence and hope. In this setting, employees are willing to go the "whole nine yards" and are continuously redefining, enlarging, and challenging the defined limits of their responsibilities. These individuals establish lofty standards of excellence for themselves and others. Empowered individuals grow to meet the increased expectations.

The leaders determine a course of action, devise a plan, and then practice the self-disciplined follow through while being cognizant of the necessity for change and the surmounting of obstacles. Although future oriented, effective leaders live one day at a time and they are aware that if they take care of the present that the care of the future will be increasingly possible and manageable.

As the decade of the 1990's yields to the twenty-first century, the role of the law enforcement "leader" will become increasingly more challenging. The workforce will be even more diverse than it is currently. The problems of the haves and have-nots in society will become accentuated. The challenges of "Justice in a Free Society (the motto emblazoned on the police cruisers in my home community of Wilmette, Illinois)" and of managing those men and women who "Serve and Protect" will intensify.

To meet the demands of the foreseeable future, the law enforcement supervisor and leader must be able to effectively diagnose, prescribe, and practice the time tested supervisory and managerial functions of planning, organizing, staffing, directing, and controlling.

The human aspects of management will command increasing amounts of the time of any supervisor, manager, or leader. Interactions with people – sworn, civilian, community resident, law abider, and law breaker, will remain one of the most critically important components of any leader's job description. Success will come only if the thirteen qualities of effective supervision and leadership are recognized, understood, mastered, practiced, and applied on a fair and equitable basis.

Bibliography

Bittel, Lester R. and Newstrom, John. *What Every Supervisor Should Know* (6th Edition). New York: McGraw-Hill Book Co., 1989.

Bittner, Egon. *Aspects of Police Work.* Boston: Northeastern University Press, 1990.

Blanchard, Kenneth H., Zigarmi, Patricia, and Zigarmi, Drea. *Leadership and the One Minute Manager.* New York: Morrow and Company, 1985.

Copeland, Lennie and Griggs, Lewis. *Going International; How to Make Friends and Deal Effectively in the Global Marketplace.* New York: Random House, 1985.

Dennis, Leslie E., and Onion, Meredith L. *Out in Front: Effective Supervision in the Workplace.* Chicago: National Safety Council, 1990.

Fournie, Ferdinand F. *Coaching For Improved Work Performance: Why Employees Don't Do What They Are Supposed To Do And What To Do About It.* Blue Ridge Summit, PA: Liberty House, 1989.

Garfield, Charles. *Peak Performers are Second to None: How Our Smartest Companies Put People First.* Homewoor, IL: Irwin Press, 1991.

Hersey, Paul. *The Situational Leader.* Escondido, CA: The Center for Leadership Studies, 1984.

Hersey, Paul and Blanchard, Kenneth H. *Management of Organizational Behavior: Utilizing Human Resources* (4th Edition). Englewood Cliffs, NJ: Prentice-Hall, 1982.

Loden, Marilyn and Rosener, Judy B. *Workforce America; Managing Employee Diversity as a Vital Resource.* Homewood, IL: Business One Irwin, 1991.

Nowicki, Ed. *True Blue.* Powers Lake, WI: Performance Dimensions Publishing, 1992

Nowicki, Ed. *Total Survival.* Powers Lake, WI: Performance Dimensions Publishing, 1993.

Osborne, David and Gaebler, Ted. *Reinventing Government.* New York: Addison-Wesley, 1992.

Sparrow, Malcolm; Moore, Mark H., and Kennedy, David M., *Beyond 911: A New Era For Policing.* New York: Basic Books, 1990.

Stoch, Ernest L. *Leadership Communication.* Chicago: Nelson-Hall, 1983.

Dr. Murlene "Mac" McKinnon

Dr. Murlene "Mac" McKinnon is CEO and lead trainer of MACNLOW Training Associates, a company specializing in criminal justice training. MACNLOW delivers on site agency analysis and problem solving and Mac works one-on-one with corporate executives and police administrators to develop interpersonal communications skills. Her background includes twenty years as professor of management communications and nonverbal behavior.

Chapter 18

Interpersonal Communications Skills for Supervisors

by Dr. Murlene "Mac" McKinnon

Supervising employees, while often difficult and sometimes frustrating, can be some of the most rewarding and fulfilling work a law enforcement officer ever does. Although often stuck in the middle, between upper management and patrol officers, the first line supervisor bears the major responsibility for how the unit and each officer in it functions.

Experienced officers frequently like to serve on specialized departmental teams because of the camaraderie, the sense of mission, the cooperative teamwork, and the recognition. Sergeants who seek success as leaders can choose to develop this very same type of teamwork on their own shifts. Law enforcement supervisors set the tone which affects the workday climate for their subordinates. No command officer ever gets closer to the actual law enforcement team than its first line supervisor.

Supervising today's workforce provides more challenges than ever before. The once effective and expected authoritarian management style, which worked fairly well with a homogeneous, less educated, and less questioning group of subordinates who were loyal to the organization and valued job security, no longer produces a smoothly, functioning team. Diversity in the workplace applies at the minimum to age, gender, education, disabilities, and values. And, because of higher educational levels (even though certain basic skills are lacking), people are freer to move.

According to Jamieson and O'Mara in *Managing Workforce 2000*, the top values that motivate this changing workforce mix include:[1]

❏ recognition for competence and accomplishment

❏ respect and dignity

❏ personal choice and freedom

❏ involvement at work

❏ pride in one's work

❏ lifestyle quality

❏ financial security

❏ self development

❏ health and wellness

At the same time, Bradford and Raines in *Twentysomething*, see the twentysomethings' core values as:[2]

❏ self-orientation

❏ cynicism

❏ materialism

❏ extended adolescence

❏ quantity time

❏ fun

❏ delayed commitment

❏ indifference to authority

The first line supervisor who recognizes and acknowledges these new value mixes possesses an enhanced ability to resolve workplace issues and appropriately reward performance.

Personal Characteristics

The overall attitude of supervisors is the most significant determinant of supervisory success and is manifested in how leaders interact and communicate with those who report directly to them.

Strasser, in *Working It Out*, links four characteristics to effectiveness in interpersonal relationships.[3]

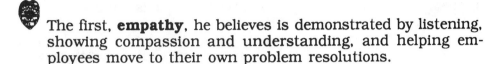 The first, **empathy**, he believes is demonstrated by listening, showing compassion and understanding, and helping employees move to their own problem resolutions.

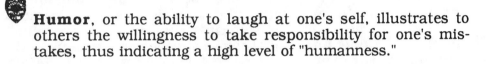 **Humor**, or the ability to laugh at one's self, illustrates to others the willingness to take responsibility for one's mistakes, thus indicating a high level of "humanness."

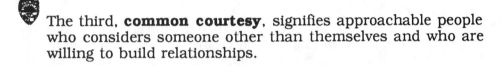 The third, **common courtesy**, signifies approachable people who considers someone other than themselves and who are willing to build relationships.

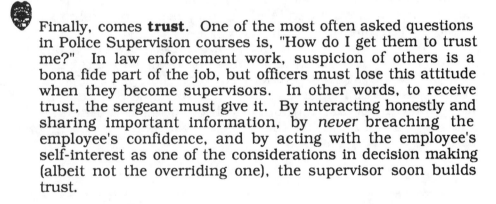 Finally, comes **trust**. One of the most often asked questions in Police Supervision courses is, "How do I get them to trust me?" In law enforcement work, suspicion of others is a bona fide part of the job, but officers must lose this attitude when they become supervisors. In other words, to receive trust, the sergeant must give it. By interacting honestly and sharing important information, by *never* breaching the employee's confidence, and by acting with the employee's self-interest as one of the considerations in decision making (albeit not the overriding one), the supervisor soon builds trust.

Three Rules

Three rules every supervisor should carry uppermost in their thoughts when dealing with problems and problem people are the following:

- ☐ don't take things personally

- ☐ don't hold grudges

- ☐ don't prejudge situations and/or people

Easier said than done! However, there is one excellent skill that will enable any supervisor to achieve the first and last rules. That skill is reflective listening, more recently known as active listening.[4]

When faced with a charge of unfairness or some other complaint that puts one on the defensive, or when the supervisor knows or suspects that he or she may prejudge a person, a situation, or a suggestion based on previous experience, it is time to be quiet and listen.

Regarding rule one, supervisors who receive complaints against themselves feel attacked, which naturally results in defensiveness. If instead of defending, the supervisors hear out the complainants without interruption, and then reflect back to the complainants their understanding of the concerns, the supervisors gain a clearer picture.

At the same time, as sergeants concentrate every effort on listening and understanding, their defensiveness lessens. Once the sergeants finish their reflections, the employees are free to agree that that is what they meant, or to disagree and then clarify the sergeants' understanding.

Continuing in this vein until mutual clarification results, enables supervisors to maintain emotional control and stay off the defensive. If the complainants become over emotional, using the reflective technique usually helps sergeants diminish it. Once the two parties achieve a common understanding, they are more likely to move on to an objective resolution of the issue.

What people often forget in an interaction which has emotional overtones, is that the emotion must be dealt with first before anyone can get on to rational problem solving. If it isn't dealt with, it just resurfaces at the next encounter until someone does handle it or until a big blowup occurs. Although a direct order could handle the situation, it is less likely that the sergeant will be seen as fair or that the issue will be truly resolved.

How to Listen Reflectively

1. Paraphrase concisely, accurately, and in a non-judgmental manner, using your own words

2. Reflect meaning

3. Reflect feelings
   - ❏ focus on feeling words
   - ❏ observe body language
   - ❏ ask yourself how you might feel

4. Reflect totally

One of the major gripes heard from employees about their bosses deals with what the employees perceive as fairness: "He never listens." "She makes up her mind before she hears my side of the story." Supervisors who

❑ suspend instant evaluation,

❑ gather pertinent facts, opinions, and information,

❑ analyze the data, and then

❑ render a judgment

are much more likely to be perceived as fair in their employees' eyes, than is the supervisor who gives a knee jerk response based on past images and evaluations of others.

Supervisors may believe that their decisions and judgments are fair, but it is what those who work for them perceive that tells the real story. If supervisors receive frequent complaints about fairness or bias, it is time to rethink the manner in which they choose to communicate. Supervisors who offer trust and respect, usually find it returned by employees. The author of *Organizational Communication* comments, "People communicate with others in accord with the way they perceive these others communicating with them."[5]

A final word about the rules; supervisors cannot afford the luxury of holding grudges. Employees are not young children to be punished for some misdemeanor. Following a reprimand or disciplinary session, employees, no matter how they may appear on the outside, are concerned with how supervisors will react on their next encounter. The supervisors' responsibility is to accept the employees back into the fold and coach them to improved work performance.[6]

If the employees perceive that the sergeants expect higher performance and will reward it in increments as it continues to improve, the employees will respond accordingly and see the supervisors as mentors who truly care about their welfare. But, when supervisors hold grudges and expect negative behavior, they set themselves up as adversaries who encourage a self fulfilling prophecy. Thus, poor performance or behavior is exactly what they will get.

Communication Barriers

Most of the significant barriers to effective workplace communication actually come from within individuals. As most people age, they become more and more like themselves. This is called perceptual constancy. According to Carl Weaver, "We tend, day after day, to perceive the world in about the same ways; that is, the incoming data are selected that fit and support our internal frame of reference . . . Thus we become, as we grow older, more and more like ourselves, stereotyping, overestimating and underestimating . . . and misperceiving because of a more and more rigid internal frame of reference."[7] That is, people resist change preferring instead their own sets of values, opinions, information, etc.. Obviously, such preference affects the way in which they perceive the world around them.

Couple this with *selectively exposing* themselves to ideas primarily similar to their own, and once having exposed themselves, then in *selectively attending* only to those things with which they already agree. Add to this, *selective perception* where humans further filter, distort, or reject facts and information disagreeable to them, and finally *selective retention* where they remember 10 to 25% of all they have "heard."

An interesting fact is that individuals can make themselves less prone to this selectivity cycle by giving themselves new experiences, interacting with diverse kinds of people, and generally maintaining a tolerant approach to others. In other words, good listeners tend to have fewer strong internal biases affecting their message reception.

Consider the communication barriers as identified by Leonard Sayles and George Strauss in *Human Behavior in Organizations*.[8]

 Hearing What We Expect To Hear. The supervisor who expects the same old "alibi" for a poorly written report bases a response on past experience with an individual. If an officer is trying to improve on report writing and the supervisor doesn't recognize and comment on even the slightest improvement, the expectation will have created not only a communication barrier, but an obstacle to future change.

 Ignoring Information That Conflicts With What We Know. Contract negotiations are a great opportunity for ignoring information. Rather than actually consider the possibility that any grievance may have merit during contract time, many managers dismiss it because "they know" that the number of grievances always increases just prior to contract negotiations.

One might note, that where management uses effective communication techniques and treats its employees with respect, the union will be far less inclined to use grievances as a weapon.

Witness Madison, Wisconsin, a department of over three hundred sworn officers: it has been working under the Total Quality Management approach (which emphasizes teamwork, interpersonal communications, and customer service, among other things) for the last several years and the union president reports just four grievances in 1991.[9] Three of those would not have been filed except the chief was out of town and the two of them could not get together within the filing time to discuss and resolve the issues.

 Evaluating the Source. Old images die hard! When officers reporting to a new shift have preconceived notions about each other, they frequently base their responses on those preconceptions (as pointed out above – filtering, distorting, and rejecting), and never give one another a fair opportunity to build trust.

Of course this works in reverse as well, with the preconceptions being so positive that a "halo effect" occurs. A chief or supervisor then sees only the good in that individual and allows inadequacies apparent to everyone else in the department to slide by.

 Differing Workgroup Perceptions. An individual's values and the working environment affect how words, actions, and events are perceived. One officer may enjoy donating his time to Little League, food kitchens and the church youth group. While his or her supervisor may notice and applaud this community time because it sheds a favorable light on the law enforcement agency, a sub group of officers may consider it an insincere attempt to win the Community Spirit Award and "brown nosing" to boot. These differing perceptions create major barriers to communication among departmental team members.

 Words That Mean Different Things To Different People. Communications instructors have taught for years, "Words don't mean – people mean," and "Meanings are in people," both of which signify that the sender and receiver in a given communication think the meaning in their head, but can never actually transmit 100% of it to another. This is because no two people have exactly the same background or set of experiences and thus cannot have identical frames of reference concerning the world.

This is another reason why the reflective listening skill is critical to clear communication. It allows for the closest approximation of meaning possible between two persons when used correctly to seek mutual understanding of the message.

 Inconsistent Nonverbal Messages. If the messages a supervisor sends are not consistent verbally (words), vocally (voice), and non-verbally (behaviors such as eye contact, facial expression, posture, and gestures), receivers will tend to believe the nonverbal. The reason for this is that nonverbal behavior makes up 55%, or the greatest part of any message that is sent,[10] and individuals do believe the old adage, "Actions speak louder than words."

Thus, baggage from supervisors' personal lives needs to be left outside the worksite, lest they appear to be sending messages which they do not intend. And of course, this presents an excellent argument against holding grudges, because they show through in nonverbal leakage!

 Effects of Emotions. The emotion of the moment affects any supervisor's interpretation of incoming messages. When a manager feels insecure, for example, nearly any message, sometimes even a compliment may cause a defensive response. First line supervisors especially need to be cognizant of emotions that are affecting them at the moment and factor that recognition in as they handle important work-place communication.

Words can also trigger emotional responses that interfere with communication. **PIG** represents an excellent example. But rather than becoming defensive and over-emotional about being referred to in this manner, police printed up T-shirts with the words **Pride - Integrity - Guts** and wear them proudly. A sense of humor wins again!

 Noise. Noise may be external (horns, phones, rattling keys) or internal (a decision that something is irrelevant, hunger pangs, a negative attitude). Subordinates quickly lock on to repetitive words, particularly ones which suggest high priority to the sergeant, when, in reality, the item does not qualify as high priority. Over time, subordinates learn to disregard these as irrelevant noise and thus may fail to carry through on an important assignment.

Sayles and Strauss suggest several methods for handling the above barriers. These include:

❏ giving and receiving feedback

❏ communicating face-to-face

❏ being sensitive to the other's world (their values, attitudes, and expectations)

❏ recognizing that the same words can have both positive and negative "meanings" depending on the individuals communicating

❏ keeping language simple and direct

❏ using redundancy (or explaining something two or more ways) in an effort to ensure receiver understanding[11]

Setting the Workplace Climate

Sergeants say that the toughest part of the job is "running interference between upper management and the troops," and conversely that the "best thing about the job is being a mentor to and role model for others' development."[12] Consider these thoughts in tandem with Goldhaber's statement, "The most important contributor to job satisfaction is the quality of the relationship employees have with their supervisors."[13] All of these make it abundantly clear that first line supervisors have a major responsibility for creating and maintaining the workplace environment.

First line supervisors can create hell on earth, a place where subordinates who are constantly on the defensive from feeling continually hassled go out on the road and take it out on the public at every opportunity. The prescription for such a defensive, repressive climate looks like this:

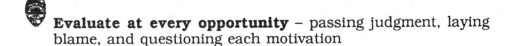

Evaluate at every opportunity – passing judgment, laying blame, and questioning each motivation

Control others – issuing direct orders even when unnecessary and attempting to coerce attitude change

Strategize each action – manipulating others into performing actions according to the supervisor's approved method only

Remain neutral – under the mistaken assumption that it is impartial and fair (when it actually demonstrates no concern for the subordinate's welfare)

Communicate an attitude of superiority – reminding others of the sergeant's rank, education, physical ability, and so forth to make subordinates feel inadequate and inferior

 Communicate an attitude of certainty – demonstrating dogmatism and the need always to be right and always to win[14]

Or, sergeants can create **A Great Place to Work**,[15] a place where subordinates are happy to be, produce their best, make the department look good, and have a little fun while doing it. The supportive climate possesses six main characteristics. *Note that these are the six opposites of the defensive climate.*

Describe behaviors they have observed and request information about actions taken while avoiding becoming judgmental.

Maintain a problem resolution orientation which aids the subordinate in resolving issues through mutual interaction as opposed to acting the supervisory "all knowing" parent.

Act spontaneously in a genuine and honest fashion which invites straight forward, honest responses (rather than manipulation).

Demonstrate empathy for subordinates by listening and respecting their worth as a human beings.

Treat others as equals in the sense of demonstrating respect and trust without allowing power, rank, or status to intrude.

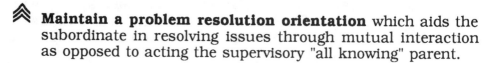 **Demonstrate provisionalism** (as opposed to certainty) by being open to others' perspectives and information and showing a cooperative attitude.[16]

During Police Supervision seminars, another question often asked is, "How can I motivate people?" The most appropriate response is, "We cannot motivate others, but we can set the workplace climate which enhances self-respect, spend 100% of the time on the positive and 90% on the negative rather than the usual reversed approach, and reward consistently efficient, productive, and people oriented performance. The result will be employees who motivate themselves."

> **Providing A Supportive Work Climate**
>
> ❑ Use descriptions of behavior rather than being judgmental.
>
> ❑ Maintain a problem resolution approach rather than a controlling approach.
>
> ❑ Behave in a spontaneous, honest, and genuine fashion rather than manipulating others to perform.
>
> ❑ Demonstrate empathy by showing respect and listening.
>
> ❑ Treat others as equals rather than pulling rank.
>
> ❑ Be open to others' perspectives rather than being dogmatic and expressing a "My way or the highway" approach.

Conclusion

Employees who are provided with a supportive climate, where they know they are valued by their supervisors and are included in the process of resolving workplace problems, are likely to maintain highly positive attitudes and deliver exceptional performance.

When first line supervisors make their people look good, they respond in kind and make the supervisors and the department look good.

Thus sergeants rise to the challenge of helping their law enforcement teams thrive and when that happens, the sergeants do more than survive – as first line supervisors, they thrive!

References

[1] David Jamieson and Julie O'Mara, *Managing Work Force 2000* (San Franciscon, CA: Jossey-Bass, Inc., 1992), 28-29.

2 Lawrence Bradford and Claire Raines, *Twentysomething: Managing and Motivating Today's New Workforce* (New York, NY: Master Media Ltd., 1992), 31-50.

3 Soundview Editorial Staff, *Skills for Success* (Bristol, VT: Soundview Executive Book Summaries, 1989), 11.

4 Robert J. Wickes, M.D., *Helping Others: Ways of Listening, Sharing and Counseling* (Rando, PA: Chilton Book Co., 1979), 65-68. See also Carl Weaver, *Human Listening: Processes and Behavior* (New York, NY: Bobbs-Merrill Co., Inc., 1972), 86-87.

5 Gary L. Kreps, *Organizational Communication* (New York, NY: Longman, 1986), 163.

6 Ferdinand Fournies, *Coaching for Improved Work Performance* (New York, NY: Van Nostrand Reinhold Co., 1978), 76-207. Coaching has come to be used (by many) as synonymous with cheering your employees on. Fournies, however, delineates a very specific way of handling performance problems. It is a positive approach to discipline, but it is not "cheerleading." MACNLOW Associates teaches this practical method in its Police Supervision course.

7 Carl Weaver, *Human Listening: Processes and Behavior*, 68-69.

8 Leonard R. Sayles and George Strauss, *Human Behavior in Organizations* (Englewood Cliffs, CA: Prentice-Hall, 1966), 238-246.

9 Detective Steve Gilfoy, Verbal communication to MACNLOW team member visiting department in June 1992.

10 Albert Mehrabian, *Silent Messages* (Belmont, CA: Wadsworth, 1981), 75-80.

11 Saynes and Strauss, *Human Behavior in Organizations*, 246-256.

12 Sgt. Darrell Ellis, Michigan State Police, Flint, MI Post, 1992. Sgt. Ellis has five years at rank and twenty years of experience. His words were chosen for inclusion because they were so succinct.

13 Gerald Goldhaber, *Organizational Communication* (Dubuque, IA: William C. Brown Publishers, 4th edition, 1986), 236.

14 Jack R. Gibb, "Defensive Communication," *Journal of Communication*, Vol. II, No. 3, 1961, 141-148.

15   Robert Levering, *What Makes Some Employers So Good (And Most So Bad)*, (New York, NY: Avon Books, 1988).

16   Op. Cit., J. Gibb, p. 141-148.

Dr. Vance McLaughlin   Stephen Smith

Dr. Vance McLaughlin was previously a police officer in Sarasota, Florida. He received his M.S. in Criminology from Florida State and his Ph.D. from Penn State. He taught the undergraduate courses in law enforcement at the University of North Carolina at Charlotte for five years. In 1987, he became the Director of Training for the Savannah Police Department. His most recent publication is, Police Use of Force: The Savannah Study, published by Praeger in 1992.

Mr. Stephen Smith is currently a Captain with the Savannah Police Department in Georgia. He has been with the Savannah Police Department for twenty years. He has served in a wide variety of assignments including Accreditation Manager. He is currently the Assistant Bureau Commander of the Management Services Bureau. He received his B.S. and M.S. from Armstrong State College in Savannah, Georgia.

Chapter 19

Preparing for Promotion

by Dr. Vance McLaughlin and Stephen J. Smith, M.S.

Introduction

Promotions in all law enforcement agencies are a time of stress to those involved. Historically, two problems have contributed to this stress. First, there are usually more officers qualified for the position than can be promoted. Law enforcement officers have few positions open to them during their careers. In fact, in some state law enforcement agencies, troopers who are promoted once to corporal during their careers are success stories. Secondly, there has not been strict criteria established that officers must meet in order to be promoted to different ranks. New officers find it difficult to chart a course on how to rise in rank within organizations.

Education, training, employee evaluations, experience in a number of different assignments, and other factors have not been predictors in the past of who advances in law enforcement agencies. In fact, political considerations (religion, race, gender, affiliation with key people or groups, etc.) have always impacted both recruitment and promotion. There has been little done to change the opportunities for promotion in most agencies (though some have adopted modular plans where classifications of Officer I, Officer II, and Officer III exist), and the political situation is always in flux.

One factor in promotions that is becoming increasingly important is *competence*. New "best friends" of the Chief, City Manager, or Mayor are officers who do their jobs properly. Top administrators want supervisors who can solve problems. The challenges of law enforcement work are always changing. Therefore, a supervisor must have the ability to adapt to new situations.

This chapter examines a number of things that can enhance officers' chances for promotion. It will discuss what type of things they can do over a long period of time to prepare for promotion, and what they can do closer to the time of evaluations.

Starting to Prepare for Promotions

Officers begin preparing for promotion the moment they start work in an agency. The following long-term strategies will be discussed and include, putting your best "self" forward, training, and education.

Putting Your Best "Self" Forward

People tend to fluctuate around what is their own "average" behavior. Sometimes they are better than their average and sometimes they are worse. Each person has done better at times than is expected by the people that know them. On the other hand, each person has done things that are not up to the level of their "true" self.

First impressions are in many cases lasting impressions. In law enforcement, officers have contact with the majority of people only a few times. It is important to keep in mind that officers should always act professionally.

When veteran officers around the United States were asked, "What is the most important factor you look for in a law enforcement officer," they invariably answered, "good judgment!" If anyone could find a method of implanting this into people, that person would have made a significant contribution to society. Judgment is improved through the experience gained from making good decisions and learning from the bad ones.

In every department there are officers at every rank who are considered competent and incompetent. Variances exist among officers about where their pears should be grouped in these two categories. There is also a broad consensus when it comes to categories of very competent and very incompetent.

Competent officers are those who do their paperwork properly, testify expertly in court, deal professionally with the public, and back other officers up on calls. These are all visible traits and they are not lost on supervisors who control the promotion process. Almost all officers have the ability to be classified as very competent if they start from day one to work toward that goal. This takes a conscious effort to *put your best "self" forward.*

Training

After officers are finished with recruit school and off probation, they should try to get as much job-related, competency based training as possible. This training will have a positive impact on their jobs in terms of productivity and efficiency.

When officers take easy courses that they enjoy, but that have no relevance to their jobs, they are working at cross purposes with their departments and their careers. Supervisors who approve any training request just so officers get their annual requirement of training hours are doing those officers a disservice. When promotions are scheduled and these supervisors are questioned on their subordinates' training files, they will not be able to offer any helpful explanation of how the training was relevant.

 ### Education

A popular concentration for law enforcement officers at both two-year and four-year colleges is criminal justice. Criminal justice programs offer students an understanding of the criminal justice system, theories of crime causation, and probably includes some courses that are akin to training.

Three areas of education needed for all law enforcement officers are English, computers, and research methods. These are three areas that many officers avoid, because they are perceived as difficult.

Officers must realize that the time they spend in class will be the same as the amount of tuition spent no matter which course they take. They should also realize that at promotion time those on the promotion board are not overly impressed with courses such as pottery making, flower arranging, and other esoteric topics.

English is vital when expressing oneself verbally or through the written word. Reports and memorandums through the chain of command must be factual and concise. All departments, with the advent of personal computers, find that first level supervisors need to understand how to operate a computer and use software. Research methods, in spite of all the "jargon" used in such courses, is basically problem solving in a scientific way. As stated in the introduction, problem solving is what chief executives are looking for in their supervisors.

Types of Promotional Processes

Invariably, chiefs of police or sheriffs are going to make the final decision of who is promoted within their departments. They will do this from a list of "qualified" applicants. The way this list is compiled varies among law enforcement agencies. Three types of promotional processes will be presented with the understanding that each agency adapts them to their own needs. These types are patronage, written tests, and assessment centers.

 Patronage

The term patronage has a "negative" connotation among most citizens, though it is actually value free. In this chapter, the term means that chief executives decide who will be promoted, based only on their own decisions, with or without consultation with their top administrators. Many sheriff's departments around the United States promote in this way.

The chief executives believe that they know more about the candidates from working with them over a period of time, than by using any other "testing" method. While the vast majority of management texts dealing with personnel find this type of promotion without merit, even those agencies that have "scientific" promotion methods use it in part. Usually, the higher officers go in rank their numerical scores on tests are not as important as other factors.

What is important to chief executives using patronage is that the applicants are loyal and help the agency reach the goals set by the chief executives. One advantage chief executives have in promoting by patronage is that the removal of officers from positions is usually much easier.

 Written Tests

Written tests were part of the first move by the civil service to take politics out of policing. It is an arguable point whether that was ever accomplished. Written tests when used by law enforcement agencies are usually either aptitude or job skills' testing. Aptitude measures officers' interests, skills in reading and writing, and intelligence. A more common test is job ability.

Job ability tests can either focus on the skills officers have gained in the positions they now occupy or in the skills they should have if promoted to the next position. The latter situation is usual in large agencies.

In a way, the use of this test is illogical. The question most often asked by applicants is, "How am I supposed to know what to do before I have been in the position or been trained?" Many agencies provide a suggested reading list for the applicants so they can prepare. These agencies test *job knowledge* instead of *job ability.*

In law enforcement agencies, this type of testing usually presents a group of *qualified* candidates from which chief executives can choose. The percentage of viable candidates will depend on where the cut-off point is placed. In many cases, the cut-off point allows for most of those taking the exam to be eligible.

Officers taking the written test should find out in advance what type of material is going to be covered and get a suggested reading list. Officers should also talk to supervisors who have taken the test and been successful in achieving high scores. Officers who are continually furthering their schooling have a distinct advantage, because they are used to taking written tests.

 Assessment Centers

Assessment centers are currently in vogue. Although they do not rely on paper and pencil tests, the passing of a written test may be a precursor to being accepted into the assessment center process in some agencies. The assessment center has become popular in law enforcement agencies because it is job-related and can stand Equal Employment Opportunity Commission (EEOC) scrutiny.

The following may be the type of exercises used by an assessment center designed for sergeants competing for the position of lieutenant. These are the proposed exercises currently used at the Savannah Police Department.

 In-Basket Exercise. This exercise is constructed to simulate the desk-work aspect of the position of shift commander. Candidates are presented with a number of items similar to those which might accumulate in the in-baskets of shift commanders. Their tasks are to take whatever actions deemed appropriate on the items, having assumed the roles of shift commanders and behaving as they would if actually in that position. At the completion of the exercise, each candidate is interviewed by an assessor to discuss the actions which were taken.

 One Hour Department Staff Meeting Exercise. Eight specific items are on the agenda for the group of candidates to discuss and offer recommendations in the absence of the superior officer. The recommendations can be used by the superior officer in reaching a decision on those items contained in the agenda. Participants are to reach a consensus on each item.

 Group Discussion Exercise. This exercise simulates a meeting of shift commanders (lieutenants and captains). To invoke competition among the members of the group, each individual is assigned a point of view which he or she is to argue. By the end of the discussion period, the group members must reach a final decision regarding the relative acceptability of the view of each member.

 Subordinate Counseling Exercise. Candidates assume the roles of newly appointed captains/lieutenants and are about to meet with law enforcement officers for their annual performance reviews. The candidates and the officers' sergeants have agreed on the performance rating of the officers. Candidates have five minutes to review the material before conducting the performance review counseling session. The counseling session with each officer lasts fifteen minutes. At the conclusion, the candidates are to either confirm the ratings or amend them, and sign them.

 Problem-Solving Exercise. Each candidate generates three simulated problems plaguing the department. They meet in sub-groups to reach a consensus of the three most critical problems. They meet in one group to further reduce to a consensus the final three most critical problems. A time limit is set for reaching and developing solutions for resolving them.

Finally each candidate has ten minutes to prepare a written list of recommendations based on their understanding of the group consensus.

There are a number of things candidates can do to improve their chances for success in an assessment center.

 First, each of these exercises is scored on certain dimensions (i.e., organizing and planning, interpersonal relations, observation skills, leadership, oral communication, written communication, decision making, and behavioral flexibility). If the candidates are aware of what dimensions are being rated during each exercise, they can make sure that these dimensions are used in their presentations.

 Second, reading books and articles on assessment centers will give the candidates an in-depth understanding of the types of questions that may be asked and strategies that may be used in formulating answers.

 Third, it is a good idea to talk to others who have successfully gone through assessments. They can offer actual examples of exercises they have gone through and responses that they have given.

Fourth, candidates must realize that their actions, from the time they enter the assessment area to the time they leave, have an impact on the impression they make on the assessors. This means that the candidates should project the image of leaders throughout the span of assessment activities (i.e., during breaks, between exercises, going and returning from lunch).

 Fifth, candidates for promotion must also be mindful that promotion time is a tense time for all the candidates.

Sometimes this tension manifests itself in subtle hostilities and undercurrents between competitors. Disciplined candidates would not become involved in such petty behavior, and not allow such behavior on the part of others to divert them from presenting themselves to the best of their abilities.

 Sixth, it is not the loudest or the most authoritarian candidates who do well in assessment centers. It is the candidates that facilitate group discussions, handle problems calmly and professionally, and present a positive image, who score well.

 Seventh, serious candidates should be aware of the "law of reverse effect." Basically, the *law of reverse effect* states that the harder you try to do something – especially if it is important to you – the more difficult it will be to accomplish (i.e., after learning to juggle in private, you attempt to show your friends).

To overcome the *law of reverse effect*, candidates should get a good nights' sleep before the assessment center and during the day eat small portions at both breakfast and lunch. In addition, candidates should practice stress reduction techniques during the session (i.e., inhale deeply and exhale slowly; consciously cause the body to relax).

Conclusion

Officers who are going to succeed in being promoted in their agencies begin to work toward that goal as soon as they are hired. They enhance their credentials through training and education and are able to present strong personnel folders. They have always tried to present themselves well to the public and their peers, which reinforces all their formal accomplishments.

Law enforcement agencies can promote on patronage, written tests, assessment centers, or any combination of the three. Officers who understand this *process* will be able to showcase the abilities that are the most important in their agencies.

Mildred K. O'Linn

Ms. Mildred K. O'Linn is an attorney with Franscell, Strickland, Roberts & Lawrence in Pasadena, California, a law firm which specializes in police defense. She is also on the board of directors of the prestigious American Society of Law Enforcement Trainers (ASLET). She was previously the Technical and Legal Adviser for the Law Enforcement Television Network (LETN) in Dallas, Texas.

Prior to that Ms. O'Linn was with the Kent State University Police Department for eight years. She moved from patrol officer to manager of the police academy, and finally to Administrative Assistant to the Director of Police.

Ms. O'Linn has an extensive defensive tactics instructor background and is an International PR-24® Instructor.

Chapter 20

Sexual Harassment

by Mildred K. O'Linn

Have you had your finger on the pulse of America lately? If you have then you know the public's attention is focused on two issues that are near and dear concerns to the law enforcement profession – police misconduct and sexual harassment.

In the fall of 1991 the world's attention was drawn to the issue of sexual harassment by the accusations of Professor Anita Hill against U.S. Supreme Court nominee, Judge Clarence Thomas. The significance of this event to the law enforcement supervisor is tantamount to another incident which occurred in 1991 – the Rodney King incident.

There is grave concern over both of these issues in the community and consequently in the minds of individuals who will comprise a jury. You just have to read the newspapers to develop an understanding of the public's sensitivity to both of these issues. The law is a people business, and it is critical that we take note not only of the law, but of the public's concern.

The recent rise in the public's sensitivity to this issue began with the Thomas Confirmation Hearings. As a result of that hearing, there has been an increase in the number of sexual harassment cases filed and consequently, the amount of monetary damages available.

The likelihood of such a trend was in fact noted in 1984 by a nationally recognized authority in the area of civil liability, Attorney Emery Plitt, then of the Maryland Attorney General's Office. Mr. Plitt predicted that sexual harassment would be the next area of contention for discrimination charges in the law enforcement community.

Given the fact that one-third of the nation's cases in this area reportedly originate in the law enforcement field, it appears that Mr. Plitt was in fact correct.

The courts' and society's views of sexual harassment have changed. The courts were once reluctant to impose liability and viewed supervisory interactions with subordinates as personally motivated and unrelated to work. Such actions were not considered to be intrinsically hostile nor offensive and conduct of a sexual nature was simply the result of the natural attraction between the sexes.

It was further believed that women should be flattered and welcome such attention. The "boys will be boys" and "there's no harm in asking" attitudes were the prevalent philosophies used to explain sexual misconduct. However, as a result of numerous studies that were done regarding the effects of sexual harassment and the legal claims which have been brought and won, a less tolerant attitude has developed towards such behavior.

On the other hand, I am less certain that the law enforcement profession's attitude has kept pace with the attitude changes of the courts and the community. Certainly, if someone was harassing a member of your family employed in any profession other than law enforcement your reaction would be unfavorable. However, within the law enforcement profession it has been my experience, and until recently even my own attitude, to take an "if you can't take the heat get out of the kitchen" position towards what I considered to be "thin skinned" or "overly sensitive" types who just happened to become cops.

Quite frankly, we all understand that within any profession there is a certain amount of camaraderie generated by what might be characterized as good natured teasing between employees and even supervisors. Law enforcement personnel often talk about how this is a form of stress relief. In fact, if an individual demonstrates an intolerance towards such teasing it is only likely to increase the volume. I remember being told as a young officer that I should worry when the kidding stopped, because the other officers didn't kid around with anyone they didn't like. I would kid back and say, "Don't like me so much." This was generally all good natured kidding and the comments were not of a sexual nature.

However, and this is a critical point – this type of attitude creates a conflict between what individuals are expected to tolerate and the legal parameters of professional conduct and liability. The point being – as members of the law enforcement profession you have to realize that the profession is comprised of individuals from varied and diverse backgrounds. Not everyone is tolerant of heckling and verbal jabs and if that heckling is of a sexual nature, the law does not require tolerance! Nor does the law have a different set of standards for evaluating the conduct of cops!

Statistical Overview of the Problem

Studies indicate that vast numbers of women have experienced sexual harassment in one form or another and the 36,000 female officers and over 100,000 women employed in law enforcement in one capacity or another are no exception.

A 1978-79 *Redbook* magazine survey indicated that 88% of their readers had experienced sexual harassment in the workplace.

Another study done in the same time frame by the Federal Merit Systems found that sexual harassment cost the federal government, and ultimately each one of us as taxpayers, $189 million in terms of lost work in that year alone. In that study, of the 20,000 federal workers surveyed, one out of every four workers reported some form of sexual harassment, including 40% of the women and 15% of the men.

In a statistically sophisticated study of Illinois state workers, the survey indicated that 51% of the workers had experienced sexual teasing and suggestive looks; 26% had experienced subtle hints and pressures; 25% had been touched or grabbed; and 2% had experienced actual coercive sex. This survey is reported to be one of the most statistically sophisticated surveys ever done.

Two more recent studies, one done in 1980 and the other in 1989, of Los Angeles county workers are of note: The 1980 study, which polled 827 female county workers, found that one out of every ten female workers had quit a job because of sexual harassment; 53% reported being sexually harassed – mostly by married men; and 33% had experienced negative job consequences because of sexual harassment.

The 1989 study figures were consistent with the 1980 findings in that one-third of the 4,826 females responding reported sexual harassment. Even more disturbing and disheartening to the County was the fact that 70% of the respondents felt that it was fruitless to report harassment and 61% feared retaliation.

Studies reported in national magazines during the Thomas Confirmation Hearings indicated that 13% of the women and 11% of the men responding to the poll had filed a sexual harassment complaint personally or knew of someone who had. Public opinion of men and women ran fairly even when asked if a man repeatedly asked a woman who works for him to have sex. In response to that question, 96% of the women and 94% of the men said it was in fact sexual harassment.

When asked if it was sexual harassment for a man to repeatedly ask a woman who works for him out for a date, 47% of the women and 48% of the men answered yes. It is worth taking note that 75% of the women and 64% of the men thought that it was sexual harassment for a man to make sexual remarks or jokes to a woman who works for him. Likewise, 72% of the women and 75% of the men believed it was sexual harassment for a man to make sexual remarks or noises at women on the street.

Management, for good reasons, should and is becoming less tolerant of sexual harassment for both economical and philosophical reasons. The effects of sexual harassment on employees are detrimental to the work environment and to employee performance. Examples of the negative effects of sexual harassment on employees include: stress, humiliation, loss of employment, lower self-esteem, lower job satisfaction, guilt, fear, feelings of powerlessness, betrayal, and anger.

Employers also suffer as a result of the effects felt by individual employees. Losses for the employer include: lower productivity, poor morale, increased use of sick leave, higher turnover and re-training costs, and legal fees.

The significance of that last item, legal fees, should not be overlooked. There have been numerous occasions when juries have awarded $1.00 to a plaintiff to vindicate the plaintiff's rights and the plaintiff's attorney fees were paid by the defendant. This, of course, usually amounts to several tens of thousands of dollars in costs. These are just a few examples of the individual and organizational costs of sexual harassment.

Legal Protections

Title VII of the Civil Rights Act of 1964, as amended by the Equal Employment Opportunity Act of 1972, broadly prohibits employment practices that discriminate because of race, sex, color, religion, or national origin. It covers all terms of employment and holds the employer responsible for such discrimination.

Equal Employment Opportunity Commission guidelines state that sexual harassment violations of Title VII are enforceable in the courts. This affords employees protection from coworkers, clients, customers, and the general public where the employer created the complained of situation. These guidelines prohibit employers, employment agencies, and unions from discrimination in hiring, promoting, and in the working conditions themselves. These guidelines also provide for up to two years in back pay to the victim employee. The EEOC has full authority to investigate complaints and violations of the Civil Rights Act of 1964. In fact the EEOC may initiate suits on its own or on behalf of an employee.

Even though Title VII has been in existence for a long time, it was the courts that were the major force in dealing with sexual harassment. The pressure was put on by members of the public to address what were primarily the concerns of female subordinates in the male dominated work environment. Sexual harassment violations were first recognized by the courts in 1972. However, it was not until 1986 in the case of *Meritor Savings Bank v. Vinson*[1] when the Supreme Court officially recognized sexual harassment as a form of sex "discrimination" under Title VII and this cause of action became a true concern for employers.

On November 21, 1991, President Bush signed into law the Civil Rights Act of 1991 making significant changes in employment law and specifically overruling some more recent Supreme Court decisions which had been favorable to employers.

Specifically, the Act expands the remedies available to an employee for intentional discrimination and unlawful harassment in the workplace. Title VII has been amended to allow general and punitive damages including damages for pain and suffering and emotional distress if the plaintiff is alleging a cause of action other than disparate impact[2] and cannot recover under §1981. If punitive damages are alleged, either party may now demand a jury trial. For punitive damages to lie it must be proven that the employer acted with malice or reckless indifference to the federally protected rights of the plaintiff.

There are limits on the amount of punitive damages available ranging from $50,000 to $300,000 depending on the size of the employer's workforce and the jury will not be told the limit on the amount of punitives.

Under the Civil Rights Act of 1991, compensatory damages available under Title VII may not include back pay, interest on back pay, or other relief already available under Title VII. A prevailing party is entitled to attorney's fees under 42 U.S.C. §1988. Under that section such fees are viewed as a bonus to plaintiff's attorney for pursuing the case. The amount awarded has nothing to do with the contract between the attorney and the client or the amount of damages awarded.

Another area of law which has been held by some courts to have application to sexual harassment claims brought by and against members of the law enforcement profession is 42 United States Code section 1983. Section 1983, as many of you are aware, specifically prohibits the deprivation of constitutional rights under the color of law.

In fact, some courts have permitted section 1983 claims and Title VII claims to co-exist. Procedurally, the impact of such a decision is negated by the enactment of the Civil Rights Act of 1991, except that the qualified immunity defense is available in section 1983 actions.

In addition to Title VII and section 1983, there are several other alternative legal remedies for alleged victims of sexual harassment to pursue. They include: state and local equal employment laws; state tort actions for such claims as constructive discharge, assault and battery, and infliction of emotional distress; worker's compensation actions; and actions brought under the Equal Pay Act and the Pregnancy Discrimination Act.

Functional Issues

What is sexual harassment? The Equal Employment Opportunity Commission defines sexual harassment as unwelcome sexual advances, requests for sexual favors, and other verbal or physical conduct of a sexual nature which constitutes sexual harassment:

 When submission to such conduct is either explicitly or implicitly a term or condition of an individual's employment;

 When submission to or rejection of such conduct has the purpose or effect of unreasonably interfering with the work performance or creating an intimidating hostile or offensive work environment.

Some of the key concepts in the Federal Equal Employment

Opportunity Guidelines are:

⪻ **Unwelcome**, meaning unwelcome to the employee from the employee's perspective;

⪻ **Term or condition of employment**, referring to whether it effects assignments, transfers, promotions, etc.;

⪻ **Purpose or effect**, referring to interfering with the employee's work performance with or without the intent or knowledge on the part of the alleged offender;

⪻ **Knew or should have known**, signifies that the courts are holding managers responsible for managing and supervisors responsible for supervising;

⪻ **Failed to take immediate and appropriate action**, indicating that departments are expected to self-enforce in a manner that serves as a deterrent to others.

Types of activities that have been taken to be sexual harassment include:

- physical contact
- off-color jokes and remarks
- propositions
- crude language
- holding an individual up for ridicule
- sexually explicit materials
- signs on bulletin boards or desks
- transfers
- demotions and dismissals
- off-duty telephone calls
- demeaning remarks

As you can see it is much more subtle than being fired for refusing to sleep with the boss. The key descriptive words here are *unwarranted, unwanted,* and *unwelcome.*

Legally, the sexual harassment problem is broken down into two basic categories: quid pro quo type harassment and hostile work environment harassment. "Quid pro quo" literally translated means "this for that" and it is the most basic type of sexual harassment. It pertains to a situation where sexual favors are requested for favorable job evaluations or employment advancement. "Hostile work environment" harassment is believed to be the most prevalent type of sexual harassment and is, from a victim's perspective, the most difficult to handle and prove.

Guidelines issued by the EEOC in March 1990 further defined what, in fact, constitutes a hostile work environment. Prior to the issuance of the March 1990 guidelines, the EEOC decisions had made it clear that acquiescence in sexual conduct at work may not mean that the conduct is welcome. Furthermore, the charging party need not have confronted the offending supervisor where the charging party feared retaliation, so long as the charging party's reactions and comments demonstrated that the conduct was unwelcome.

The March 1990 guidance document supplements previous guidelines and states that circumstances must be viewed as a whole. If there is an indication of welcomeness, the charging party's claim will be strengthened if there was a contemporaneous complaint filed. Use of sexually explicit language does not negate a claim that sexual conduct is unwelcome, but it may be considered in deciding whether the conduct was unwelcome. Additionally, sexually aggressive behavior, such as discussions of sexual fantasies and inquiries into the sex lives of coworkers may be factors indicating welcomeness. Finally, general character evidence and evidence of sexual behavior with individuals other than the harasser is given little weight in determining welcomeness.

With regard to when a work environment is "hostile," the 1990 guidelines state that behavior must be sufficiently severe so as to alter the terms of employment. Sexual flirtation, innuendo, or vulgar language that is trivial or merely annoying is insufficient to constitute a hostile environment. The standard to be used is that of the "reasonable woman." The reasonable woman is used as a measure from the perspective of the claimant and is not merely the application of societal notions of acceptable behavior. Unless conduct is quite severe, isolated incidents of sexual conduct or statements do not create a hostile environment.

Generally, a pattern of conduct is required, but certain behavior is considered so offensive that it is presumptively illegal. A single touching of intimate body parts would be one example. If the conduct involves verbal sexual harassment alone, the nature, frequency, context, and target of the remarks will be considered in deciding whether a hostile environment has been created. When verbal conduct is combined with non-intimate physical contact, a hostile environment is more likely to be found.

Who may be classified as a victim of sexual harassment? A man as well as a woman may be the victim, and conversely, the harasser. The harasser need not be a supervisor, but this does make the case stronger and easier to prove. The crucial question is whether the harasser treats a member, or members of one sex not necessarily the opposite sex, differently. A third party who is indirectly effected, such as an employee who feels that a hostile environment has been created by the sexual harassment imposed on another, may also file a complaint. Title VII also governs sexual discrimination where a qualified employee is discriminated against in favor of an individual that provided sexual favors to the person granting the employment opportunity or benefit.

If the harasser is a supervisor who is acting within the course and scope of his or her responsibility as a supervisor, liability for those actions will be imputed to the employer. The Supreme Court in *Meritor* rejected the notion that employers are always automatically liable for hostile environment sexual harassment by supervisors. Lower courts have imposed the strict liability standard on employers in the quid pro quo cases involving a loss of a tangible job benefit. Such cases include those where the supervisor relies on their apparent authority to extort sexual favors from an employee.

In hostile environment cases, "agency" principles are used as a foundation for employer liability. The legal principle of agency law permits employer liability where the employer has either actual or constructive notice of the misconduct. Thus, the employer is liable with regard to hostile environment claims if the employer knew or should have known of the harassment in question and failed to take prompt and effective remedial action.

Remember, to prove a charge of sexual harassment an employee must show that unwelcome, unsolicited verbal or physical conduct of a sexual nature:

- ☐   is a condition of employment;
- ☐   is the basis of an employment decision;
- ☐   interferes with work performance;
- ☐   creates a hostile and intimidating work environment; and
- ☐   was actually or constructively known by the agency, which then failed to take appropriate remedial action.

If there is a loss of a tangible job benefit and a supervisor/subordinate relationship exists, strict liability will be imposed. Remember, there is no requirement that the victim complain or report sexual harassment for the employer to be held responsible.

As mentioned earlier in this discussion, an employee who believes that they have been the victim of sexual harassment has several options available to redress the situation. The employee may bring an inter-departmental complaint; file a bargaining unit grievance; file a compliant with a local or state deferral agency; file a complaint with a federal agency; file a state or federal civil suit; or even file criminal charges, such as sexual battery or rape. The remedies available to the plaintiff in a sexual harassment claim include: injunctive relief; reinstatement or forced hiring; back-pay or other equitable relief; and punitive damages in some states. In addition, attorney's fees are applicable under Title VII and section 1983.

Prevention and Defenses: An Action Plan

To protect the agency, they must have a valid policy prohibiting sexual harassment. That policy must, in turn, be supported in spirit and should define sexual harassment as an offense, not only against the individual employee, but as an offense against the employer. The policy must be disseminated to all members of the agency and training provided on the topic. The policy should provide a way for victims to go around their chain of command, if necessary, to report a policy violation. It should also include a step-by-step reporting procedure.

Prompt investigation should be conducted of any complaints and prompt resolutions sought. Then if the employer has a mechanism in place and the employee fails to take advantage of it, the employer is protected, unless the employer knew or should have known about the problem. However, if the policy is ineffective, and it is the custom or informal policy of the agency to ignore or mishandle such complaints, the written policy is not worth the paper it is written on.

Agencies must provide training and hold all employees responsible for reporting violations and supervisors responsible for supervising. When a complaint is received, investigators should access the credibility of the report, obtain the facts, and deal with the concerns of the complainant with regard to confidentiality and reprisals. Once a determination is made, speedy and fair actions to resolve the situation must be taken. The policy must be enforced or it does not, in fact, exist.

An employer's defenses to charges of sexual harassment are numerous. Employers showing that they took appropriate and immediate action is a strong defense. This would include corrective action which administratively addresses the problem. Employers should follow the departmental policy and meet with both the accused and any percipient witnesses. Sanctions on the offender if the allegations are confirmed might include anything from an apology and mandatory counseling to termination. Sanctions should be consistent with other administrative discipline procedures. It may be appropriate in some cases to inquire of the victim what he or she believes is an appropriate remedy both for the record and to access the seriousness of the offense from his or her perspective.

Another defense for an employer is to prove that the "victim" voluntarily participated in the conduct. Remember, however, if duress is shown this defense will fail. In this area, evidence of "trolling" is admissible. The employer may show that an employee voluntarily participated in a relationship. Thereafter, the employee had an affirmative duty to notify the employer that the attention was no longer welcome.

Other defenses to sexual harassment accusations include proving that the terms and conditions of the employment were in no way effected, or that the conduct was part of customary business practices, such as working undercover vice. The lack of a nexus – a relationship between the conduct and the employment, is also a viable defense. Also a lack of notice to the employer is a feasible defense where the offender is a subordinate. Of course proving that the complaint is false is another alternative. Finally, the initiation of a criminal investigation is prudent and should be strongly considered if the allegations suggest that a crime may have been committed.

As a supervisor, it is important that you take prompt action when a problem comes to your attention and to inquire when you believe there may be a potential problem. Documentation of your actions and inquiries is as essential in this area as it is in other areas of your supervisorial responsibilities.

Be aware of the areas and times when this type of problem is likely to occur. Areas of frequent concern include the roll call area, work-out areas, off-duty contacts which spill over into an on-duty context, and basic academy and in-service training sessions. Training sessions require additional attention when you bring in outside personnel to instruct and they choose to conduct themselves in a less than professional manner.

I know of one situation where a department was stuck with a less than acceptable recruit. A number of guest instructors had given this recruit such a strong basis for a sexual harassment complaint that extensive remedial training was the department's only viable alternative. It is truly unfortunate when a department feels forced to keep a poor recruit to avoid facing charges of sexual harassment.

As a supervisor, it is critical that you act promptly in response to these issues and that you take all complaints seriously. Document your investigation even when an employee tries to tell you something "off the record." The best response in this situation is to explain before the employee tells you the problem that nothing can be *off the record*. You may be asked under oath if you knew about the problem before a certain day and time. Unless you are willing to commit perjury, you can't have off the record conversations. You are not a priest or an attorney – you are a supervisor.

In closing, I would like to make a suggestion to supervisors and to officers who are concerned about individual liability. Professionalism is the key word for all involved. The "Appropriateness Test" was a concept developed by the 3M Corporation as a quick way for individuals to access potential offensiveness of their own conduct. The elements of this test are:

 Would I be embarrassed to discuss my language and behavior at work with my family?

 Would a newspaper account of my behavior or language at work embarrass my family or me?

 Would I be embarrassed to discuss my language or behavior with my supervisor or management?

Footnotes

1   *Meritor Savings Bank, FBS v. Vinson*, 477 U.S. 57 (1986).

2   Where a particular practice has a discriminatory impact on one or more minority groups.

Chapter 21

Supervisory Liability

by Barbara E. Roberts

So now you're a supervisor! Congratulations! You're off the streets (for the most part) and seldom (if ever) get involved in confrontations with suspects and citizens, reducing the risk of injury to you and also lessening the odds of getting sued. *Not!*

While the odds of incurring *direct* liability for use of excessive force, false arrest, civil rights violations, and such may be reduced, rather than limiting liability exposure, promotion to supervisor in many ways *expands* the possibilities. Supervisors may be exposed to liability not only for their own acts and omissions, but for the acts and omissions of those they supervise.

The possible areas of liability are many, and most overlap to some extent, but can all generally be placed into three primary categories: common law torts, Civil Rights Act violations, and employment-related claims.

Before the specific supervisory liability traps can be examined, however, the elements of the most common types of law enforcement liability in general must first be understood.

Liability Principles

Use of Force

As a Civil Rights Act Violation

Until 1985, in most federal circuits there could be no recovery for the use of excessive force as a constitutional violation unless the force used was grossly disproportionate to the need for action under the circumstances, and was inspired by malice rather than mere careless or unwise excess of zeal so that it amounted to an abuse of official power that shocks the conscience, and caused severe injuries.[1]

This principle was adapted as part of a four-prong test for resolving all 42 U.S.C. § 1983 force claims in *Johnson v. Glick*,[2] and subsequently adopted as the rule of law in many other circuits.[3]

In 1985, the Supreme Court considered the question of whether or not the use of deadly force is a seizure under the Fourth Amendment, and thus to be judged by that section's reasonableness standard. Finding in the affirmative, the court stated that,

☐   "Whenever an officer restrains the freedom of a person to walk away, he has seized that person . . . there can be no question that application of deadly force is a seizure subject to the reasonableness requirement of the Fourth Amendment."[4]

Extending this analysis further, in 1989[5] the Supreme Court held that,

☐   "Today we make explicit what was implicit in *Garner's* analysis and hold that *all* claims that law enforcement officers have used excessive force – deadly or not – in the course of an arrest, investigatory stop, or other 'seizure' of a free citizen should be analyzed under the Fourth Amendment and its 'reasonableness' standard."[6]

Thus, the ultimate test to be applied to a claim of excessive force is whether or not the force used was reasonable under all the circumstances known to the officer at the time the officer acted.[7]

That question does not complete the analysis, however, as there must first be a seizure under the Fourth Amendment.[8] The test to be applied to make that determination is three-fold and requires finding a

☐   governmental
☐   termination of freedom of movement
☐   through means intentionally applied.[9]

Thus, if officers are not performing a governmental function at the time they allegedly use excessive force upon a plaintiff, any "seizure" that occurs is not within the parameters of the Fourth Amendment and does not permit redress under 42 U.S.C. § 1983.

Without this element, there would be little distinction, if any, between a state tort and a claim of constitutional deprivation. The latter simply cannot occur by a merely neglient act.[10]

Moreover, the argument can be made that there must also be proof of a "significant injury" approximately caused by the deprivation.[11] This requirement is consistent with the analysis of Graham:

☐ "The Fourth Amendment is not violated by an arrest based on probable cause, even though the wrong person is arrested, (citation) nor by the mistaken execution of a valid search warrant on the wrong premises (citation). With respect to a claim of excessive force, the same standard of reasonableness at the moment applies: 'Not every push or shove, even if it may later seem unnecessary in the peace of a judge's chambers,' (citation) violates the Fourth Amendment."[12]

These holdings also distinguish the importance attached to constitutional rights, as opposed to the lesser degree of culpability attached to mere torts:

☐ "Injuries which result from, for example, an officer's justified use of force to overcome resistance to arrest do not implicate constitutionally protected interests. An arrest is inevitably an unpleasant experience. An officer's use of excessive force does not give constitutional import to injuries that would have occurred absent the excessiveness of the force, or to minor harms. Nor can transient distress constitute a significant injury."[13]

Finally, since there is no direct action under the Fourth Amendment and recovery is permissible only under 42 U.S.C. § 1983, the requirements of that statute must also be met. This requires a finding that the officer was acting "under color of law" at the time of the events or, put another way,

☐ "The unlawful acts must be done while the official is purporting or pretending to act in the performance of his official duties; that is to say, *the unlawful acts must consist of an abuse or misuse of power which is possessed by the official only because he is an official;* and the unlawful acts must be of such a nature, and be committed under such circumstances, that they would not have occurred but for the fact that the person committing them was an official, purporting to exercise his official powers.[14]

As a Common Law Tort

A "tort" is a civil – as opposed to criminal – act or omission that causes harm. Torts are redressed by a civil lawsuit which can result in compensatory (i.e., reimbursement) damages for medical and related expenses, lost earnings, property damage, and "pain and suffering" (emotional distress), as well as punitive (i.e., punishment) damages to punish or make an example of the person who commits the tort (the "tortfeasor").

"Common law" torts are those whose primary antecedents are not statutory, but are based upon principles developed over years (often centuries) of Anglo-American jurisprudence. The precise details of common law torts vary from state to state, but a number of common principles have evolved over the years defining the essential elements of each tort.[15]

Actions for use of force incidents as common law torts primarily rely upon civil claims of battery or simple negligence. Subject to statutory immunities which vary from state to state,[16] an officer, and his employing entity, may be held liable for force that meets the following tests and causes injury:

☐ "A battery is an intentional, unlawful and harmful or offensive contact by one person with the person of another.

The intent necessary to constitute battery is not an intent to cause harm, but an intent to do the act which causes the harm.[17]

A plaintiff who suffered any bodily harm as a legal result of a battery committed upon him by a defendant is entitled to recover damages for such injury from that defendant."[18]

☐ "Negligence" is a more general concept, and imposes liability for acts that are contrary to those things a reasonable person would or would not do under the same circumstances.

Implicit in both of these instances, however, is that *privileged conduct* is not actionable. An officer is privileged to use whatever force is *reasonably necessary* to effect an arrest or overcome resistance or prevent escape.[19] Concomitantly, in most jurisdictions the person being arrested has a duty not to resist arrest or detention. If the person resists, then obviously the degree of force that may lawfully be used may escalate to overcome the resistance.[20]

First Amendment Retaliation

One particular type of claim frequently given short shrift in discussions of civil liability, but which is more and more often becoming a problem as demonstrations and civil disobedience again become common, occurs when an officer acts in response to the legitimate exercise of First Amendment rights. This usually occurs during an arrest for "obstructing, delaying or interfering with an officer in the performance of his duties" or "resisting arrest."

Generally, to constitute an offense, a person must willfully resist, delay or obstruct a public officer in the discharge or attempted discharge of his duty.[21] There are four basic elements to such a violation:

- willfulness,
- resistance, delay, or obstruction of
- a public officer, and
- some official duty which the officer is discharging or attempting to discharge.

However, a person cannot be punished for failing to obey the command of an officer if that command violates the federal Constitution.[22] For example, speech is generally protected by the First Amendment *even if it is intended to interfere with the performance of an officer's duty*, provided no physical interference results.[23] With that in mind, the arrest of a person who refuses to desist from verbally "chipping" at an officer (even if the chipping is *intended* to interfere with the officer's duties), without more, is probably a "bad" arrest which will subject the officer and the department to civil liability.

In a recent case,[24] an intoxicated individual directed a series of expletives and obscene hand gestures at a police officer who responded by detaining and arresting the plaintiff and his wife. Plaintiff sued under 42 U.S.C. § 1983. Cross-motions for summary judgment were filed. The officers defended on the grounds that they were qualifiedly immune from suit because they acted in the good faith belief their actions were reasonable.[25] The district court ruled in favor of plaintiff, and the defendants appealed.

The appellate court held that "mere boisterous conduct," although tasteless and crass, was alone insufficient to give a police officer any cause to detain plaintiff. Absent such cause, the stop and detention were illegal and could subject the defendant to liability. Further, the court noted that if the officer intended retaliation for plaintiff's method of expressing his opinion, this was a violation of § 1983 and squarely within First Amendment protection.

The court further reasoned that government officials in general, and police officers in particular, may not exercise authority for personal motives (i.e., anger, vengeance, spite, etc.), particularly in response to real or perceived slights to their dignity, and concluded that no matter how peculiar, abrasive, unruly, or distasteful a person's conduct may be, it cannot justify a police stop *unless* it suggests that some specific crime has been, or is about to be, committed, or that there is imminent danger to persons or property.

Thus, as stated above, it is clear that mere verbal interference or harassment, without more, cannot justify an arrest or detention for "resisting, delaying, or obstructing." Should the offending party, however, stray beyond the bounds of "innocent," constitutionally-protected speech, and thereby violate a statute such as challenging to fight or inciting a riot, or engage in some *physical interference* with the officer's duties, detention and arrest become appropriate.[26]

Employment-Related Actions

In addition to various state prohibitions, Title VII[27] prohibits – as a federal cause of action – discrimination in employment conditions on the basis of sex, race, religion, ethnicity, alienage, age, or disability. Discrimination may take the form of an employment practice that has a disparate impact on a particular protected group, denies a particular individual equal rights and opportunities as enjoyed by his or her coworkers, or that has the effect of creating a hostile working environment.

Employees will be held personally liable to coworkers for harassment or discriminatory conduct. This liability, when found during an action under the Civil Rights Act, may include compensatory and pain and suffering damages, as well as punitive damages and attorney's fees.

When the discriminatory or harassing event(s) is a practice of the employer, the employer will also be held liable. Employers will additionally be held liable if they "knew or should have known" the conduct was occurring and failed to take "immediate and appropriate action."[28]

Direct discrimination or harassment is fairly easy to define, but what is a "hostile working environment?" It is an environment where discrimination or harassment is so severe or pervasive as to create an *offensive* or *abusive* environment.[29] The conduct need not be directed specifically at the plaintiff, but it is sufficient if it infects the working atmosphere. It need not be sexual in nature.[30]

These issues may also be addressed as common law torts (typically a claim of battery), but as the (financial) rewards are greater under Title VII or the Civil Rights Act, the greater exposure is to be found in these federal claims.

Supervisory Concerns

Common Law Torts

Supervisors may, of course, be exposed to liability on any or all of the above theories for their own tortious acts, but they may also be held liable when their subordinates commit tortious acts if the trier of fact (judge or jury) determines there was a failure to adequately supervise the subordinate.

Inadequate supervision can be demonstrated in one of several different ways:

 By far the most common is the **failure to discipline,**[31] that is, having knowledge that a subordinate is incompetent or a danger, and doing nothing about it. Sometimes this tort is referred to as "negligent" supervision, but regardless of name, the elements are the same.

Suppose, for example, that every Hispanic arrested by a particular officer comes in with injuries requiring at least some degree of medical treatment; few others arrested by this officer seem to have the "balance problems" demonstrated by this officer's Hispanic suspects that cause them to trip over curbs or into car doors and fall into cell bars.

As the supervisor, if you do not take action and the attorney for the next "clumsy" Hispanic arrestee learns of this pattern, there may well be *inadequate supervision* liability in your future.

 The **failure to adequately train** officers is a close relative of the failure to discipline, only under this title liability can attach where there has been a training, rather than a supervision, lapse.

For example, if narcotics' officers in an area with a lot of methamphetamine labs are not trained to recognize the symptoms of phosgene poisoning,[32] then seize such a laboratory and fail to recognize the symptoms in a suspect who dies, liability may be imposed on the officer, the agency, and possibly the supervisor in charge of training.

 Failure to intervene. While not as common (yet) and not the subject of a large body of case law (yet), more and more attention is being paid to the on-scene supervisor. If an officer uses excessive force, for example, in front of a supervisor who fails to step in and stop it, the supervisor may end up just as liable (and potentially more so) than the officer wielding the PR-24®.[33]

 Ratification comes in many forms. It has been found, for example, when a police chief, after a finding of liability against arresting officers for excessive force, publicly says, "Plaintiff's lucky he only got a broken nose."[34]

In its simplest form, *ratification* occurs when, having all available facts, the supervisor agrees with (or praises) the conduct at issue. This is not to say that line officers should not be praised for doing a good job in an aggressive manner, even in "high profile" cases. They should. It is only to point out that doing so (particularly in a confrontational manner) may generate even more second-guessing than usual.

If the confidence is misplaced, it may lead to liability. More important, there are ways of supporting the officers without adding gasoline to a flame, such as statements like, "The officers had a difficult job to do under difficult circumstances; if a jury looking at the evidence years later in the calm of a courtroom finds that they were wrong, that does not necessarily mean that they are evil, cruel, or unfit. It means they are human."

Civil Rights Violations

Supervision brings its own bag of mixed blessings in this area. As a general rule, there is no "group" liability for civil rights violations[35] and no liability on the basis of *respondeat superior*.[36] Perhaps not surprisingly, however, there are exceptions to these "general rules."[37]

 The "custom-policy-practice" conundrum
Until 1978 and *Monell v. Department of Social Services*,[38] neither public entities nor supervisory personnel could be held liable under the Civil Rights Act (42 U.S.C. § 1983, *et seq.*). Since *Monell*, municipalities and policy making personnel may be held liable to the same extent as their employees *if* the employee violates the civil rights of the plaintiff *and* the violation was proximately caused by an unconstitutional custom, policy, or practice of the municipality or that person whose acts "can be said to represent a decision of the government itself."[39] Without those two elements established, the entity and supervisor are not directly liable under the Civil Rights Act.[40]

 Training
Liability for failure to train as a Civil Rights violation is more complex than under a common law negligence principle. For one thing, it is not enough for a plaintiff to prove

that an injury or accident could have been avoided if an officer had had better or more training sufficient to equip him or her to avoid the particular injury-causing conduct.[41]

Instead, there must be proof that the failure to train, as a cause of a civil rights violation, resulted from a *deliberate indifference* to the rights of the citizenry, or a particular class of citizens. Returning to the earlier example of a failure to train narcotics' officers to recognize the symptoms of phosgene poisoning, if methamphetamine has not been a substance of choice in the area before, there would be no need to provide such training, and the failure to provide such training could probably not be characterized as a *deliberate indifference* to a problem that does not exist.

Employment-Related Issues

Supervisors who actively participate in discriminatory or harassing practices will obviously be held personally liable for any resulting damages. One frequent form of liability peculiar to supervisory personnel is *"quid pro quo"* harassment: "You engage in sexual relations with me and I'll (promote you) (give you a raise) (keep you from being laid off) (select one or more)."

A more subtle basis for liability, however, exists where the supervisor knows (or, in the language of Title VII, *should have known*) of discriminatory or harassing conduct and fails to take *"immediate and appropriate remedial action"* designed to (a) punish the misconduct, (b) remedy the harassment, and (c) notify other employees that such conduct will not be tolerated.[42] One circuit has gone so far as to say that a failure to impose strict disciplines may be a sufficient basis for liability.[43]

To avoid liability, then, it is in the supervisor's best interests to ensure that the entity has a policy that prohibits harassment and discrimination, provides for a complaint process that does *not* require adherence to the chain of command, provides for *prompt* investigations, and provides for the imposition of sanctions on an escalating scale.[44] In addition, whenever the supervisor becomes aware of harassing or discriminatory conduct, *from any source*, intervention *must* take place, even in the absence of a complaint, to avoid eventual liability.

A final tip on protection from the departing employee: oftentimes the complaint of discrimination or harassment, whether based on sex, race, age or any other category, comes from a *former* employee. One of the best, and easiest, protection from such a claim is a well-structured exit interview, taped if possible, where the departing employee is asked how they liked their time with the entity, why they are leaving, and what their opinion is of the entity's supervision. The answers to these questions will either uncover a previously-unidentified problem, or serve as a defensive shield in the future should a different claim be made.

Footnotes

[1]   *Rochin v. California*, 342 U.S. 165, 172-173, 96 L.Ed. 183, 72 S. Ct. 205 (1952).

[2]   481 F.2d 1028 (2nd Cir., 1973), *cert. den.*, 414 U.S. 1033.

[3]   See, e.g., *Meredith v. State of Arizona*, 523 F. 2d 481, 484 (9th Cir., 1975); *Rutherford v. City of Berkeley*, 780 F.2d 1444, 1446 (9th Cir., 1986).

[4]   *Tennessee v. Garner*, 471 U.S. 1, 7, 85 L.Ed 1, 7, 105 S. Ct. 1694 (1985).

[5]   *Graham v. Connor*, 490 U.S. 386, 104 L.Ed.2d 443, 109 S. Ct. 1865.

[6]   Id., 104 L.Ed.2d at 454, emphasis original.

[7]   Id., 104 L.Ed.2d at 455-456.

[8]   *Brower v. County of Inyo*, 489 U.S. 593, 103 L.Ed.2d 628, 635, 109 S. Ct. 1378 (1989).

[9]   *Reed v. Hoy*, 909 F.2d 324, 329 (9th Cir., 1990), emphasis added.

[10]   *Brower v. County of Inyo, supra*, 103 L.Ed.2d at 635-636; *Daniels v. Williams*, 474 U.S. 327, 88 L.Ed.2d 662, 106 S. Ct. 668 (1986); *Davidson v. Cannon*, 474 U.S. 344, 88 L.Ed.2d 677, 106 S. Ct. 662 (1986).

[11]   *Johnson v. Morel*, 876 F.2d 477, 480 (5th Cir., 1989); *Brown v. Glossip*, 878 F.2d 871 (5th Cir., 1989).

[12]   *Graham, supra*, 104 L.Ed.2d at 455-456.

[13]   *Johnson v. Morel, supra*, 876 F.2d at 480; see also, *Hay v. City of Irving*, Texas, 893 F.2d 796 (5th Cir., 1990).

14 Devitt, Blackmar and Wolff, *Federal Jury Practice and Instructions*, Inst. 103.04, and cases cited therein, emphasis added.

15 Readers are advised to review the statutes of their own states for individual exceptions and immunities.

16 Some jurisdictions still subscribe to the common law principles of sovereign immunity; that is, the "sovereign" (state) can do no wrong. Many, however, have codified those principles of immunity. They have elected to retain and have expressly provided for liability in other areas. Local statutes should be consulted.

17 *California Basic Jury Instructions*, Civil (BAJI), 7.51, restating basic common law principles of battery.

18 *Id*, BAJI 7.50.

19 See, *e.g., Pierson v. Ray*, 386 U.S. 547, 18 L.Ed.2d 288, 87 S. Ct. 1213 (1967).

20 *E.g., Arnsberg v. United States*, 757 F.2d 971, 979 (9th Cir., 1985), cert. den., 475 U.S. 1010 (1986).

21 See, e.g., *19 Cal Jur 3d* § 1738, p. 28-29.

22 *Wright v. Georgia*, 373 U.S. 284, 10 L.Ed.2d 349, 83 S. Ct. 1240 (1963).

23 *Houston v. Hill*, 482 U.S. 451, 96 L.Ed.2d 398, 107 S. Ct. 2502 (1987).

24 *Duran v. City of Douglas*, 904 F.2d 1372 (9 Cir., 1990)

25 *Malley v. Briggs*, 475 U.S. 335, 89 L.Ed.2d 271, 106 S. Ct. 1092 (1986); *Anderson v. Creighton*, 483 U.S. 635, 97 L.Ed.2d 523, 107 S. Ct. 3034 (1987); *Floyd v. Laws*, 929 F.2d 1390 (9th Cir., 1991).

26 Even physical interference may not always be enough, however; *e.g., People v. Wetzel* (1974), 11 Cal.3d 104, 108, holds that the test is whether or not the officers were in fact obstructed in carrying out their duties.

27 42 U.S.C. § 2000e.

28 *Meritor Savings Bank v. Vinson,* 477 U.S. 57, 91 L.Ed.2d 49, 106 S. Ct. 2399 (1986).

29 *Hall v. Gus Construction Co.,* 842 F.2d 1010, 1014 (8th Cir., 1988); *Andrews v. City of Philadelphia,* 895 F.2d 1469, 1485 (3rd Cir., 1990); *Ellison v. Brady,* 924 F.2d 872 (9th Cir., 1991).

30 See, *e.g., E.E.O.C. v. Hacienda Hotel,* 881 F.2d 1504, 1508 (9th Cir., 1989); *Rogers v. E.E.O.C.,* 454 F.2d 234 (5th Cir., 1971), *cert. den.,* 406 U.S. 957 (1972), but *cf, Scott v. Sears, Roebuck & Co.,* 798 F.2d 210, 212 (7th Cir., 1986); *Rabidue v. Osceola Refining Co.,* 805 F.2d 611 (6th Cir., 1986), *cert. den.,* 481 U.S. 1041 (1987).

31 In this regard, see also the discussion under employment-related claims, *infra.*

32 An often-fatal "side effect" of a poorly-ventilated methamphetamine laboratory.

33 *Ting v. United States,* 927 F.2d 1504 (9th Cir., 1991).

34 See, *e.g., Larez v. City of Los Angeles,* 946 F.2d 630 (9th Cir., 1991).

35 See, *e.g., Ting v. United States, supra.*

36 *Monell v. Department of Social Services,* 436 U.S. 658, 56 L.Ed.2d 611, 98 S. Ct. 2018 (1978).

37 Readers are again directed to the section on employment-related claims, *infra,* which have different rules for supervisory liability although they can sometimes be framed as civil rights violations.

38 See, fn. 32, *supra.*

39 *City of St. Louis v. Praprotnik,* 485 U.S. 112, 99 L.Ed.2d 107, 120, 108 S. Ct. 915 (1988); *Pembaur v. Cincinnati,* 475 U.S. 469, 89 L.Ed.2d 452, 106 S. Ct. 1292 (1986).

40 This is, of course, except to the extent that in some states the entity may be required to defend and indemnify the employee.

41 *City of Canton v. Harris,* 489 U.S. 378, 391, 103 L.Ed.2d 412, 109 S. Ct. 1197 (1989).

42 See, *e.g., Meritor Savings Bank v. Vinson, supra; Ellison v. Brady, supra.*

[43] *Intlekofer v. Turnage*, 1992 W.L. 201088, docket 90-16793 (9th Cir., 1992).

[44] *Meritor Savings Bank v. Vinson, supra.* In this regard, it should also be noted that even the Ninth Circuit does not object to informal counselling as a remedy, provided it is a *first step* and provided it is reasonably calculated to end the conduct. *Intlekofer v. Turnage, supra.*

About the Author

Ms. Barbara E. Roberts received her B.S., cum laude, from California State University in Los Angeles and her J.D., cum Laude, from Loyola University School of Law. She is admitted to the State Bar of California; the United States District Courts of the Central, Southern, and Eastern Districts of California; the United States Court of Appeals, Ninth Circuit; and the United States Supreme Court.

Ms. Roberts is a frequent guest lecturer and speaker before government and law enforcement organizations nationwide on tort liability, employment issues, training, policy development, and related topics for law enforcement agencies. She also speaks at seminars for senior law enforcement management, security directors, risk managers, and personnel managers.

Ms. Roberts is also an adjunct professor of Criminal Justice for California State University at Los Angeles, and chair of the firm's State Bar certified continuing legal education committee.

Hillary M. Robinette

Mr. Hillary M. Robinette is a twenty-year veteran Special Agent of the FBI, and former FBI National Academy and University of Virginia faculty member. He presently operates Quantico Group Associates, Inc., a training and consulting firm for criminal justice and public safety agencies.

Mr. Robinette travels throughout the U.S. and abroad to present training seminars in professional ethics, management, and supervision. His company also provides training in forensic fingerprint training and disaster planning for public safety agencies. He is a director of the Prince William County (VA) Chamber of Commerce, and is listed in the 23rd edition (1993) of Marquis Who's Who in the South and Southwest.

Mr. Robinette is the author or co-author of several police management textbooks, one of which, Burnout in Blue, won the Jefferson Award from the University of Virginia for its "contribution to criminal justice education."

Chapter 22

Supervising Tomorrow

by Hillary M. Robinette

Policing methods are changing in the United States. Criminal justice academics and practitioners alike write and talk about community policing, problem oriented policing, neighborhood partnerships, and civilian empowerment. Civilian activists, politicians and government officials seek an energetic role in law enforcement oversight and activity.

In New York City each of the 75 precincts has a Precinct Management Team that includes civilians from the community. Police Commissioner Lee Brown says, "The team has the responsibility of identifying problems and developing strategies to solve the problems using law enforcement and other resources."[1]

In a much smaller jurisdiction, law enforcement in Dumfries, Virginia, cooperate with a local church for a new presence in a high crime neighborhood. A townhouse has been rented by the church and the initiative, partially funded and operated by parishioners, provides for town and county law enforcement officers to use the residential facility as a place to write reports, interview neighbors, and converse with community youth.

Community empowerment policing in Washington DC's 3rd District has officers leading neighborhood kids on nature hikes and taking them out to pick up trash. Working within the neighborhoods on foot, they develop contacts ranging from civic leaders to merchants and drug dealers. "People are more willing to come forward when they know the officers personally," said Hubert Williams, president of the Police Foundation and an advocate of the community empowerment approach. "It allows you to get information so you can get convictions, not just arrests."[2]

Harvard scholars Mark Moore and George Kelling add an academic voice and say that law enforcement methods are changing in major ways and that a new law enforcement strategy is in formation throughout the land.[3]

Such changes in the law enforcement role have important implications for the nature and quality of law enforcement supervision in the future – and in some departments, the future is now.

The traditional law enforcement first-line supervisor, shift commander, or mid-level executive is unprepared in training and experience for the requirements of the new strategy.   Classical management theory, heavily influenced by the mass-production industry and the wartime experience of the military, dominates traditional law enforcement supervisory practice.

The command and control model of policing during the past fifty years measured supervisors' successes in the statistical accomplishments of their units.   Arrests made, citations issued, calls for service answered, response times, and case closings were all counted. They became the criteria of successful law enforcement work. A good law enforcement officer, like a good soldier, followed orders and stayed out of trouble, filled out forms and reports correctly, and didn't steal or hurt people unnecessarily.

Supervision by rule was the mode; orders came down from the top and reports went back up the chain in accordance with regulations and sound administrative practice. Sergeants checked spelling, form, and compliance of the paper going up the chain and found themselves handling more and more of the lieutenants' administrative work and spending less and less time on the streets. On an average day, supervisors saw all of their people only once at roll call in the ritual formality of organizational efficiency. It worked well. The brass made the decisions in a closed system and sergeants were semi-members of their units and semi-members of the command structure, often accountable to neither.

Diversity and the New Leadership Model

The new strategy calls for a different leadership methodology. Diversity rather than homogeneity will characterize the law enforcement work group of the future as well as the community it serves. Cultural, gender, and ethnic diversity in work teams will make it difficult for new supervisors to manage according to traditional standards.

Executives will demand more team-building from subordinates in the chain; there will be more ambiguity as managers experiment with structure. The downsizing and restructuring which characterized the late eighties and early nineties will be followed by decentralization and the introduction of civilian participants in problem-solving and decision-making at unprecedented organizational levels.

Part of the diversity will dictate flexible work schedules for subordinates that will require computer skills of the new supervisors to help keep in real-time touch with many people over a distance. What is now being called "groupware" technology with local area network PC's (LAN's)[4] joined in overlapping webs will affect organizational communications. Therefore, future supervisors will need specific training and hands-on experience with technology to the same degree that they now need proficiency in firearms and defensive tactics.

Primary communications will be through interlocking webs of LAN's with different kinds of information being swept from each to be stored in central electronic files— precinct intelligence, criminal incident files, personnel, performance, and research. Some units will even develop an artificial intelligence capacity to help solve problems and make decisions that require examination of high volume data.

Electronic Bulletin Boards will enable users to exchange information, post notices, send and receive electronic mail (E–Mail), share software, and query on-line data bases. As it does now, technology will drive the organizational communications system. Supervisors will need the technical skills in order to be proficient.

Supervisory performance will be evaluated from a variety of sources. Even now, so-called "360 degree feedback" is in practice in some private sector organizations. It will come to law enforcement work quickly as departments restructure to implement new strategies for community policing.

Individual performance will be measured by many who have contact with supervisors and their self-directed work teams. They will also be evaluated on their performance by seniors – several rather than by one as is traditional – and also by their peers in the organization. Performance appraisal will not only be top/down, but down/up, across and through the organization and its clientele – the public.

Values, quality of community and organizational life, and consensus will become more important than the traditional order giving and statistical measurements of productivity. This change in the law enforcement role will be very difficult for those in the transition. New supervisors will have to deal with difficult attitude and behavior changes during the transition. Also, supervisors in the new strategy of policing will have to demonstrate and teach the new values of high performance policing.

In the New York City Police Department, quality of life in the neighborhoods is a new value. A department value statement calls for each member to promise "to protect lives and property, . . . to impartially enforce the law, . . . to maintain a higher standard of integrity than is generally expected of others," and finally, "our pledge is to value human life, respect the life of each individual, and render our services with courtesy and civility."[5]

In Boston the law enforcement commitment is "to the positive evolution, growth, and livability of our city.[6] And in Rochester, New York, officers "pledge and subscribe to the dignity of the person, the Constitution and laws, our community, leadership and personal character, and organizational excellence."[7]

The Burden of Change

The transition to the new strategy will place the highest burden of change on the supervisor.

In the New York City Police Department where "beat cops" are the new strategy officers, they are resented by the "radio car cops" because of the department's preferential attitude towards the beat cops assigned to the neighborhood teams. One radio car officer explained, "While I'm out here doing all the grunt work and risking my life, they're playing with the neighborhood kids or attending some community meeting." Another officer observed, "I know a community patrol officer (beat cop) who spends most of his day hiding out in a store. I guess he's getting to know the merchants or helping them solve their problems."[8]

The new strategy has so split the NYPD that there are reports of locker room incidents of name-calling, shouting matches, and overturned lockers. The events are long over before the brass has to deal with them – if, indeed, at all – but the supervisor must face them daily. Truly "in the middle," sergeants in departments undergoing such transformational changes have the toughest jobs.

Value oriented policing places a high burden on the supervisor to understand, accept, demonstrate, and teach the law enforcement behaviors that come about because of the values. The supervisor needs the skills to convert the concept into action. Thinking, writing, and speaking skills shall be at least as important as tactics, arrest techniques, administrative, and operational procedures.

Tomorrow's supervisors will be team builders. In those departments that implement the new strategy, supervisors will have more freedom to intervene, innovate, and reallocate resources and task personnel. They will need to set clear do-able goals and define outcomes, recognize the beauty of differences, and provide recognition, visibility, celebration, and reward for team accomplishment. They will design collaborative programs and services based on department values and neighborhood needs in order to move from internal and external turfdom to a unity of performance of larger and longer term benefit than traditional bureaucracy allows.

Tomorrow's supervisors will need team-building skills to clarify member tasks and roles, and to encourage participation by all and prevent domination by any one. They must share information, facilitate learning, engage in joint problem solving, and establish norms that support the expansion of different viewpoints within sound legal and ethical limits. Finally, they must provide the team members with the resources needed to do their jobs. Traditional supervisory training (when it occurs) does not teach such skills. Paramilitary model methodology does not include such active supervisory responsibilities.

Improvement in the quality of organizational and community life will become a primary supervisory goal. New supervisors will be in the neighborhood talking to people, taking reports, and meeting with policing team members on a regular basis. They will focus their energy on knowing what is going on in the place – what their people are saying and doing. They will be precinct chiefs who are expected to make referrals to other public agencies on behalf of their neighborhood clients to remove the direct and indirect breeders of crime and disorder.

In 1982, the federal Victim and Witness Protection Act directed all federal law enforcement agencies to develop and implement consistent guidelines for the fair treatment of federal crime victims and witnesses. Federal law enforcement agencies since that time have worked to meet the law's requirements. The U.S. Capitol Police has 18 specially trained officers and detectives spread through each department division who respond to the scene of serious crimes to assist victims and witnesses. New strategy supervisors will manage similar programs as more jurisdictions legislate requirement akin to the federal law.[9]

Research in the Santa Monica (CA) Police Department during the first five months of 1990 revealed that about 27% of the calls for service involved homeless persons as criminal victims, suspects, or involved parties. Thirty-five percent of the people booked in the Santa Monica jail during the period were homeless. Over one-third of law enforcement patrol services were generated by, and for, less than 2% of the resident population.

The impact the homeless have had on law enforcement operations led to the creation of the Homeless Enforcement Liaison Program (HELP), and the department gained authorization for seven more officers to work specifically with the homeless. Santa Monica Lieutenant Barney Melekian writes, "The dimensions of the (homeless) problem are national in scope, but local in impact. Every jurisdiction in the nation will have to deal with the homeless in some form during the remainder of this century. Until such time as public policy decisions have been made at the local, state, and national levels with respect to mental health facilities and detoxification centers, the problem will fall largely on the shoulders of local law enforcement."[10]

Law enforcement actions such as the Victim-Witness Assistance Program and the Homeless Enforcement Liaison Program represent problem oriented policing at its best. Such programs become community policing when the underlying strategic philosophy and values are implemented by neighborhood law enforcement supervisors and their teams.

Quality of Life

Quality of life *within* the department will present new supervisory challenges. The median age of the workforce will be almost forty in 2000. The increase in older workers in the national workforce will be reflected in the law enforcement workforce. Older officers will be less willing to change tasks or assignments. Rungs will be cut off career ladders as more officers reach the structural plateau earlier in a law enforcement career than before.[11]

As openings at the top decrease, career development will move laterally requiring officers to develop multiple competencies to qualify for salary increases. Supervisors will be the ones who will advise and assist their team members in their self-development education and professional growth. Some of their charges will need remedial reading help; others, help in learning a second language; all will need training in technology, the law, and human skills. Supervisors will be expected to help manage learning and obtain resources to do it.

Retirement planning, health, and child care will become more important quality of life issues for employees than they have been in the past. Management training for newly promoted or promotable supervisors will be critical to the success of quality of life in the department. Promotion based exclusively on written test taking, or on an aggressive reputation, or through the "old boy network" is doomed to fail in the new strategy. Department executives must commit to long term development and training for supervisory leadership.

The agency of the future will develop horizontal fast-tracks for the ambitious and gifted. Broad knowledge secured with depth will be the key to success. Eighty percent of all jobs will require mental rather than physical skills and those with brain power will command premium pay.

Authors Jamieson and Harrison predict that about half of the workforce in the year 2000 will be female.[12] A vast store of human brain power never previously tapped is beginning to swell in the ranks of law enforcement. Between 1978 and 1986 the number of women law enforcement officers in municipal departments more than doubled, and continues to grow at an increasing rate.[13]

Supervisors in traditionally male-dominated institutions are just beginning to struggle with the notion of working with women as peers, let alone working under their supervision and management. In a recent study on women in law enforcement, "75 percent of the women interviewed indicated that they had experienced some form of sexual harassment, including 49 percent who had been pressured for sexual favors by a supervisor or fellow officer."[14]

The San Francisco Police Department had the profession's equivalent of the Navy's 1991 Tailhook Convention in its infamous Rathskeller Sex Scandal in 1984. The ten-year veteran officer who reported the incident involving sexual misadventure at a police academy graduation party said she was the object of repeated sexual pranks and abuse during her service as a police woman. The event was a source of major reform in the department, as the Tailhook Convention incident has been for the Navy.

The clear lesson that comes from such events is that supervisors and managers of the future need to break old attitudes and habits that are offensive. They must root out the hidden inconsistencies of past practices. They need to teach new manners and civility, and require behavior that does not demean nor offend, and do it in an atmosphere of pop culture and violence that flies in the face of civility, dignity, and respect for authority.

Law enforcement and other public service managers might

think that because of the discontinuous nature of the changes that are forecast that it is impossible to plan for them. It is impossible to foretell the precise impact of such changes, but tomorrow's supervisor can better prepare for uncertainty by having a deep well of principles upon which to draw as new challenges approach.

Basic Principles

Basic principles do not change. Form and method do. Policing in democratic societies is based on fundamental principles that, in the United States, are anchored in the Constitution. *Free and equal access* to law enforcement service, fidelity to the public *trust, balancing* the needs of safety and security with the needs of enforcement, *cooperation and coordination* of activity with the community and other public agencies, and *objectivity* are Constitutional principles of policing that do not change.[15]

Tomorrow's supervisors can examine their actions and plans in the light of the five principles. They guide as lighthouse beacons through the rocks and shoals of contemporary supervision. To reflect on the daily application of *free and equal access*, the supervisor tests each decision against its equity effect. Is the action or decision I am about to take equitable? Is it fair to those affected? Can I explain how it is fair? This type of preliminary consideration will prevent insensitive behavior and unintended consequences and applies to behavior inside as well as outside the department.

The second question to ask, "Is it the right thing to do?" The answer here is embedded in the principle of *trust.* Supervisory – as well as all Constitutional authority – is based on trust; trust that each will examine individual choices of actions in light of personal and organizational integrity. Does the action or decision I choose support and demonstrate the values to which I am pledged by my oath of office?

The third managerial question deals with danger and the needs of the law. Is my choice lawful? Are there any unnecessary risks to life and property? Am I willing to do myself what I am asking of others? Are there safer alternatives? Is time truly an urgent factor or can I wait for better conditions? The answers to these questions give guidance according to the principle of *balance in enforcement* action.

The fourth test of managerial action is that of *cooperation and coordination.* Is my choice of action or decision based on the best possible beneficial outcome for all the parties involved? Does it fit the requirements of teamwork? Can I defend it in the public forum? Can I correct misperceptions with adequacy and force?

And finally the supervisory test of *objectivity* (which may be the most difficult) examines one's personal motives for choice and action. Why am I choosing this action or decision over others? Are my intentions good and honorable? Can I clearly define them? Do my intentions fit well with my duties and obligations?

Meeting the high standards of law enforcement management is not easy and will become more difficult as social, technological, and political change happens. Tomorrow's best supervisors and managers will be both realists and idealists. They will have multiple competencies developed through enthusiastic pursuit of learning both inside and outside the profession. They will practice the skills of consensus generation and develop a consultative approach to directing and controlling. They will be reflective and sensitive men and women of action with a commitment to service. And finally, they will be leaders with a clear sense of fundamental ideals that will serve as "a moral and professional compass." A commitment to respect for the dignity of others, to integrity, to authority of law, and to accountability can keep an institution or an individual on the right course, just as a helmsman's compass keeps a ship on course.

But a compass is not enough. In addition, a helmsman must know the waters, the tides, the currents, the shifting shoals and sands beneath the waters, the weather and the climate, the winds, the channels, and the rules of the sea. A helmsman cannot secure the safety of the ship and its passengers, crew, and cargo without attention to changes in the environment and the conditions of their voyage.

So, too, with a police department. Though the right ideals are permanent, they must be applied with a clear eye for the changing problems the public faces, the corresponding changes in needs or service, and fluctuations in the conditions of the department."[16]

Methods change; ideals and principles remain. Tomorrow's supervisors will *know* more than their predecessors, will be both flexible *and* principled, will be a careful listener with high mental and physical energy, and have confidence in their decisions.

This may be a daunting vision of the law enforcement supervisors of tomorrow. These are people dedicated to the service of others, and committed to a professional career with few external rewards and many hazards. But in the long blue line of men and women who have risen to law enforcement leadership, the successful ones have taken the hard jobs, given their best, and served their community. "It goes with the stripes."

Footnotes

[1] "An Interview with Commissioner Lee P. Brown of New York," *Law Enforcement News*, May 15, 1992, Vol. XVIII, No. 358, p.11.

[2] Quoted by Ruben Castaneda in *The Washington Post*, July 2, 1992, p. D1.

[3] See "The Evolving Strategy of Policing," by George L. Kelling and Mark H. Moore, Perspectives in Policing, No. 4, *National Institute*

of Justice, November 1988.

4   A Local Area Network (LAN) is a series of personal computers connected with each other.

5   Lee Brown, *Law Enforcement News*, p. 14.

6   See Robert Wasserman and Mark H. Moore in "Values In Policing," Perspectives on Policing, No. 8, November 1988, U.S. Department of Justice, *National Institute of Justice*, p. 5.

7   Rochester Police Department Pledge Card and Mission Statement.

8   As quoted by Angelo L. Pisani in "Dissecting Community Policing," *Law Enforcement News*, May 31, 1992, Vol. XVIII, No. 359, p. 8.

9   See "Victim-Witness Assistance," by Joseph R. Luteran, FBI *Law Enforcement Bulletin*, March 1991, Vol. 60, Nr. 3, p. 1.

10   "Police and the Homeless," by Lt. Barney Melekian, Santa Monica Police Department, *FBI Law Enforcement Bulletin*, November 1990, Vol. 59, No. 11, p. 7.

11   The "structural plateau" is the point in a police career after which there will be no more promotion.   Judith M. Bardwick describes the effect on individuals and organizations in her book, *The Plateauing Trap* (New York: Amacom, 1986).

12   see *Managing Workforce 2000* by David Jamieson and Julie O'Mara (San Francisco: Josey-Bass, 1991).

13   *On the Move: The Status of Women in Policing* by Susan E. Martin (Washington, DC: The Police Foundation, 1990). p. 185.

14   Martin, p. 140.

15   These five moral principles of police behavior were developed by Howard S. Cohen and Michael Feldberg and are the subject of their book, *Power and Restraint: The Moral Dimension of Police Work* (New York: Praeger Publishers, 1991).

16   Edwin J. Delattre and Cornelius J. Behan, "Practical Ideals for Managing in the Nineties," *Local Government and Police Management*, Third Edition, ed. William A. Geller (Washington, DC: International City Management Association, 1991). P. 549.

Neal E. Trautman

Mr. Neal E. Trautman is National Director of the Law Enforcement Career Development Center. You may know Mr. Trautman as a founder of the Law Enforcement Television Network (LETN), the nation's largest provider of enforcement training. As the Network's Director of Training, he was responsible for all aspects of training provided to 120,000 officers daily.

Mr. Trautman was founder and charter president of the nationally respected Florida Criminal Justice Trainer's Association. He served as editor of the Florida Police Training Officer's Association Newsletter for three years and has written numerous articles and books relating to law enforcement training and professionalism. He has written the following textbooks: A Study of Law Enforcement; Law Enforcement In-Service Training Programs; Law Enforcement Training; Law Enforcement - The Making of a Profession; Standards for Security and Law Enforcement Agencies; and 50 Things Teens Can Do to Fight Drugs.

Chapter 23

Supervisory Ethics

by Neal E. Trautman

Supervisors face many challenges. No challenge is greater than molding those whom they supervise into truly great officers.

Pride, dedication, and ethics are crucial ingredients for being great. Supervisors must instill a sense of tradition, but to do so requires that they understand the history of law enforcement supervision and its struggle for ethics.

The History of Law Enforcement Supervision Ethics

The 1800's

These were difficult times for law enforcement leadership. The badge was looked upon in a degrading manner. Corruption and graft became widespread as political interference and manipulation grew.

Strength and size were the only employment standards. Police chiefs did not have the authority to appoint, assign, or terminate officers. Discipline could not be enforced because of political protection. Extortions of citizens, drunkenness on duty, and assaulting superior officers were common.

The lack of employment requirements other than political friendship also resulted in relatively low salaries. Officers wore no uniforms. The numbers on their copper badges were the only means of identification. Political favoritism continued to prosper.

Law enforcement on state and federal levels was growing. In 1835 the Texas Rangers organized to fight Indians, outlaws, and Mexicans. The International Association of Chiefs of Police was founded in 1893 to advance law enforcement service. The mid to late 1800's witnessed the creation of the United States Secret Service and the

Internal Revenue Agency. The U.S. Department of Justice was established in 1870.

The Early 1900"s

The early 1900"s was a time when many officers were voicing their dissatisfaction with work conditions. The famous Boston Police Strike of September 9, 1919 originated from union sentiment.

Local police unionization had begun by the turn of the century. The Boston Union had requested to become affiliated with the American Federation of Labor. The police commissioner refused and suspended several officers for their union activities. The union reacted by voting to strike. Thousands of officers walked off their assignments, sending Boston residents into panic.

August Vollmer was a domineering force in leadership. He established a law enforcement training school using the facilities of the University of California at Berkeley.

The 1920's

While law enforcement leadership was struggling during the 1920's, social unrest was placing great demands on policing. In addition to the new Eighteenth Amendment which prohibited the manufacture, sale, import, and export of liquor, the Volstead Act of 1919 made provisions for enforcement of the Eighteenth Amendment.

Prohibition created a great deal of difficulty for administrators and their departments. When the majority of citizens chose to ignore the prohibition laws, the police became extremely unpopular.

Law enforcement professionalism got a great "shot in the arm" when J. Edgar Hoover established the Federal Bureau of Investigation in 1924. His pursuit of excellence and exceedingly high standards were tremendous examples for all to follow. However, Hoover's far-reaching benefits of leadership in law enforcement training and professionalism were yet to be realized.

Graft, political influence, and corruption substantially increased because officers were so frustrated. Leadership had to deal with the public's feeling of apathy toward law enforcement authority due to the belief that officers could be bought. This resulted in low morale and self-respect among officers.

The 1930's

J. Edgar Hoover's untiring pursuit of professionalism was demonstrated in 1932 with the development of the Law Enforcement

Bulletin. The bulletin's objective was simply to further the advancement of law enforcement service.

An advancement in leadership occurred in 1935 when the FBI created their National Academy. The academy has played a crucial role in upgrading law enforcement service. It has trained thousands of administrative and supervisory officers from all levels of law enforcement.

The George-Dean Act of 1936 marked the first form of financial support for law enforcement. The act was intended to assist vocational education. However, section 6 of the act specifically provided for funds that could be used by law enforcement agencies. These early educational programs gradually evolved into college credit programs.

The 1940's and 50's

This was an era of only mediocre leadership advancement. The International Association of Chiefs of Police conducted a survey which indicated that officers throughout the nation were dissatisfied with their working conditions. Unsatisfactory working hours, salaries, pensions, and other employment benefits had resulted in forty-four police unions in operation by 1956.

The late 50's marked a renewed interest in law enforcement leadership. In 1959, California passed legislation establishing the Commission on Police Officer Standards and Training (POST). Its purpose was to provide technical resources, economic support, training and educational standards to local law enforcement. The commission was the first of its kind in America. Every state now has some form of similar regulating body.

The 1960's

Unlike the 40's and 50's, the 1960's was a time when municipal forces found themselves the recipients of a tide of criticism. Student unrest exploded in the streets as out nation's colleges protested social conditions and the war in Vietnam. Civil rights' demonstrations became ugly and violent. Riots were almost common in some major cities. The crime rate skyrocketed and drug addiction climbed to unprecedented heights.

Law enforcement leadership was caught poorly equipped, unprepared, and untrained during the 60's. The front line of defense against a population which increased approximately 13 percent and reported crimes that rose 148 percent was struggling to keep its head above water. Serious crime increased at a staggering rate; aggravated assault was up 102 percent, robbery rose 177 percent, and forcible rape climbed 16 percent during the decade.

The mid 60's crime surge resulted in a staggering amount of research and leadership at the federal political level. Released in 1967, the President's Commission on Law Enforcement was a two year study conducted by more than 250 advisers, consultants, and staff members. An incredibly extensive collection of surveys, reports, and statistical information was compiled and is used as a resource even today.

An indication of how badly leadership in the area of law enforcement training was needed during this era is found in the International City Management Associations Municipal Yearbook for 1968. It reported police recruits in cities of 10,000 or more received no academy training in:

- 7 percent of the largest agencies,

- 11 percent of suburban agencies,

- 32 percent of agencies having just over 10,000 population.

In smaller cities, almost 50 percent of new officers did not attend a police academy.

Leadership and professionalism were truly struggling during this period. Many agencies failed to ensure that their officers knew basic criminal justice skills. Most departments were forced to place emphasis on surviving in the streets rather than focus their efforts on professionalism.

Federal leadership took the lead as President Lyndon Johnson established the Commission on Law Enforcement and the Administration of Justice in 1965. The Law Enforcement Assistant Administration and The Omnibus Crime and Safe Streets Act were born from the Presidential Commission. America's "war on crime" was declared. Nearly eight billion dollars was directed toward the battle against crime from 1968 through 1978.

The President's Commission published their extensive report, The Challenge of Crime in a Free Society, in 1967. It set forth comprehensive goals and standards which called for monumental changes and the implementation of many new programs to further professionalism. Some innovative and progressive law enforcement administrators initiated similar standards and goals at the state and local levels, yet the impetus soon diminished.

Great technological landmarks came about from massive funding. As an example, 1965 marked the development of the National Crime Information Center (NCIC). By 1967, NCIC was alive and running. Nationwide computerized information concerning wanted persons, stolen vehicles, stolen property, etc., was now available to officers across the nation. NCIC spurred on the creation of similar information systems at the state and local levels.

As the 1960's came to an end, the social troubles which plagued all law enforcement agencies had prompted extensive internal improvements for the same agencies. Education and training levels moved ahead significantly. Technology was implemented and leadership was strengthened.

Although it was one of law enforcement's most difficult periods, it was also one in which tremendous advancements were realized.

The 1970's and 80's

Federally funded college programs during the 1970's had dramatic, wide sweeping effects on the quality of college level law enforcement education. While most officers do not have a bachelor's degree, the majority have attended at least some college. The term "law enforcement professionalism" became synonymous with higher education during the 70's.

Leadership and professionalism were enhanced by the insight and progressiveness of several administrators and scholars. An intellectual foundation was established through the untiring efforts of authors such as August Vollmer, O. W. Wilson, V. A. Leonard, and James Q. Wilson.

In 1979, The Commission on Accreditation for Law Enforcement Agencies, was created through the efforts of many law enforcement executives and organizations. Its goal is law enforcement professionals through the overall improvement in the delivery of services. Professionalism will be achieved through agencies voluntarily meeting exceedingly high standards of operation. The standards were established by the Commission.

State of the Art Law Enforcement Supervisory Ethics

Contemporary American law enforcement administrators are faced with frequent criticism of their agencies. Citizen complaints, misleading newspaper articles, and insensitive elected officials are quick to pinpoint any departmental weaknesses, especially ethical ones.

The fallacy of some of these accusations is that they ignore the social and political influences which often create the same ethical problems law enforcement is criticized for not correcting. Thus, being knowledgeable of law enforcement history allows supervisors to repute many criticisms by placing some of the responsibility on the true guilty party, society.

Unlike past decades, some administrators realize the management style of our nation's "best run" corporations can be adapted to law enforcement. Due to bureaucracy, the managerial effectiveness of law enforcement has lagged behind the leadership within most Fortune 500 companies.

Many highly acclaimed management texts point out that it's the nature of a bureaucracy to generate stagnation and inefficiency. They also advise highly effective organizations to develop employee skills, abilities, and knowledge. It should become one of their highest priorities. For many agencies, this will mean a major transformation of leadership style.

The Police Executive Research Forum clearly summarized the importance of management style in their publication, How To Rate Your Local Police. The book emphasizes that law enforcement response times, crime rates, arrest rates, and the percentage of investigative clearances are important, but should not be a community's primary concern.

The initial consideration should focus on the agency's management style. When a department treats its employees as their most important resource, crime and arrest rates will have a tendency to improve naturally.

Supervisors can make an ethics' difference by promoting a philosophy which is people oriented and participatory, instead one that is strict authoritarian. In doing so, a working atmosphere which encourages unethical conduct will be eliminated and replaced with one that generates teamwork, comradeship, and ethical cops.

In all probability, most departments will need the expertise of a management consultant to transform its management style. Regardless of the difficulty involved, an agency cannot be truly ethical if poor leadership constantly eats away at the dedication and loyalty needed to be truly professional.

Although complicated and difficult, the change in leadership will help slice through the bureaucracy. The "search for excellence" is essentially over when an organization really is "people oriented."

Innovative problem solving, a sincere desire to do the best possible job, and a substantial improvement in performance spreads throughout the agency. Internal communication and personal relationships have a tone of togetherness. Shifts and divisions will thrive on teamwork. Officers will be proud to be ethical.

Easier Said Than Done

What's the most difficult part of developing such a tremendous ethical leadership style? It is the courage to take the first step, and a sincere commitment. Some agencies have already developed an ethical leadership style. They're glad they did, but none would say it was easy. In a sense, it's like any great achievement – only hard work makes it happen.

> **Leadership** — The processes through which supervisors motivate, direct, influence, and communicate with subordinates to get them to perform in ways that will help the organization to achieve its goals.
>
> **Power** — The ability to influence others in an organization has many levels and sources. It is exercised in many ways and has led to the development of a variety of leadership techniques and theories.
>
> **Ethics** — A code or system of conduct that has universal moral obligations and duties that explain how to act.

The path to become an agency with great ethical leadership begins with taking one giant step – a sincere commitment. Making the commitment may be more difficult than it appears.

At first glance, most administrators believe that they have already made this commitment. After all, they are dedicated, sincere, and loyal to the highest ideals of law enforcement, and they attend numerous seminars and management training courses.

Administrators have learned rational management practices and principles. They ensure that middle management and line supervisors attend appropriate supervision courses. Virtually all the staff is versed on the traditional fundamentals of management and supervision.

As expected, it is traditional management that generates difficulty in carrying out the commitment. Since the commitment involves restructuring the managerial philosophy of the organization, traditional principles, especially the semi-military structure, must be transformed. Remember, teamwork and people-oriented management are the qualities needed to promote high quality performance.

Law enforcement administrators must commit themselves and their staff to a leadership style which develops skills, abilities, and the potential within all employees of the organization. At the same time they must always be ethical role models.

Ethics — A Matter of Attitude

In addition to being necessary for becoming a great leader, law enforcement supervisors will reap tremendous benefits from a participatory leadership style. A total revitalization of attitude can filter throughout an organization.

Problems such as unethical conduct, apathy, absenteeism, poor communication, poor interpersonal relationships, and high turnover will begin to improve. Officers in every department across the nation

Neal E. Trautman

are filled with unleashed potential. The key to unlocking this potential is the chief administrator.

The Key to Success

Chiefs of Police or Sheriffs are the keys to success or the catalysts for failure, because it is they who control the tone of the organization. They are the ones who set the ethics' atmosphere.

Motivation starts at the top. Subordinates can be motivated by dedication to the agency or driven by self-serving interests. The staff will follow the policies and examples set by the chief administrator. Subordinates follow the examples of their immediate supervisors.

It is obvious which leadership style is compatible with an excellent department. Fear and intimidation have no place in a professional law enforcement agency. Domineering and inflexible supervisors will counteract any benefits derived by more enlightened supervisors.

Inherently motivating supervisors are those who:

- Convey a sincere interest in others.
- Satisfy the needs of subordinates.
- Develop an organizational commitment.
- Are honest and open in dealings with fellow employees.
- Allow officers to play an active role in decision making.
- Provide challenges and responsibilities for officers.
- Convey trust and understanding.
- Assist officers in their personal development.

Leadership Styles

Leadership styles are generally classified by who makes the decisions and when the work group becomes involved in the decision-making. Some styles promote good ethics more than others.

Autocratic

Autocratic supervisors make decisions to inform their groups after decisions are made. On the surface this appears to be a very simple and effective style for supervisors. However, it is best used with new officers or in an emergency situation, because it can be perceived as a "dictatorial" approach.

Four Leadership Styles

Style	Approach	When Group Gets Involved
Autocratic	Tell	After the decision is made by supervisor.
Benevolent Autocratic	Sell	After the decision is made to be persuaded to accept supervisor's decision.
Democratic	Consult	Prior to the decision being made. Group expresses opinions about issues.
Participative	Join in	During the decision-making process to mutually arrive at a group decision.

Benevolent Autocratic

Leaders with this style make decisions, then try to persuade their subordinates to support them because they were fair and necessary decisions. This style does not encourage sound ethics.

Although the group is involved in discussions about the issues, they don't have any ability to influence the decision. Pride is not instilled.

Democratic

Subordinates are permitted to express their opinions prior to a decision being made. Employees appreciate this leadership style, because they can influence decisions that may effect them.

Participative

Supervisors allow employees to have a major role in decisions. Supervisors discuss facts related to current questions with subordinates and invite them to have equal authority to make the decision.

This style is more complicated and difficult. Group decision-making requires patience and understanding. Employees appreciate being allowed to have some control over their future. Dedication and good ethics are enhanced.

Mid and upper management also have specific ethics' responsibilities and roles. Their roles include:

- Being supportive of sound ethics, but not controlling,

- Responding promptly to ethics assistance requests,

- Making resources available for ethics' training when needed,

- Doing MBWA (Management By Walking Around),

- Recognizing, appreciating, and reinforcing ethics' efforts,

- Emphasizing team effort over individual effort.

Life in the Department

Most officers face more stress from within their own agency than they do from "working the streets." While this is sad but true, it does not mean things can't change.

The following are merely a few examples of the things we, as supervisors, need to change, and how to change them:

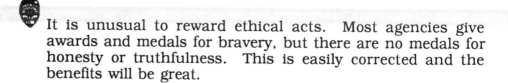 It is unusual to reward ethical acts. Most agencies give awards and medals for bravery, but there are no medals for honesty or truthfulness. This is easily corrected and the benefits will be great.

Ethics are the subject of jokes. Simply don't let people make fun of ethics, honesty, and dedication. Hundreds of great cops have died for these things.

Negative views and attitudes often become a way of life within an organization. It doesn't have to be like this. In fact, administrators and supervisors usually create an "atmosphere" which results in either good or bad attitudes among employees. Changing the "organizational climate" within an agency is complex and difficult, however, and will probably require a good consultant.

 Role models are the greatest factor to determine the atmosphere, attitude, and ethical views within any organization. Although it seems very simple, most organizations have found this a very difficult task. The reason? It all comes back to attitude, anger, lust, and greed. You see, to be a great role model you have to rise above these temptations just like everyone else.

 Few departments have policies and procedures that provide constant "checks and balances" related to ensuring ethical conduct.

Concluding Guidelines That Work:

• Don't pass the buck.

• Find the solution, not excuses.

• Look for the ethical way.

• View every difficult ethical decision as an opportunity to do the right thing instead of a crisis.

• Don't give up – few ethical dilemmas just go away.

Life isn't always fair. The future will hold difficulties in both your career and your personal life. Accepting disappointment as merely a temporary setback will allow you to be a much happier person.

Every agency faces far too many problems on the streets to be bickering and spending time fighting among themselves. Developing and maintaining a good public image takes a never-ending effort.

Everyone needs to pull together. A single act of corruption can destroy the entire image of a department. Making a commitment to be an ethical, conscientious cop is an important ingredient for keeping the image of your department shining bright. There is no way anyone can control everything that's going to happen on the streets, but the one thing you can control is yourself.

> *Don't spend time regretting or living*
> *in the past . . . live for the future.*
>
> *Don't develop a habit of criticizing*
> *others . . . concentrate on becoming*
> *the best you can be.*
>
> *Don't be a burden by nagging or*
> *arguing . . . search out your own*
> *shortcomings and improve yourself.*
>
> *Don't sit in judgment of others . . . allow*
> *them to be human and control their*
> *own destinies.*

Once sincere ethics are ingrained throughout an agency, the entire organization develops a new tone. Togetherness and teamwork suddenly become a real part of everyone's life.

It takes guts to make sure the badge doesn't become tarnished. If yours is to shine, the courage to stand up for what's right must be strong within you. Every officer across the nation has a reputation to earn and maintain. All of us must do something about that!

Professional Image

Attorneys and physicians provide services that usually go unquestioned by their clientele. An assumption of professionalism exists before individuals ever walk into their offices. Law enforcement officers, on the other hand, don't enjoy the luxury of working in an atmosphere of assumed faith.

Professional image will come in accordance with the degree to which it is deserved. If achieved, the following accomplishments will create a professional law enforcement image.

 Officers at all levels must exhibit professional attitudes and conduct. A positive, professional attitude by individual officers is essential for society to accept them as professionals. Officers who are driven by high esteem, pride, and sound moral values will have no problem in sustaining conduct consistent with the highest ideals of the profession.

 Professionalism must be instilled and reinforced throughout an officer's entire career. Law enforcement agencies often fail to establish sincere respect within officers for law enforcement tradition, purpose, and value. The police academy, in-service training, and daily reinforcement by immediate supervisors are logical opportunities for ingraining and maintaining the values of loyalty, dedication, service to others, respect, and pride in one's self and agency.

 A high education level is a fundamental prerequisite for recognition of professionalism. Chiefs and sheriffs should immediately move to impose a two or four-year college degree hiring requirement.

Initially, the sacrifice will be great. Higher standards of employment will mean a smaller recruitment "pool" from which recruiting agencies have to choose. The sacrifice, however, will be a wise investment in the long haul, because educated officers really are better prepared to perform their duties.

 Training must be enhanced for professionalism to become a reality. Historically, law enforcement training has been terribly neglected. The advent of innovative technology has resulted in marked improvements, however. Nationwide standardization of in-service training is nonexistent.

 Standards of employment must be raised and adhered to if society can accept law enforcement as professionals. Maintaining high standards of employment is, of course, much easier said than done.

Some administrators argue that this belief is naive and unrealistic since law enforcement salaries and benefits are lower than other accepted professions. The irony of such logic is that justification for improved salaries and benefits may only be substantiated when law enforcement earns these benefits, as demonstrated by raising standards of employment and education.

 The law enforcement code of ethics must become meaningful. Although the code is already established, it doesn't play an important role in the daily lives of officers.

Officers don't receive regular reinforcement on the importance of the code of ethical conduct. Both individual officers and agency leadership must take responsibility for changing this.

⚝ An increased emphasis on human resource development must take place. The most valuable resource in any organization is its employees. Law enforcement neglects to fully appreciate or develop the abilities of law enforcement personnel.

⚝ Management style must undergo a significant change for law enforcement to keep pace with the efficiency of other organizations. Currently, most departments have bureaucratic-paramilitary management and leadership.

Overwhelming evidence indicates a participatory-people-oriented style of management yields much higher levels of quality performance and effectiveness.

⚝ Improved career development will enhance professional image. It must play a more important role within law enforcement agencies. Many departments don't have a formal career development function. As such, they are missing a tremendous opportunity for improvement.

⚝ Lateral entry is a way of life in the corporate world. Successful businesses seek the best people, wherever they might be. Law enforcement exists in the dark ages when it comes to ensuring the most qualified and proficient individual is placed in a particular position. Many business organizations would go bankrupt if they operated this way.

⚝ Without strong and harmonious community relations, police departments won't be recognized as professional. The significance of community support will be appreciated when agencies fully understand their role as community servants.

It is certainly possible to be a public servant and a professional. Examples are physicians and the ministry.

⚝ The most beneficial use of manpower is critical to reaching maximum efficiency. The future must include increased use of civilian community service officers, selecting the right person for every position, effective manpower allocation of all patrol officers, and less anti-productive bureaucracy.

⚝ Little standardization presently exists within law enforcement. This must change for proficiency of services to occur. State and national organizations must take more of a lead in this regard.

 The national accreditation process should be viewed as the vehicle to be used in establishing nationwide standardization and improvement. Agencies that refuse to acknowledge the wisdom of accreditation will eventually be forced to become accredited by community pressure and civil liability.

 How law enforcement perceive their own role in society is critical to future change. Currently, most officers envision their role as that of "crime fighters." Actually, they are highly specialized public servants more than crime fighters.

 Enhancing the organizational climate within police departments is necessary to achieve a high level of productivity. When a pleasant working environment does not exist, employees usually have low levels of morale and pride. The absence of pride equals an absence of quality.

 A professional association having all officers across the nation as members does not exist. Unlike many other countries, America has chosen not to regulate mandatory membership in a single, nationwide law enforcement association.

Employees and Leadership by the Year 2000

Law enforcement agencies should consider the following ways to adapt to this increasingly diverse work force:

Minority Recruiting
Within the corporate world, as many as 75 percent of organizations in major industries will implement special minority recruiting programs during the next five years. Law enforcement should consider the need and benefits of doing the same. Such programs would define recruiting goals, recruit in selected cultural communities, and train managers how to recruit minorities.

Cultural Sensitivity Training
The need for cultural sensitivity training by law enforcement is highlighted by the news media on a regular basis. The cultural differences between citizens and offi-

cers, or even among officers can result in devastating consequences. All departments need training that will pro-vide officers with knowledge about other cultures and the skills required to effectively interact with them.

 Employee Teams

Focus groups have been proven to be a good way of generating feedback on diversity issues, testing programs, and offering ideas on critical concerns. They are comprised of a cross section of employees within the agency.

By the year 2000, the American labor force will be comprised of:

- 40 percent white males

- 47 percent women

- 10 percent blacks

- 10 percent Hispanics

- 4 percent Asians

Leadership Test

Answer "True" or "False" to the following questions about the workforce and leadership:

Within the next several years

1. True   False   Virtually half of the workforce will be women.

2. True   False   Less than half of the workforce will be white men.

3. True   False   Hispanics will comprise more than 20 percent of the workforce.

4. True   False   Blacks will account for more than 25 percent of the workforce.

5. True   False   Almost 5 percent of the workforce will be Asian.

6. True   False   75 percent of the corporations in some industries will have cultural diversity training.

7. True   False   Over 75 percent of the corporations in some industries will develop and implement customized minority recruiting programs.

8. True   False   Approximately 15 percent of the net addition of employees will be white men.

9. True   False   More than 60 percent of women over the age of 16 will be working.

10. True   False   Most of the population growth will take place in the West.

Leadership Test

Answer Sheet

1. True

2. False (40 percent)

3. False (10 percent)

4. False (11 percent)

5. True

6. True

7. True

8. True

9. True

10. True

Source: *The Monthly Labor Review*

Bibliography

Killinger, George G. and Paul F. Cromwell, Jr. *Issues in Law Enforcement.* Boston, MA: Holbrook Press, 1975

Editor's Biography

Ed Nowicki

Ed is a leading law enforcement trainer in the nation. He is also the former Executive Director of the nation's largest law enforcement training association, the prestigious American Society of Law Enforcement Trainers (ASLET).

A continuously sworn police officer since 1968, and survivor of six separate shooting incidents, he began his law enforcement career with the Chicago Police Department, where he served for more than ten years. He has held the ranks of patrolman, detective, lieutenant, and Chief of Police with four law enforcement agencies.

Ed has been employed full-time as a Police Training Specialist with Milwaukee Area Technical College since 1981, and serves part-time as a sworn police officer for the Twin Lakes (WI) Police Department. He is an international trainer and has trained thousands in law enforcement around the world.

Ed is a regularly featured speaker at a number of professional conferences. There have been articles written about him, and he has frequently appeared on television. He has been judicially recognized and declared an expert on police training and has received numerous awards for his contributions to law enforcement training.

A widely published and respected author for various law enforcement publications, he serves as a contributing editor to *Law Enforcement Technology* magazine. He is one of two technical advisors for *Police* magazine, and is an advisor to *The Police Marksman* magazine. In addition to *Supervisory Survival*, he has written three other books. A former Municipal Judge, he holds a Bachelor of Science degree in Criminal Justice and a Master of Arts degree in Management.

Contact Information for the Authors

Berry, Dean, Dean Berry Associates, Inc., P.O. Box 4490, St. Paul, MN 55104, (612) 222-4168.

Berry, Stan, Dean Berry Associates, Inc., P.O. Box 4490, St. Paul, MN 55104, (612) 222-4168.

Blume, John, Management Specialist, Institute of Police Technology and Management, University of North Florida, 4567 St. Johns Bluff Road, South, Jacksonville, FL 32216, (904) 646-2722.

Bock, Wally, Bock Information Group, Inc., 1441 Franklin Street, Suite 301, Oakland, CA 94612, (510) 835-8522.

Bonshire, Jr., Robert L., Supervisory Special Agent, FBI Academy, Quantico, VA 22135.

Bunting, Stephen M., Executive Director, American Society of Law Enforcement Trainers (ASLET), 102 Dock Road, P.O. Box 361, Lewes, DE 19958-0361, (302) 645-4080.

Carpenter, Michael J., Professional Training Resources, P.O. Box 291, Shaftsbury, VT 05262, (802) 447-2577.

Carvino, James J., Chief of Police, Boise Police Department, 7200 Barrister Drive, Boise, ID 83704-9217, (208) 377-6670.

Chandler, Dr. James T., 206 Twin Oaks Drive, Rochester, IL 62563, (217) 498-8889.

Christenberry, Thomas, Supervisory Special Agent, FBI Academy, Quantico, VA 22135.

Crouse, Robert C., Associate Director, Southern Police Institute, University of Louisville, Louisville, KY 40292, (502) 588-0328.

Eden, Jr., Gorden E., Bureau Chief, New Mexico Department of Public Safety, Training and Recruitment Division, 4491 Cerrillos Road, Santa Fe, NM 87505, (505) 828-2480.

Field, Ginny, Communications Instructor, FBI Academy, Quantico, VA 22135.

Grossi, David M., Senior Instructor, Calibre Press, Inc., 666 Dundee Road, Suite 1607, Northbrook, IL 60062-2727, (708) 498-5680.

Hasting Craig V., Deputy Inspector, Milwaukee Police Department, 6680 North Teutonia Avenue, Milwaukee, WI 53209, (414) 935-7562.

Kolpack, Bryce D., Deputy Chief, Appleton Police Department, 222 S. Walnut Street, Appleton, WI 54911-5899, (414) 832-5500.

Kondracki, Edward N., Chief of Police, La Crosse Police Department, 400 La Crosse Street, La Crosse, WI 54601, (608) 789-7200.

MacHovec, Dr. Frank J., Clinical Psychologist, 3804 Hawthorne Avenue, Richmond, VA 23222, (804) 329-9418.

Mazur, Dr. Edward H., Mazur & Associates Training and Development, 1033 New Trier Court, Wilmette, IL 60091, (312) 251-2460.

McKinnon, Dr. Murlene E., CEO, MACNLOW Associates, 1116 Boulder Court, Lansing, MI 48917, (517) 323-0740.

McLaughlin, Dr. Vance, Savannah Police Department, P.O. Box 8032, Savannah, GA 31412, (912) 651-6667.

Nowicki, Edward J., Police Training Specialist, Milwaukee Area Technical College, 6665 S. Howell Avenue, Oak Creek, WI 53154, (414) 768-5725.

O'Linn, Mildred K., Attorney, Franscell, Strickland, Roberts & Lawrence, 225 S. Lake Avenue, Pasadena, CA 91101-3005, (818) 304-7830.

Roberts, Barbara E., Attorney, Franscell, Strickland, Roberts & Lawrence, 225 S. Lake Avenue, Pasadena, CA 91101-3005, (818) 304-7830.

Robinette, Hillary M., Quantico Group Associates, Inc., 3904 Lansing Court, Dumfries, VA 22026-2460, (703) 221-0189.

Smith, Stephen, Savannah Police Department, P.O. Box 8032, Savannah, GA 31412, (912) 651-6667.

Trautman, Neal E., President, National Institute of Law Enforcement Ethics, 135 E. Bahama Road, Winter Springs, FL 32708, (407) 699-4012.

Suggested Reading

Berry, Dean and **Berry, Stan**
   Action Writing for the '90s
   Business Grammar & Style

Berry, Dean
   A Workbook of Writing Models
   The Officer As Writer
   Report Writing
   Writing Skills for Command Personnel

Chandler, Dr. James T.
   Modern Police Psychology

Kondracki, Edward N.
   A Practitioner's Field Guide to Problem Solving

MacHovec, Dr. Frank J.
   Interview and Interrogation

McLaughlin, Dr. Vance
   Police Use of Force: The Savannah Study

Nowicki, Edward J.
   Total Survival

Robinette, Hillary M.
   Burnout in Blue

Trautman, Neal E.
   A Study of Law   Enforcement
   Law Enforcement In-Service Training Programs
   Law Enforcement Training
   Law Enforcement - The Making of a Profession
   Standards for Security and Law Enforcement Agencies
   50 Things Teens Can Do to Fight Drugs.

Suggested Video Viewing

Berry, Dean and **Berry, Stan**
   Report Writing,
   Writing Skills for Command Personnel

Nowicki, Edward J.
   Interpersonal Communication Skills

Index

A

F

G

M

N

O

Q

S

T

Other Books and Videos Available from Performance Dimensions Publishing

Con Games and Con Artists (Video): This program shows how some of the most popular confidence games are used on unsuspecting and trusting victims. Racine County, Wisconsin, Sheriff Eric Johnson, provides valuable insight into the methods and motivation of con artists.
ISBN: 1-879411-21-0. 27 minutes. $29.95.

Courtroom Skills and Tactics (Video): This video is meant to improve an officer's skills and abilities on the witness stand. Mark Baganz and John Livingston, two nationally known and well respected practicing attorneys, are featured. Meant for new and experienced officers alike, viewers are taken through a number of courtroom re-enactments that actually take place in a courtroom with an officer giving testimony. You have survived the streets, now learn how to survive the courts.
ISBN: 1-879411-16-4. 31 minutes. $29.95.

Crisis Intervention (Video): This program provides information on how to recognize and effectively intervene in a crisis situation. This program features Paul Roemer, a skilled and experienced hostage negotiator formerly with the Federal Bureau of Investigation. Viewers are also shown methods to de-escalate and resolve conflict that, if left unresolved, can lead to a crisis.
ISBN: 1-879411-20-2. 28 minutes. $29.95.

Interpersonal Communications Skills (Video): This video features one of law enforcement's most respected names, Ed Nowicki. This informative program shows how to use and recognize voice inflection, body language, and proper distance to enhance the interpersonal communications' process. Learn why some of the most effective law enforcement officers are also great communicators.
ISBN: 1-879411-19-9. 29 minutes. $29.95.

Law Enforcement Ethics (Video): This video emphasizes the value of ethics for today's law enforcement professional. Containing live footage and interviews, the program offers much needed "food for thought." Neal Trautman, Director of the National Institute of Law Enforcement Ethics, is featured.
ISBN: 1-879411-17-2. 28 minutes. $29.95.

Management of Aggressive Behavior (Book): This book was written by Roland Ouellette, a retired lieutenant with the Connecticut

State Police and an expert on how to manage aggressive and violent behavior. This practical book contains 20 informative chapters that show how to recognize and manage aggressive behavior. Written in an easy to comprehend fashion with extensive photos.
ISBN: 1-879411-22-9. 200+ pages. $14.95.

Street Signs (Book): Written by Mark S. Dunston, this is the most comprehensive identification manual ever written on symbols of crime and violence used by street gangs, hate groups, motorcycle gangs, prison gangs, and others as a secret method of communications. These street signs may be present in the form of tattoos, graffiti spray painted on walls, patches worn on clothing, or in many other ways. Street signs communicate a great deal about an entire group, or an individual group member. The *Street Signs* manual can be used alone, but it is best used in conjunction with *Street Signs: The Video* as a complete training and information package.
ISBN: 1-879411-13-X. 232+ pages. $14.95.

Street Signs (Video): This video visually dramatizes how many of the street signs shown in the book may put the uninformed at risk. Realistic and graphic portrayals will enlighten and amaze viewers. Although it can be used alone, this video is best used as part of a complete training and information package along with the book, *Street Signs.*
ISBN: 1-879411-12-1. 30 minutes. $29.95.

Street Weapons (Book): An identification manual for improvised, unconventional, unusual, homemade, disguised, and exotic personal weapons. *Street Weapons* is widely recognized as the most authoritative book ever written on these highly unusual weapons. This comprehensive manual contains hundreds of photos and drawings along with descriptions that clearly explain how these weapons can be used and carried covertly. Written by Ed Nowicki and Dennis A. Ramsey, two of the leading experts on these types of weapons. You will discover how a normal looking ring can turn into a deadly flesh tearing instrument, or how the stems to a pair of glasses can deliver deadly wounds. A companion to *Street Weapons: The Video.* Must reading for every law enforcement officer.
NOTE: This book will only be sold to law enforcement, security, corrections, or military personnel — proper identification required when ordering.
ISBN: 1-879411-11-3. 240+ pages. $19.95.

Street Weapons (Video): A companion to the book, *Street Weapons.* This fast paced video dramatizes the deadly potential of some of the weapons that are included in the book. Viewing this video should be mandatory for every law enforcement officer. Although this video can be used alone, it is most effective when used in cooperation with the book for a complete training and information package.

NOTE: This video will only be sold to law enforcement, security, corrections, or military personnel — proper identification required when ordering.
ISBN: 1-879411-12-1. 22 minutes. $29.95.

Total Survival (Book): One of the most unique books ever written about the important topic of officer survival. It is not meant to compete with, or to replace, any other books dealing with officer survival. It is meant to be a part of each law enforcement officer's survival library. The pages of *Total Survival* reads like a "Who's Who" in law enforcement training and writing. Over 45 authors contributed to this comprehensive survival source.
ISBN: 1-879411-23-7. 544+ pages. $24.95.

True Blue (Book): This critically acclaimed book contains "true stories about real cops." Written by one of the most respected law enforcement writers, Ed Nowicki, a twenty-four year law enforcement veteran who survived six shootings. *True Blue* contains an assortment of some of the most fascinating and compelling stories about the realities of being a law enforcement officer. This revealing book never lets up and will take you on a trip through the full range of human emotions. *True Blue* will have you uncontrollably laughing while reading one story and shedding tears while reading another. A provocative and sometimes shocking look into the extraordinary world of law enforcement. There's nothing quite like it!
ISBN: 1-879411-15-6. 255+ pages. $14.95.

Why Not Save Time and Order Now with Your MasterCard or Visa?
Call TOLL FREE
1-800-877-7413

Order Form

Telephone Orders: Call 1-800-877-7413. Have your MasterCard or Visa ready.

Postal Orders: Performance Dimensions Publishing, P.O. Box 502, Powers Lake, WI 53159-0502, U.S.A., (414) 279-3850.

FAX Orders: Fax your purchase orders to (414) 279-5758.

Quant.	Title	Price Each	Total
	Con Games and Con Artists (Video)	29.95	
	Courtroom Skills and Tactics (Video)	29.95	
	Crisis Intervention (Video)	29.95	
	Interpersonal Communications Skills (Video)	29.95	
	Law Enforcement Ethics (Video)	29.95	
	Management of Aggressive Behavior (Book)	14.95	
	Street Signs (Book)	14.95	
	Street Signs: The Video (Video)	29.95	
	Street Weapons (Book)	19.95	
	Street Weapons: The Video (Video)	29.95	
	True Blue (Book)	14.95	
	Supervisory Survival (Book)	17.95	
	Total Survival (Book)	24.95	

Shipping & Handling (a flat charge for any quantity)   3.00

Total Enclosed $

☐ Please send FREE information about other books and videos when published.

☐ I would like to host a Seminar.

Method of Payment:
☐ Check   ☐ Money Order   ☐ MasterCard   ☐ VISA

If credit card: Card Number _____

Name on Credit Card _____

Signature _____ Expires _____

Send to my :   ☐ Work   ☐ Home

Name _____ Title _____

Agency/Company _____

Address _____

City _____ State _____ Zip _____

Agency/Company Phone (   )_____

Home Phone (   ) _____

WHY WAIT?
Call your
order in to
us RIGHT
NOW!
Call Toll
Free at 1-
800-877-
7413